OVID, *METAMORPHOSES*, 3.511–733

Ovid, *Metamorphoses*, 3.511–733

Latin Text with Introduction, Commentary, Glossary of Terms, Vocabulary Aid and Study Questions

Ingo Gildenhard and Andrew Zissos

https://www.openbookpublishers.com

© 2016 Ingo Gildenhard and Andrew Zissos.

This work is licensed under a Creative Commons Attribution 4.0 International license (CC BY 4.0). This license allows you to share, copy, distribute and transmit the text; to adapt the text and to make commercial use of the text providing attribution is made to the authors (but not in any way that suggests that they endorse you or your use of the work). Attribution should include the following information:

Ingo Gildenhard and Andrew Zissos, *Ovid, Metamorphoses, 3.511–733. Latin Text with Introduction, Commentary, Glossary of Terms, Vocabulary Aid and Study Questions*. Cambridge, UK: Open Book Publishers, 2016. http://dx.doi.org/ 10.11647/OBP.0073

In order to access detailed and updated information on the license, please visit https://www.openbookpublishers.com/isbn/9781783740826#copyright

Further details about CC BY licenses are available at https://creativecommons.org/licenses/by/4.0/

All external links were active on 26/8/2016 unless otherwise stated and have been archived via the Internet Archive Wayback Machine at https://archive.org/web

Updated digital material and resources associated with this volume are available at https://www.openbookpublishers.com/isbn/9781783740826#resources

Every effort has been made to identify and contact copyright holders and any omission or error will be corrected if notification is made to the publisher.

This is the fifth volume of the Classics Textbooks series:

ISSN: 2054-2437 (Print)
ISSN: 2054-2445 (Online)

ISBN Paperback: 978-1-78374-082-6
ISBN Hardback: 978-1-78374-083-3
ISBN Digital (PDF): 978-1-78374-084-0
ISBN Digital ebook (epub): 978-1-78374-085-7
ISBN Digital ebook (mobi): 978-1-78374-086-4
DOI: 10.11647/OBP.0073

Cover image: Central panel of the Pentheus mosaic depicting Pentheus being killed by Theban maenads, an episode in Euripides' play *The Bacchae*, excavated in Nîmes in 2007, 2nd half of 2nd century AD/3rd century AD, Nîmes Archaeology Museum. Photo by Carole Raddato, https://www.flickr.com/photos/carolemage/16382722126, CC BY-SA 2.0.

All paper used by Open Book Publishers is SFI (Sustainable Forestry Initiative), PEFC (Programme for the Endorsement of Forest Certification Schemes) and Forest Stewardship Council(r)(FSC(r) certified.

Printed in the United Kingdom, United States, and Australia
by Lightning Source for Open Book Publishers (Cambridge, UK)

Contents

Acknowledgements	vii
Abbreviations	ix
Symbols and Terms	ix
Reference Works	ix
Grammatical Terms	x
Ancient Literature	x
Introduction	1
1. Ovid and His Times	3
2. Ovid's Literary Progression: Elegy to Epic	9
3. The *Metamorphoses*: A Literary *Monstrum*	13
3a. Genre Matters	14
3b. A Collection of Metamorphic Tales	16
3c. A Universal History	19
3d. Anthropological Epic	25
3e. A Reader's Digest of Greek and Latin Literature	27
4. Ovid's Theban Narrative	31
5. The Set Text: Pentheus and Bacchus	39
5a. Sources and Intertexts	39
5b. The Personnel of the Set Text	45
6. The Bacchanalia and Roman Culture	65

Text	69
Commentary	115
511–26: Tiresias' Warning to Pentheus	119
527–71: Pentheus' Rejection of Bacchus	135
531–63: Pentheus' Speech	137
572–691: The Captive Acoetes and his Tale	163
692–733: Pentheus' Gruesome Demise	207
Appendices	223
1. Versification	225
2. Glossary of Rhetorical and Syntactic Figures	235
Bibliography	241

Acknowledgements

The present volume joins other commentaries in the OBP Classics Textbook Series, which is designed to offer support and stimulation to student-readers. We would like to express our gratitude to Alessandra Tosi for her patience throughout a longer gestation period than she must have initially hoped for and Inge Gildenhard for supplying the illustrations. A special thanks goes to John Henderson, who twice, virtually overnight, supplied us *per litteras* with copious notes of nonpareil insight. We have incorporated a number of his notes into the Introduction and the Commentary, attributing these simply to 'John Henderson' (to be distinguished from A. A. R. Henderson, whose commentary on *Metamorphoses* 3 we occasionally cite as 'Henderson 1979'). He tried his best to inject the project with an appropriate dose of Dionysiac spirit, and if readers don't find the final product as tipsy as it ought to be, the blame's on us.

* * *

Note on translations: unless indicated otherwise, translations of Greek and Latin texts are from the Loeb Classical Library, often somewhat modified.

Statue of Ovid in Constanța, Romania. https://commons.wikimedia.org/wiki/File:Constanta_-_Ovid-Platz_-_Statue_des_Ovid.jpg

Abbreviations

Symbols and Terms

§	Indicates a section (e.g. of the Introduction or of a reference work).
*	Indicates a term defined in either Appendix 1 (Versification) or Appendix 2 (Glossary of Rhetorical and Syntactic Figures).
˘	Indicates a syllable that scans short (for details of scansion, see Appendix 1).
—	Indicates a syllable that scans long (for details of scansion, see Appendix 1).
CE/BCE	Common Era/Before Common Era (a designation for the calendar year, equivalent to AD/BC). In this volume CE should be assumed when no indication is provided.
Comm.	Refers to the Commentary in this volume.
Intro.	Refers to the Introduction (normally with following section specification).
n.	Refers to an entry in the Commentary (normally with preceding line specification).

Reference Works

AG	*Allen and Greenough's New Latin Grammar for Schools and Colleges*, edited by J. B. Greenough, G. L. Kitteredge, A. A. Howard, and B. L. D'Ooge (Boston, 1903).
CIL	*Corpus Inscriptionum Latinarum* (Berlin, 1862).
L-S	*A Latin Dictionary*, edited by C. T. Lewis and C. Short (Oxford, 1879).

LSJ	*A Greek-English Lexicon*, 9th edition, with Supplement, edited by H. J. Liddle and R. Scott, revised by H. S. Jones (Oxford, 1968)
OLD	*Oxford Latin Dictionary*, edited by P. G. W. Glare (Oxford, 1968–82).
TLL	*Thesaurus Linguae Latinae* (Leipzig, 1900).

Grammatical Terms

abl.	ablative (similarly nom. = nominative; gen. = genitive; dat. = dative; acc. = accusative)
act.	active voice (similarly pass. = passive voice)
fut.	future tense (similarly perf. = perfect; pres. = present; etc.)
indic.	indicative (similarly subjunct. = subjunctive)
part.	participle
pers.	person
pl.	plural (similarly sing. = singular)

Ancient Literature

Apollod.	Apollodorus, *Bibliotheca* (*Library*)	
Ap. Rhod.	Apollonius Rhodius, *Argonautica*	
Apul.	Apuleius	
	Met.	*Metamophoses* (or *Golden Ass*)
Arat.	Aratus	
	Phaen.	*Phaenomena*
Cat.	Catullus, *Carmina* (*Poems*)	
Cic.	Cicero	
	Fam.	*Epistulae ad Familiares* (*Letters to his Friends*)
	Leg.	*De Legibus* (*On the Law*)
	Nat. D.	*De Natura Deorum* (*On the Nature of the Gods*)
Enn.	Ennius	
	Ann.	*Annales* (*Annals*)

Eur.	Euripides	
	Bacch.	*Bacchae*
Hdt.	Herodotus, *Histories*	
Hes.	Hesiod	
	Op.	*Opera et Dies (Works and Days)*
Hom.	Homer	
	Il.	*Iliad*
	Od.	*Odyssey*
Hor.	Horace	
	Carm.	*Carmina (Odes)*
	Epod.	*Epodes*
Hyg.	Hyginus	
	Fab.	*Fabulae*
Hymn. Hom.	Homeric Hymns	
Liv.	Livy, *Ab urbe condita*	
Luc.	Lucan, *Bellum Civile (Civil War)*	
Lucr.	Lucretius, *De Rerum Natura*	
Mart.	Martial	
	Ep.	*Epigrams*
Ov.	Ovid	
	Am.	*Amores*
	Ars	*Ars Amatoria (The Art of Love)*
	Fast.	*Fasti*
	Her.	*Heroides*
	Met.	*Metamorphoses*
	Trist.	*Tristia*
Plaut.	Plautus	
	Cas.	*Casina*
	Merc.	*Mercator*
Plin.	Pliny (the Elder)	
	NH	*Naturalis Historia (Natural History)*

Plut.	Plutarch	
	Caes.	Caesar
Prop.	Propertius, *Carmina (Poems)*	
Sen.	Seneca (the Younger)	
	Oed.	Oedipus
Serv.	Servius	
Stat.	Statius	
	Ach.	Achilleid
	Silv.	Silvae
	Theb.	Thebaid
Suet.	Suetonius	
	Aug.	Divus Augustus (Life of Augustus)
Theoc.	Theocritus	
	Id.	Idylls
Val. Max.	Valerius Maximus	
Val. Flacc.	Valerius Flaccus, *Argonautica*	
Varr.	Varro	
	Ling.	De Lingua Latina (On the Latin Language)
Virg.	Virgil	
	Aen.	Aeneid
	Ecl.	Eclogues
	G.	Georgics

INTRODUCTION

1. Ovid and His Times

Ovid, or (to give him his full Roman name) Publius Ovidius Naso, was born in 43 BCE to a prominent equestrian family in Sulmo (modern Sulmona), a small town about 140 km east of Rome. He died in banishment, a resident of Tomi on the Black Sea, in 17 CE. Ovid was one of the most prolific authors of his day, as well as one of the most controversial.[1] He had always been constitutionally unable to write anything in prose — or so he claims in his autobiography (composed, of course, in verse). Whatever flowed from his pen was in metre, even after his father had told him to put an end to such nonsense:

> saepe pater dixit 'studium quid inutile temptas?
> Maeonides[2] nullas ipse reliquit opes'.
> motus eram dictis, totoque Helicone[3] relicto
> scribere temptabam verba soluta modis.
> sponte sua carmen numeros veniebat ad aptos,
> et quod temptabam dicere versus erat.
> (*Trist.* 4.10.21–26)

---

1   Introductions to Ovid abound. See e.g. Mack (1988), Holzberg (2002), Fantham (2004), Volk (2010), Liveley (2011). There are also three recent 'companions' to Ovid, i.e. collections of papers designed to enhance our understanding and appreciation of the poet and his works. See Hardie (2002b) (by far the best and most affordable), Weiden Boyd (2000) and Knox (2009).
2   *Maeonides* means 'a native of Maeonia', a region in Asia Minor, from which Homer was in antiquity believed to have hailed: hence *Maeonides* = Homer.
3   Mount Helicon in Boeotia is said to be the place where the Muses do dwell; hence *toto Helicone relicto* = 'all Helicon abandoned' = 'having abandoned the writing of poetry'.

> My father often said, 'Why try a useless
>   Vocation? Even Homer left no wealth'.
> So I obeyed, all Helicon abandoned,
>   And tried to write in prose that did not scan.
> But poetry in metre came unbidden,
>   And what I tried to write in verses ran.
> (tr. Melville)

Students of Latin may well be familiar with Naso senior's banausic attitude: classics graduates, some wrongly assume, have similarly dismal career prospects. But eventually Ovid would shrug off paternal disapproval in pursuit of his passion. After dutifully filling certain minor offices, he chose not to go on to the quaestorship, thereby definitively renouncing all ambition for a senatorial career. In his case, the outcome was an *oeuvre* for the ages. For quick orientation, here is a time-line with the basics:[4]

Time-line	Historical Events	Ovid's Biography	Literary History
50s BCE			Catullus, Lucretius
44	Julius Caesar murdered		
43	Cicero murdered	Ovid born	
30s			[Gallus *Amores* 1–4 (lost)], Horace *Epodes*
35			Virgil *Eclogues* Horace *Satires* 1
31	Battle of Actium		
29			Virgil *Georgics*
27	Octavian becomes 'Augustus'		

---

4   A good way to get a sense of his life and career is to read his highly spun autobiography *Trist.* 4.10, which begins with a charming couplet addressed to *you*: *Ille ego qui fuerim, tenerorum lusor amorum, | quem legis, ut noris, accipe posteritas* … ('That you may know who I was, I that playful poet of tender love whom you read, hear my words, you of times to come …')

Time-line	Historical Events	Ovid's Biography	Literary History
Early 20s			Livy 1–10
20s			Propertius 1–3, Tibullus 1, Horace *Odes* 1–3, *Epistles* 1
19			Virgil *Aeneid*, Tibullus 1–2
18	*Leges Iuliae* (initial Augustan marriage legislation)		
17	Secular Games; Augustus adopts Gaius and Lucius		Horace *Carmen Saeculare*
16			Propertius 4
10s–0s		*Amores* 1–3, *Heroides*, *Medicamina faciei femineae*, *Medea* (a lost tragedy)	Horace *Ars Poetica*, *Epistles* 2, *Odes* 4
2 BCE		*Ars Amatoria* 1–2	
1 CE	Birth of Jesus		
2		*Ars Amatoria* 3 and *Remedia Amoris*	
4	Augustus adopts Tiberius		
8	Scandal at court; Augustus relegates Ovid to Tomi on the Black Sea	Finished just before the relegation (?): *Metamorphoses* 1–15, *Fasti* 1–6	
8–17		*Tristia* 1–5, *Epistulae ex Ponto* 1–4, *Ibis*, *Double Heroides*	
14	Augustus dies; Tiberius accedes		
10s			Manilius *Astronomica*
17 (?)		Ovid dies	Livy dies

Ovid was born when the Republic, the oligarchic system of government that had ruled Rome for centuries, was in its death throes. He was a teenager at the time of the Battle of Actium, the final showdown between Mark Antony and Octavian that saw the latter emerge victorious, become the first *princeps*, and eventually take the honorific title 'Augustus' by which he is better known to posterity. Unlike other major poets of the so-called 'Augustan Age' — Virgil, Horace, Propertius, Tibullus — Ovid never experienced a fully functional form of republican government, the *libera res publica* in whose cause figures like Cato and even Cicero ultimately died. There is another important difference between Ovid and most of the other major Augustan poets: he did not have a 'patron-friend', such as Maecenas (a close adviser of the *princeps* who, in the 30s, 'befriended' Virgil, Horace and Propertius) or Messalla, the amateur poet and power-politician to whom Tibullus dedicates his poetry. Ovid came from a prominent family and was financially self-sufficient: this left him free — or so he must have thought — to let rip his insouciant imagination.

A consummate urbanite, Ovid enjoyed himself and was an immensely popular figure in the fashionable society of Augustan Rome. He was more than happy to endorse the myth that the founding hero Aeneas and thus the city itself had Venus in their DNA (just spell Roma backwards!). For him Rome was first and foremost the city of Love and Sex and his (early) verse reads like an ancient version of 'Sex and the City'.

Eventually, though, Ovid ran afoul of the regime. In 8 CE, when he was fifty years old, Ovid was implicated in a lurid court scandal that also involved Augustus' niece Julia and was relegated by the emperor to Tomi, a town on the Black Sea (the sea-port Constanța in present-day Romania).[5] The reasons, so Ovid himself tells us, were a 'poem and a mistake' ('*carmen et error*', *Trist*. 2.207). He goes on to identify the poem as the *Ars Amatoria* — which had, however, been published a full ten years earlier — but declines to elaborate on the 'mistake', on the grounds

---

5 Technically speaking, Ovid suffered the punishment of *relegatio* ('deportation') rather than the more severe penalty of *exilium* ('exile') — the poet himself stresses the distinction at *Trist*. 2.137. This meant that Ovid retained citizenship and many of the rights that went with it, and his property was not confiscated. His (third) wife Fabia did not accompany him to Tomi, but seems to have remained faithful to him.

that it would be too painful for Augustus. He maintained this reticent pose for the rest of his life, so what the *error* was is now anybody's guess (and many have been made). In any event, despite Ovid's pleas the hoped-for recall never came, even after the death of Augustus, and he was forced to pine away the rest of his life far from his beloved Rome. He characterizes Tomi as a primitive and dreary town, located in the middle of nowhere, even though archaeological evidence suggests that it was a pleasant seaside resort. And while his poetry continued to flow, it did so in a very different vein from the light-hearted exuberance that characterizes his earlier 'Roman' output; the *Tristia* and *Epistulae ex Ponto* explore the potential of the elegiac distich (a verse-form consisting of a six-foot hexameter and a five-foot pentameter in alternation: the metre of mourning as well as love) to articulate grief. But on his career trajectory from *eros* to exile, Ovid made forays into non-elegiac genres: tragedy (his lost play *Medea*) and, of course, epic. In the following section we will explore Ovid's playful encoding, in a range of texts, of his longstanding epic ambition and its final realization in the *Metamorphoses*.

2. Ovid's Literary Progression: Elegy to Epic

When the first edition of the *Metamorphoses* hit the shelves in the bookshops of Rome, Ovid had already made a name for himself in the literary circles of the city.[6] His official debut, the *Amores* ('Love Affairs') lured his tickled readers into a freewheeling world of elegiac love, slaphappy hedonism, and (more or less) adept adultery.[7] His subsequent *Heroides* ('Letters written by Heroines to their absent Hero-Lovers') were also designed to appeal to connoisseurs of elegiac poetry, who could here share vicariously in stirring emotional turmoil with abandoned women of history and myth: Ovid, well attuned to female plight, provided the traditional heroes' other (better?) halves with a literary forum for voicing feelings of loss and deprivation and expressing resentment for the epic way of life. Of more practical application for the Roman lady of the world were his verses on toiletry, the *Medicamina Faciei* ('Ointments of the Face, or, How to Apply Make-up'). Once Ovid had discovered his talent for didactic exposition, he blithely continued in that vein. In perusing the urbane and sophisticated lessons on love which the self-proclaimed *erotodidaskalos* ('teacher of love') presented in his *Ars Amatoria* ('A — Z of Love') his male (and female) audience could hone their own amatory skills, while at the same time experiencing true 'jouissance' (the French term for orgasmic bliss, for the sophisticates

---

6 The following is adapted from Gildenhard and Zissos (2000b).
7 You can read the first book of the *Amores* on-line in another OBP edition. See http://www.openbookpublishers.com/product/348

among you) in the act of reading a work, which is, as one critic put it, 'a poem about poetry, and sex, and poetry as sex'.[8]

After these extensive sessions in poetic philandering, Ovid's ancient readers, by then all hopeless and desperate *eros*-addicts, surely welcomed the thoughtful antidote he offers in the form of the therapeutic *Remedia Amoris* ('Cures for Love'), a poem written with the expressed purpose of freeing the wretched lover from the baneful shackles of Cupid. To cut a long story short: by the time the *Metamorphoses* were published, Ovid's devotees had had ample opportunity to revel in the variety of his literary output about the workings of Eros, and each time, the so-called elegiac distich provided the metrical form. Publius Ovidius Naso had become, apart from a brief flirtation with the genre of tragedy (the lost *Medea*, written in Latin iambic trimeters), a virtual synonym for the composition of erotic-elegiac verse. But picking up and un-scrolling any one of the fifteen books that contained the *Metamorphoses*, a reader familiar with Ovid's literary career is in for a shock. Here are the first four lines of the work, which make up its proem:

> In nova fert animus mutatas dicere formas
> corpora; di, coeptis (nam vos mutastis et illa)
> adspirate meis primaque ab origine mundi
> ad mea perpetuum deducite tempora carmen.
> (*Met.* 1.1–4)
>
> My mind compels me to sing of shapes changed into new bodies: gods, on my endeavours (for you have changed them too) breathe your inspiration, and from the very beginning of the world to my own times bring down this continuous song.

A mere glance at the layout (no indentations in alternate lines!) suffices to confirm that Ovid has definitively changed poetic metiers (as the 'change' of verse between *formas* and *corpora* makes a 'new' syntactical role for the opening phrase *In nova*).[9] In his newest work the foreshortened

---

8   Sharrock (1994) vii.
9   Initially, the reader might be inclined to take the first four words (*In nova fert animus*: 'my mind carries me on to new things', with the adjective *nova* used as a noun) as a self-standing syntactic unit; only after reaching the opening of line 2 do we realise that *nova* in fact modifies *corpora* and the phrase goes with the participle *mutatas* ('forms changed into new bodies').

pentameters, which until now had been a defining characteristic of his poetry, have disappeared. Instead, row upon steady row of sturdy and well-proportioned hexameters confront the incredulous reader. Ovid, the celebrated master of the distich, the notorious *tenerorum lusor amorum* ('the playboy of light-hearted love-poetry' as he calls himself), the unrivalled champion of erotic-elegiac poetry, has produced a work written in 'heroic verse' — as the epic metre is portentously called.

But once the initial shock has worn off, readers familiar with Ovid's earlier output are bound to experience a sense of *déjà vu* (as the French say of what they have seen before). Ovid, while devoting his previous career to versifying things erotic, had always shown an inclination towards epic poetry. Already in the introductory elegy to the first book of the *Amores*, the neophyte announced that he was writing elegies merely by default. His true ambition lay elsewhere; he had actually meant to write an epic:

> Arma gravi numero violentaque bella parabam
>   edere, materia conveniente modis.
> par erat inferior versus — risisse Cupido
>   dicitur atque unum surripuisse pedem.
> (*Am.* 1.1.1–4)
>
> About arms and violent wars I was getting ready to compose in the weighty hexameter. The material matched the metrical form: the second verse was of equal length to the first — but Cupid (they say) smiled and snatched away one of the feet.[10]

As can be gathered from pointed allusions to the *Aeneid* (which begins *Arma virumque cano*: 'I sing of arms and the man') at the opening, the poem Ovid set out to write before Cupid intervened would have been no routine piece of work, but rather an epic of such martial grandeur as to challenge Virgil's masterpiece. Ovid's choice of the hexameter for the *Metamorphoses* signals that he has finally realized his long-standing ambition to compose an epic. But already the witty features of the proem (starting with its minuscule length: four meagre lines for a work of fifteen

---

10 By removing one of the feet from the second verse, Cupid in effect changed the genre of the poem Ovid was composing from epic (in which all verses are hexametric — i.e. contain six feet) to elegy (in which every second verse contains five feet).

books!) indicate that his embrace of the genre is to be distinctly double-edged. And, indeed, his take on epic is as unconventional as his efforts in elegiac and didactic poetry had been. Just as the *Amores* spoofed the more serious output of his elegiac predecessors Propertius and Tibullus and his string of didactic works (the *Ars Amatoria*, the *Remedia Amoris*, the *Medicamina Faciei*) spoofed more serious ventures in the genre such as Virgil's *Georgics* (a poem on farming), so the *Metamorphoses* has mischievous fun with, while at the same time also outperforming, the Greco-Roman epic tradition from Homer to Virgil. It is arguably the most unusual epic to have come down to us from antiquity — as well as one of the most influential.

3. The *Metamorphoses*: A Literary *Monstrum*

In the *Metamorphoses*, Ovid parades a truly dazzling array of mythological and (as the epic progresses) historical matter before his audience. Aristotelian principles of narrative unity and 'classical' plotting have clearly fallen by the wayside. In breathtaking succession, the fast-paced narrative takes his readers from the initial creation myths to the gardens of Pomona, from the wilful intrusion of *Amor* into his epic narrative in the Apollo and Daphne episode to the ill-starred marriage feast of Pirithous and Hippodame (ending in an all out brawl, mass-slaughter, and a 'Romeo and Juliet' scene between two centaurs), from the Argonauts' voyage to Colchis to Orpheus' underworld descent (to win back his beloved Eurydice from the realms of the dead), from the charming rustic couple Philemon and Baucis to the philosopher Pythagoras expounding on nature and history, from the creative destruction of Greek cultural centres such as Thebes in the early books to the rise of Rome and the apotheosis of the Caesars at the end. As Ovid proceeds through this remarkable assortment of material, the reader traverses the entire cosmos, from the top of Mount Olympus where Jupiter presides over the council of the gods to the pits of Tartarus where the dreadful Furies hold sway, from far East where, at dawn, Sol mounts his fiery chariot to far West where his son Phaethon, struck by Jupiter's thunderbolt, plunges headlong into the Eridanus river. Within the capacious geographical boundaries of his fictional world, Ovid's narrative focus switches rapidly from the divine elegiac lover Apollo to the resolute virgin Diana, from the blasphemer Lycaon to the boar slaying Meleager, from the polymorphic sexual exploits of *Pater Omnipotens* to the counterattacks of his vengeful wife Juno. At one point the poet flaunts blameless Philomela's severed tongue waggling disconcertingly on the ground, at another he recounts the dismemberment of the Thessalian tyrant Pelias at the hands of his devoted daughters. On a first encounter the centrifugal diversity of the narrative material which Ovid presents in his *carmen perpetuum* ('continuous song') is bound to have a disorienting, even unsettling effect on the reader. How is anyone to come to critical terms with the astonishing variety of narrative configurations that Ovid displays in this ever-shifting poetic kaleidoscope?[11]

3a. Genre Matters

The hexametric form, the cosmic scope and the sheer scale of the *Metamorphoses* all attest to its epic affiliations. As just discussed, the poem's opening verses seem to affirm that Ovid realized his longstanding aspiration to match himself against Virgil in the most lofty of poetic genres. But as soon as one scratches the surface, myriad difficulties emerge. Even if we choose to assign the *Metamorphoses* to the category of epic poetry, idiosyncrasies abound. A tabular comparison with other well-known instances of the genre brings out a few of its fundamental oddities:

Author	Title	Length	Main Theme	Protagonist
Homer	*Iliad*	24 Books	Wrath and War	Achilles
Homer	*Odyssey*	24 Books	Return/Civil War	Odysseus
Apollonius Rhodius	*Argonautica*	4 Books	Travel and Adventure	Jason
Ennius	*Annals*	15/18 Books	Men and their deeds	Roman nobles
Virgil	*Aeneid*	12 Books	Arms and the Man	Aeneas
Ovid	*Metamorphoses*	15 Books	Transformation	?

---

11 On *varietas* ('variety') in Latin literature more generally see now Fitzgerald (2016).

The tally of fifteen books, while deviating from the 'multiple-of-four-or-six' principle canonized by Homer, Apollonius Rhodius, and Virgil, at least has a precedent in Ennius' *Annals*.[12] But Ovid's main theme and his choice of protagonist are decidedly peculiar (as will be discussed in the following sections). And then there is the playfulness of the narrative, its pervasive reflexivity, and its often arch or insouciant tone — elements largely absent from earlier instantiations of the genre. 'The *Metamorphoses* is perhaps Ovid's most innovative work, an epic on a majestic scale that refuses to take epic seriously'.[13] Indeed, the heated and ultimately inconclusive debate that has flared up around the question of whether the *Metamorphoses* is an epic, an eroticization of epic, a parody of epic, a conglomeration of genres granted equal rights, an epic *sui generis* or simply a poem *sui generis* might seem to indicate that Ovid has achieved a total breakdown of generic conventions, voiding the validity of generic analysis altogether. Karl Galinsky once cautioned that 'it would be misguided to pin the label of any genre on the *Metamorphoses*'.[14] But does Ovid, in this poem, really dance outside genre altogether? Recent scholarship on the *Metamorphoses* suggests that the answer is 'no'. Stephen Hinds articulates the issue at stake very well; in reconsidering the classic distinction between Ovidian epic and elegy, he remarks that

> ... in the opening lines [of the *Metamorphoses*], the epic criterion is immediately established as relevant, even if only as a point of reference for generic conflict ... Boundaries are crossed and recrossed as in no poem before. Elements characteristic of elegy, bucolic, didactic, tragedy, comedy and oratory mingle with elements variously characteristic of the grand epic tradition and with each other ... However, wherever its shifts may take it, the metre, bulk and scope of the poem ensures that the question implied in that opening paradox will never be completely eclipsed: namely in what sense is the *Metamorphoses* an epic?[15]

In other words, denying the *Metamorphoses* the status of epic (or at least epic aspiration) means depriving the text of one of its most intriguing constitutive tensions. Ovid needs the seriousness, the ideology and the

---

12 *Annals*, as the name suggests (from *annus* = year), are year-by-year chronicles. Ennius (c. 239–c. 169 BCE) wrote his epic history of Rome towards the end of his life.
13 Mack (1988) 27.
14 Galinsky (1975) 41.
15 Hinds (1987) 121.

reputation of epic as medium for his frivolous poetics, as the ultimate sublime for his exercise in generic deconstruction and as the conceptual matrix for the savvy of his metageneric artistry (i.e. artistry that self-consciously, if often implicitly, reflects on generic matters). Within this epic undertaking, most other genres find their place as well — not least in the set text where elements of epic, oratory, hymnic poetry, tragedy, and bucolic all register (and intermingle).

Scholars are again divided on how best to handle the multiplicity of generic voices that Ovid has included in the *Metamorphoses*. Are we perhaps dealing with 'epic pastiche'? One critic answers in the affirmative: 'For my purposes ... the long poem in hexameters is a pastiche epic whose formal qualities are shaped by an invented genre that is at once *ad hoc* and *sui generis,* one with no real ancestors but with many and various offspring'.[16] But another objects that 'it is a mistake often made to identify one section of the *Metamorphoses* as "elegiac", another as "epic", another as "comic", another as "tragic", as if Ovid put together a pastiche of genres. Actually, elements of all these genres, and others as well, are as likely as not to appear together in any given story'.[17] Arguably a more promising way to think critically about the generic presences in Ovid's poem is to see the genres *in dialogue* with one another in ways that are mutually *enriching*.[18] All genres have their own distinctive emphasis and outlook, and to have several of them at work at the same time challenges us, the readers, to negotiate sudden changes in register and perspective, keeping us on our toes.

3b. A Collection of Metamorphic Tales

Its hexametric form aside, the most striking formal feature of the *Metamorphoses* is that, as its title announces, it strings together a vast number of more or less distinct tales, each of which features a metamorphosis — that is, a magical or supernatural transformation of some kind. In composing a poem of this type, Ovid was working within a tradition of metamorphic literature that had blossomed a few centuries

---

16 Johnson (1996) 9.
17 Tissol (1996) 151–52.
18 For generic dialogue see Farrell (1992); for 'generic enrichment' Harrison (2007).

earlier in Hellenistic culture. In terms of his apparent generic aspirations, Ovid's main theme (and hence his title) is unequivocally — and shockingly — unorthodox: before him, 'transformative change' was a subject principally cultivated in Hellenistic catalogue poetry, which is about as un-epic in scope and conception as literature can get.[19]

Nicander's *Heteroeumena* ('Changed Ones'), datable to the 2nd century BCE, is the earliest work dedicated to metamorphosis for which we have reliable attestations. The surviving fragments are scant, but valuable testimony is preserved in a prose compendium written by Antoninus Liberalis. The *Heteroeumena* was a poem in four or five books, written in dactylic hexameters, which narrated episodes of metamorphosis from disparate myths and legends, brought together in a single collection. An overarching concern was evidently to link tales of metamorphosis to the origin of local landmarks, religious rites or other cultural practices: Nicander's stories were thus predominantly aetiological in orientation, very much like Callimachus' *Aetia*. At the close of the Hellenistic period, Greek metamorphosis poetry evidently found its way to Rome, along with its authors. So, for example, Parthenius, the Greek tutor to Virgil, who came to Rome in 65 BCE, composed a *Metamorphoses* in elegiacs, about which we unfortunately know next to nothing.

Considered against this literary backdrop, Ovid's initial announcement in the *Metamorphoses* that this would be a poem about 'forms changed into different bodies' (*in nova ... mutatas formas | corpora*, 1.1–2) might well have suggested to a contemporary reader that Ovid was inscribing himself within a tradition of metamorphosis poetry *tout court* — setting himself up, that is, as the Roman exemplar of the sub-genre of Hellenistic metamorphosis catalogue poetry represented by such works as Nicander's *Heteroeumena*. But Ovid's epic was vastly more ambitious in conception, and proved to be no less revolutionary in design. Nicander's *Heteroeumena* and other 'collective' metamorphosis poems from the Hellenistic period are characterized by a discontinuous narrative structure: each included tale constitutes a discrete entry, sufficient unto itself, so that the individual stories do not add up to an organic whole. Ovid's *Metamorphoses* marks a radical departure from

---

19   Gildenhard and Zissos (2013) 49–51.

these predecessors: while each individual tale sports the qualities we associate with the refined and sophisticated, as well as small-scale and discontinuous, that Callimachus and other Hellenistic poets valued and cultivated, the whole is much more than the sum of its parts.

What distinguishes the *Metamorphoses* from these precursors is that it is chronologically and thematically continuous. In strictly formal terms, it is this chronological framework that constitutes Ovid's innovation within the tradition of ancient catalogue poetry. He marshals into a continuous epic narrative a vast assortment of tales of transformation, beginning with the creation of the cosmos and ending in his own times. Every 'episode' within this narrative thus needs to satisfy two conditions: (i) it must follow on from the preceding episode in some kind of temporal succession; (ii) it must contain a metamorphosis. The second condition is sometimes met by resort to ingenious devices. The set text is a case in point: the story of Pentheus, as inherited from Euripides and others, did not contain an 'orthodox' instance of metamorphosis, i.e. of a human being transforming into flora, fauna, or an inanimate object (though of course it does feature the changeling god Bacchus in human disguise and hallucinating maenads who look at Pentheus only to see a wild animal). To make good this deficiency, Ovid includes an inset narrative told by the character Acoetes, who delivers, as a cautionary tale for Pentheus, a long-winded account of how Bacchus once transformed a group of wicked Etruscan pirates into dolphins. Now some readers, particularly those coming to Ovid from the earlier tradition of metamorphic catalogue poetry, might regard this as 'cheating'; others, however, might appreciate the ingenuity with which Ovid explores the limits and possibilities of metamorphosis, combining orthodox instances of transformative change with related phenomena, such as divine allophanies ('appearances in disguise') or hallucinations ('transformations in the eyes of a beholder, based on misperception of reality that is nevertheless frightfully real in its consequences'). What is at any rate remarkable is that such 'tricks' as Acoetes' inset narrative are comparatively rare: on the whole, the *Metamorphoses* meets the daunting, seemingly impossible, challenge of fashioning, in the traditional epic manner, an 'unbroken song' (*perpetuum ... carmen*, 1.4) from disparate tales of transformation.

3c. A Universal History

Ovid's epic is a work of breathtaking ambition: it gives us nothing less than a comprehensive vision of the world — both in terms of nature and culture (and how they interlock). The *Metamorphoses* opens with a cosmogony and offers a cosmology: built into the poem is an explanation (highly idiosyncratic, to be sure) of how our physical universe works, with special emphasis on its various metamorphic qualities and possibilities. And it is set up as a universal history that traces time from the moment of creation to the Augustan age — or, indeed, beyond. In his proem Ovid promises a poem of cosmic scale, ranging from the very beginning of the universe (*prima ab origine mundi*) down to his own times (*ad mea tempora*).[20] He embarks upon an epic narrative that begins with the creation of the cosmos and ends with the apotheosis of Julius Caesar. The poet's teleological commitment to a notional 'present' (the Augustan age in which the epic was composed) *qua* narrative terminus is subtly reinforced by frequent appeals to the contemporary reader's observational experience. The result is a cumulatively compelling sequence that postures, more or less convincingly, as a chronicle of the cosmos in all its pertinent facets.

Taken in its totality, Ovid's epic elevates the phenomenon of metamorphosis from its prior status as a mythographic curiosity to an indispensable mechanism of cosmic history, a fundamental causal element in the evolution of the universe and the story of humanity: the *Metamorphoses* offers not a mere concatenation of marvellous transformations, but a poetic vision of the world conceived of as fundamentally and pervasively metamorphic.

The claim that the *Metamorphoses* amounts to a universal history may well sound counterintuitive, and for two reasons in particular. First, chronology sometimes seems to go awry — not least through the heavy use of embedded narrative — so that the audience is bound to have difficulty keeping track of the trajectory that proceeds from elemental chaos at the outset to the Rome of Augustus at the end. But upon inspection, it turns out that Ovid has sprinkled important clues into his narrative that keep the final destination of his narrative in the

---

20   Or, by a pun on *tempora*, to Ovid's 'temples' (i.e. to his cranium).

minds of (attentive) readers.[21] The second puzzle raised by the historical orientation of Ovid's epic concerns its principal subject matter: instances of transformative change that are clearly fictional. Ovid himself concedes as much. In one of his earlier love elegies, Amores 3.12, he laments the fact that, owing to the success of his poetry, his girlfriend Corinna has become the toast of Rome's would-be Don Giovannis. Displeased with the prospect of romantic competition, he admonishes would-be rivals to read his love elegies with the same incredulity they routinely bring to bear on mythic *fabulae* — and proceeds to belabour the point in what almost amounts to a blueprint of the Metamorphoses (*Am.* 3.12.19–44). Ovid's catalogue of unbelievable tales includes Scylla, Medusa, Perseus and Pegasus, gigantomachy, Circe's magical transformation of Odysseus' companions, Cerberus, Phaethon, Tantalus, the transformations of Niobe and Callisto, Procne, Philomela, and Itys, the self-transformations of Jupiter prior to raping Leda, Danaë, and Europa, Proteus, and the Spartoi that rose from the teeth of the dragon slain by Cadmus at the future site of Thebes. The catalogue culminates in the punchline that just as no one really believes in the historical authenticity of such tales, so too readers should be disinclined to take anything he says about Corinna at face value:[22]

> Exit in inmensum fecunda licentia vatum,
>   obligat historica nec sua verba fide.
> et mea debuerat falso laudata videri
>   femina; credulitas nunc mihi vestra nocet.
> (*Am.* 3.12.41–43)
>
> The creative licence of the poets knows no limits, and does not constrain its words with historical faithfulness. My girl ought to have seemed falsely praised; I am undone by your credulity.

---

21 More on this matter below; for detailed discussion see Gildenhard and Zissos (2004).

22 Any mention of *Amores* 3.12, as John Henderson reminds us, has also to invoke the Liar's Paradox at work here: the person whose only true claim is that he is lying is — lying. 'So whatever else Ovid "challenges" us to read, it is all tainted with mendacity. There is *no* true instruction for the reader coming from this author: I'd be lying, wouldn't I, if I said that we're on our own, with "myth", fictions that (like histories) tell truths by lying (esp. by telling [hi]stories)'.

The same attitude towards tales of transformative change informs his retrospect on the *Metamorphoses* at *Trist.* 2.63–64, where Ovid adduces the implausibility of the stories contained within his epic: *Inspice maius opus, quod adhuc sine fine tenetur, | in non credendos corpora uersa modos* ('Look at the greater work, which is as of yet unfinished, bodies transformed in ways not to be believed'). As one scholar has observed, 'a critic could hardly wish for a more explicit denial of the reality of the myth-world of the *Metamorphoses*'.[23]

In light of how Ovid presents the theme of metamorphosis elsewhere (including moments of auto-exegesis, where he tells his own story), it comes as no surprise that 'the *Metamorphoses*' challenges to our belief in its fictions are relentless, for Ovid continually confronts us with such reminders of his work's fictional status'.[24] But this feature of his text is merely the result of his decision to write *fiction as history*. Put differently, what is so striking about his project is not that Ovid is writing self-conscious fiction. Rather, it is his paradoxical insistence that his fictions are historical facts. From the start, Ovid draws attention to, and confronts, the issue of credibility. A representative instance comes from his account of how Deucalion and Pyrrha replenish the earth's human population after its near extermination in the flood by throwing stones over their shoulders:

> saxa (quis hoc credat, nisi sit pro teste vetustas?)
> ponere duritiem coepere ...
> (*Met.* 1.400–01)

> The stones (who would believe this if the age of the tale did not function as witness?) began to lose their hardness ...

In his parenthetical remark Ovid turns *vetustas* ('old age') into a criterion for *veritas* ('truth'), slyly counting on, while at the same time subverting, the Roman investment in tradition, as seen most strikingly in the importance afforded to *exempla* and *mores maiorum* (that is, 'instances of exemplary conduct and ancestral customs'). His cheeky challenge to see fictions as facts (and the ensuing question of belief) accompanies Ovid's characters (and his readers) throughout the poem, including the set

---

23 Little (1970) 347.
24 Feeney (1991) 229 with reference to earlier scholarship in n. 152.

text, where Pentheus refuses to believe the cautionary tale of Bacchus' transformation of the Tyrrhenian pirates into dolphins — with fatal consequences.

The situation is further complicated by the fact that some of the narrative material is historical. The reader must remain ever alert to the programmatic opening declaration that the *Metamorphoses* will proceed chronologically from the birth of the universe to the poet's own times (*Met.* 1.3–4, cited and discussed above). Ovid is, in other words, combining myth *and* history, with the latter coming to the fore in the final books, which document the rise of Rome. The end of the *Metamorphoses* celebrates the ascendancy of Rome to world-empire: *terra sub Augusto est* ('the world lies under Augustus', 15.860) observes Ovid laconically of the comprehensive sway of Roman rule in his own day (15.876–77). This is presented as a culminating moment in world history.

The combination of myth and history was, of course, hardly new. The Hebrew Bible, to name just one precedent, began in the mythological realm with Genesis, proceeded to the Garden of Eden, Adam and Eve, the deluge, and so on before moving on to more overtly historical material. And whereas this was long considered (and in some quarters still is considered) a historical document throughout, Ovid, as we have seen, is more willing to probe the implausibility of the traditional mythological tales that he has placed side-by-side with historical material. But readers of the *Metamorphoses* should be wary of placing too much stock in the dichotomy of myth and history. From an ideological perspective, the real issue is less the truth-value of specific events narrated in the epic, than the way they make sense of — and shape perceptions of — the world. The subtle anticipations of Roman geopolitical domination in Ovid's early books are scarcely less significant for being embedded in Greek mythology. A case in point arises in the opening book, where Jupiter summons all the gods in assembly in reaction to perceived human depravity, as epitomized in the barbarous conduct of Lycaon. Here, it would appear, Ovid puts on display his generic *bona fides*: any ancient epic worthy of the name could hardly omit a *concilium deorum*. From Homer onwards an assembly of the gods had been an almost compulsory ingredient of the genre.[25] But for all the seeming conventionality of his

---

25 Lee (1953) on *Met.* 1.167ff., citing Hom. *Il.* 8.1ff., 20.1 ff.; *Od.* 1.26ff., 5.1ff; Enn. *Ann.* 51–55 Sk; *Aen.* 10.1ff. One could add Lucilius, who, in his *Satires*, also featured a

set-up, Ovid provides a decidedly eccentric rendition of the type-scene. The oddities begin with a striking account of the summoned divinities hastening along the Milky Way to the royal abode of Jupiter:

> Est via sublimis, caelo manifesta sereno;
> lactea nomen habet, candore notabilis ipso.
> hac iter est superis ad magni tecta Tonantis
> regalemque domum: dextra laevaque deorum
> atria nobilium valvis celebrantur apertis.
> plebs habitat diversa loca: hac parte potentes
> caelicolae clarique suos posuere penates;
> hic locus est, quem, si verbis audacia detur,
> haud timeam magni dixisse Palatia caeli.
> (*Met*. 1.168–76)

> There is a highway, easily seen when the sky is clear. It is called the Milky Way, famed for its shining whiteness. By this way the gods come to the halls and royal dwelling of the mighty Thunderer. On either side the palaces of the gods of higher rank are thronged with guests through folding-doors flung wide. The lesser gods dwell apart from these. In this neighbourhood the illustrious and mighty heaven-dwellers have placed their household gods. This is the place which, if I made bold to say it, I would not fear to call the Palatine of high heaven.

In these lines, Ovid describes a celestial Rome. Jupiter's abode, the palace of the great ruler, is situated on a heavenly Palatine; the Milky Way is like the *Sacer Clivus* which led from the *Via Sacra* to the Palatine Hill in Rome, where of course Augustus lived. As with the Romans, the gods are divided into nobles and plebeians; the former have magnificent and well-situated abodes, complete with *atria* teeming with *clientes*; the latter must make do with more humble and obscure quarters. More strikingly, celestial patricians and plebs alike have their *penates* (household gods).[26] And the analogies don't end there. The assembly that meets in Jupiter's palace follows procedures that are recognizably those of the

---

concilium deorum ('Council of the Gods'), at which an individual called Lupus (Latin for 'wolf' — a distant intertextual relative of Ovid's Lycaon, surely) was put on trial. Ovid here follows the example of Homer's *Odyssey* and Ennius' *Annales* in placing his *concilium deorum* at the beginning of his narrative.

26   Lee (1953) on *Met*. 1.167ff.

Roman Senate.[27] Indeed, 'the correspondence with Augustan Rome is particularly close at this point, since we know that Augustus held Senate meetings in the library attached to his temple of Apollo on the Palatine, which was itself intricately linked with his residence'.[28]

The comical audacity of this sequence has elicited reams of commentary. Since Homer, the traditional epic practice was to model divine existence on human analogy, but to attribute household gods (*penates*) to the Olympian gods themselves is humorously to extend and expose the convention.[29] At the same time, though, Ovid achieves a more profound effect, for the episode hints at a kind of politico-historical telos: the Olympian political structures and those of contemporary Rome are in homology. For all the humorous touches — and we certainly do not wish to deny them — Ovid has inscribed Augustan Rome into the heavens. Since Jupiter's rule is to be eternal, there is an implication, by association, of a corresponding political-historical closure in human affairs. From the very beginning, then, the disconcerting thematic implications of potentially endless metamorphosis — which Pythagoras will assert as axiomatic for geopolitical affairs — are being countered or 'contained' with respect to *Roma aeterna*. Heaven has stabilized — the final challenges to the Jovian cosmos, those of giants and their like, are now 'in the books' — and will suffer no further political upheavals of significance. An equivalent state of affairs is subsequently to be achieved on the terrestrial level. The human realm will, over the course of Ovid's narrative, evolve into the Jovian paradigm — which is already, by the comic solipsism just discussed, the Roman paradigm. The majestic declaration in the final book *terra sub Augusto est* (15.860) neatly signals that the *princeps* has achieved the Jovian analogy; this is the language of divine power, which is to say, the earth being 'beneath' Augustus makes both his power and figurative vantage point god-like.[30]

---

27 Ginsberg (1989) 228.
28 Feeney (1991) 199, citing Suet. *Aug.* 29.3 and the discussion of Thompson (1981).
29 The notion of *penates* makes a suggestive appearance in the set text as well: see Comm. on 538–40.
30 Which is not, of course, to deny the rich ironies inherent in Ovid's parallelism between Jupiter and Augustus: see e.g. Johnson (1970), 146. John Henderson offers some characteristically trenchant observations here: 'The ugly indiscriminate speciescide perpetrated by the Almighty is ... just the first modelling of the exercise of autocratic power in Ovid's poem: the set text will picture one young monarch among the horde populating mythland attempting to play the tough guy. In the Julio-Claudian Rome of the Caesars, myths were becoming (a way to get) real, all over again'.

In writing a universal history, its eccentric narrative voice and hexametric form notwithstanding, Ovid is performing a peculiarly Roman operation. For some scholars, indeed, history first became universal in Roman times; on this view it was the creation of the Roman Empire that allowed history to become 'global' in a geographical sense.[31] This version of history adopted more or less consciously an ethnocentric or 'Romanocentric' perspective that freely incorporated mythical elements in explaining Roman supremacy in terms of both surpassing *virtus* (making the Romans superior imperialists) and surpassing *pietas* (guaranteeing them the privileged support of the gods).

Together, the record of supernatural powers and transformed human beings that the *Metamorphoses* chronicles adds up to a unique combination of 'natural' and 'universal' history, in which cosmos and culture evolve together and eventually (in the form of a Roman civilization that has acquired global reach under Augustus) coincide.

3d. Anthropological Epic

To use the theme of metamorphosis as the basis for a universal history did not just strain, it shattered prevailing generic norms. From Homer to Virgil, the stuff of epic was war and adventure, heroes and their deeds; in Ovid, it is — a fictitious phenomenon.[32] A related curiosity arises over the question of protagonist. In the other epics of our tabular comparison (see above, §3a), it is a simple matter to identify the main character or characters.[33] That is decidedly not the case in the *Metamorphoses*: Ovid's frequently un-heroic personnel changes from one episode to the next, to the point that some scholars have suggested that the hero of the poem is the poet himself — the master-narrator who holds (and thinks) everything together and, in so doing, performs a deed worthy of immortality.[34] There is, to be sure, much to be gained from focusing on the 'composition myth' in this way, but it does not rule out pinpointing

---

31 Ingelbert (2014) 256.
32 That Ovid chose to write, for the most part, fiction did not prevent him from presenting his fictions as facts: see the previous section on 'universal history'.
33 Ennius' *Annals* features several main characters, and a case could be made for Apollonius Rhodius' *Argonautica* featuring a collective protagonist, i.e. the Argonauts as a group.
34 For this approach to the poem, see Solodow (1988) 37–55, also discussed at Comm. on 568–69.

a protagonist on the level of plot as well. As Ernst Schmidt has argued, a plausible candidate for this designation is 'the human being'.[35]

There are some difficulties with this suggestion (one might well ask: what about the gods?); but all in all the thesis that humanity *as such* takes centre-stage in the *Metamorphoses* is attractive and compelling. At its core, the poem offers a sustained meditation on what it is to be human within a broader cosmic setting shaped by supernatural agents and explores the potential of our species for good and for evil. These concerns (one could label them 'anthropological') are set up by the various forms of anthropogenesis ('accounts of the origins of humanity') in the early episodes, which trace our beginnings to such diverse material as earth and a divine spark, stones cast by mortal hands, and the blood of slain giants. From an ethical point of view, the outcomes are as diverse as the material: Ovid explores a wide gamut of possibilities, covering the full range from quasi-divine and ethically impeccable human beings (witness the blissful rectitude of the golden age at 1.83–112) to bestial and blasphemous (the version of our species that descended from the blood of giants, described at 1.156–62). In the Deucalion and Pyrrha story (a 'pagan' variant on the tale of Noah's ark), Ovid makes the aetiological connection between the kind of material from which humanity is manufactured and our respective qualities explicit: originating from stones, 'we are hence a hard race, experienced in toil, and so giving testimony to the source of our birth' (*inde genus durum sumus experiensque laborum | et documenta damus, qua simus origine nati*, 1.414–15). As the reader proceeds through the poem, encounters with such atrocious human beings as Tereus or such admirable individuals as Baucis and Philemon serve as vivid reminders that accursed and salvific elements are equally part of our DNA. A 'rhetoric of origins' also plays an important role in the set text: Pentheus tries to rally the citizens of Thebes against Bacchus and his entourage by reminding them of their descent from the teeth of the dragon of Mars (3.543–45) — a belated anthropogenesis on a local scale that re-enacts the opening theme at a later stage of cosmic history.

In line with both Ovid's elegiac past and his 'anthropological' interest in humanity, the *Metamorphoses* is chock-full of sex and

---

35 Schmidt (1991).

gender issues — though readers will have to venture beyond the set text to discover this: the chosen episode is relatively free from erotic entanglements. In fact, Ovid has in many ways 'de-eroticized' earlier versions of the Pentheus-myth, such as the one we find in Euripides' *Bacchae*, which features cross-dressing, prurient interest in orgiastic sexuality, and voyeurism. But browse around a bit before or after the set text and you'll see that Ovid never departs for long from erotic subject matter. You'll find that, as discussed below (§5b-i), the sober figure of the blind seer Tiresias who introduces the Pentheus-episode first features in the poem as a divinely certified 'sexpert' on male and female orgasms. More generally, sex and gender are such pervasive preoccupations that one scholar has plausibly characterized the *Metamorphoses* as a 'hymn to Venus'.[36]

3e. A Reader's Digest of Greek and Latin Literature

In the process of laying out a vast body of mythic tales, both well known and recondite, Ovid's *Metamorphoses* produces something like a 'reader's digest' of Greek and Latin literature. Whichever authors came before him — Homer, Euripides, Callimachus, Apollonius Rhodius, Theocritus, Ennius, Lucretius, Catullus, Virgil, you name them — he worked their texts into his own, often with a hilarious spin or a polemic edge. In Ovid, the literary heritage of Greece and Rome begins to swing. His poetics — his peculiar way of writing poetry — is as transformative as his choice of subject matter. In the *Metamorphoses*, one intertextual joke chases the next as Ovid puts his predecessors into place — turning them into inferior forerunners or footnotes to his own epic mischief. To appreciate this dimension of his poem requires knowledge of the earlier literature that Ovid engages with. In the set text, Ovid's partners in dialogue include, but are by no means limited to, Homer, the author of the *Homeric Hymn to Dionysus*, Euripides, pseudo-Theocritus, Pacuvius (a 2nd-century BCE Roman tragic playwright whose work survives only in scant fragments), and Virgil. Even this partial enumeration, consisting as it does of authors and texts that have come down to us more or less intact as well as those that have all but vanished, points to

---

36   Barchiesi (1999).

an occupational hazard for anyone interested in literary dialogue: so much ancient literature that Ovid and his readers would have known intimately is lost to us. Literary critics (including the present writers: see below, §5a) will inevitably tend to stress the intertextual relationships between texts that have best survived the accidents of transmission (in our case: the *Odyssey*, Euripides' *Bacchae*, the *Homeric Hymn to Dionysus*, the pseudo-Theocritean *Idyll* 26, and Virgil's *Aeneid*). So it is worth recalling that, as far as, say, tragic plays about Bacchus and Pentheus are concerned, Ovid would have had at his disposal not only Euripides' *Bacchae*, but a number of other scripts that are lost to us or have only survived in bits and pieces, notably Pacuvius' *Pentheus*. This does not invalidate the exercise of comparing Euripides and Ovid — far from it. Even if it is salutary to bear in mind that we are almost certainly seeing only part of the full network of intertextual relationships, we should take solace from the fact that, as John Henderson points out, 'plenty of ancient Roman readers were in the same boat as us: Ovid catered for all levels, from newcomers to classical studies to impossibly learned old-stagers. And the main point remains, that, just as verse form always brings change to a tale, so too a myth can never be told in anything but a new version — stories forever mutate'.

The 'reader's digest' effect of the *Metamorphoses* works in tandem with its cosmic scope, totalizing chronology and encyclopaedic ambition to endow it with a unique sense of comprehensiveness. More fundamentally still, Ovid's epic codified and preserved for evermore one of antiquity's earliest and most important ways of making sense of the universe: myth. As a result, it has become one of the most influential classics of all time: instances of reception are legion, as countless works of art that engage with the mythic heritage of antiquity found their ultimate inspiration in Ovid's poetry. The *Metamorphoses* has been called 'the Bible of artists and painters' and 'one of the cornerstones of Western culture'.[37] It is virtually impossible to walk into any museum of note without encountering artworks that rehearse Ovidian themes; and his influence on authors, not least those of the first rank — from Dante to Petrarch, from Shakespeare to Milton — is equally pervasive.[38]

---

37 Brown (1999) 1.
38 For specific examples in the set text, see Comm. on 568–71 (Shakespeare) and 664–65 (Seneca); 670–72 (Marlowe).

'Bible' and 'cornerstone', though, with their implications of ponderous gravity and paradigmatic authority, are rather odd metaphors to apply to Ovid's epic: they capture its importance through the ages, but unwittingly invert why the *Metamorphoses* has continued to resonate with so many creative geniuses (as well as the average reader). After all, Ovid's intense exploration of erotic experience in all its polymorphous diversity and his vigorous celebration of transformative fluidity (or, indeed, eternal flux) in both nature and culture make of the poem a veritable counter-Bible, offering a decidedly unorthodox vision of the universe and its inhabitants.

It is a fundamental principle of narration, as John Henderson reminds us, that 'a tale tells on its teller — all these stories came into Ovid's mind-and-repertoire, and these are his versions, so "about" Ovid'. And (he adds) 'tales mean to have designs on those on the receiving-end, and now that includes us, and that means you. There are many reasons why the *Metamorphoses* (plural) keep bulldozing their way through world culture, but this (singular) is what counts the most. As Horace put it: *de te fabula narratur*'.[39]

---

39 For the cautionary tale of how some classical students took the Euripidean Bacchus all too close to heart, see Donna Tartt's *The Secret History*.

4. Ovid's Theban Narrative

While some themes can be encountered virtually anywhere in the *Metamorphoses*, others cluster in certain parts and generate a distinctive narrative ethos. The first two books, for instance, have attracted the label 'Divine Comedy': they feature various sexual adventures of the Olympian gods — mostly rapes of mortal women. All cry out for a feminist critique, even if — or, better, because — the narrative tone remains fairly light throughout. With the beginning of Book 3, Ovid's literary universe takes on a darker complexion. The first protagonist of the book is the Phoenician prince Cadmus, whose appearance is a carry-over from the concluding rape/abduction tale of the previous book. At the behest of his father Agenor, Cadmus attempts to track down his sister Europa, whom Jupiter had carried off at the end of Book 2 — a veritable mission impossible. Unsuccessful in his search and forbidden by his father to return home empty-handed, Cadmus heads into voluntary exile. His wanderings bring him to Boeotia where he founds Thebes, a city in which tragic and ultimately hellish energies are unleashed.[40]

Considered from the perspective of the ancient literary tradition, it is hardly coincidental that Ovid's epic takes a 'tragic' turn as it turns to Theban myth. For in Attic drama, as Froma Zeitlin has demonstrated in a seminal essay, 'Thebes consistently supplies the radical tragic terrain where there can be no escape from the tragic in the resolution of conflict or in the institutional provision of a civic future beyond the world of the play'.[41] The city indeed epitomizes what Greek tragedy is all about. Judging from the surviving scripts of Athenian playwrights, daily life in ancient Thebes featured incessant civil strife, repeated

---

40 See Comm. on 513–14 for a fuller account of these preliminaries.
41 Zeitlin (1990) 131.

autochthonous disaster, miscellaneous forms of sexual perversion (rape, sodomy, incest), and even the occasional human dismemberment (*sparagmos*) — in short, the entire range of transgressions that upset the normal order of things. To quote Zeitlin again: 'Thebes, we might say, is the quintessential "other scene", as Oedipus is the paradigm of tragic man and Dionysus is the god of the theatre. There Athens acts out questions crucial to the polis, the self, the family, and society, but there they are displaced upon a city that is imagined as the mirror opposite of Athens'.[42] Ovid's version of Thebes fully lives up to the anticipation of calamity evoked by the city's longstanding tragic associations. As the fates of Cadmus and Harmonia, Actaeon, Semele, Narcissus, Pentheus, and Ino and Athamas show, the myths that Ovid here incorporates into his epic world have lost none of the sinister and fateful character that they had acquired on the tragic stage. These *dramatis personae* embark once more on a literary destiny within a tragic dystopia that inexorably leads them to their doom.

There is, indeed, a striking coherence to *Met.* 3.1–4.603, the narrative stretch that begins with Cadmus' exile and ends with his and his wife Harmonia's transformation into snakes (stories concerning the city's founder and his offspring are in *italics*):

3.1–137	*Foundation: Cadmus, his companions, the dragon of Mars, the Spartoi*
3.138–252	*Actaeon, son of Autonoe*
3.253–315	*Semele (birth of Bacchus)*
3.316–38	Teiresias (and his sex-changes)
3.339–510	Echo and Narcissus
3.511–733	*Pentheus, son of Agave* (including the inset tale of *Bacchus and the Tyrrhenian sailors*)
4.1–415	The daughters of Minyas and *Bacchus*
4.55–388	Tales of the Minyeides:
	4.55–166 Pyramus and Thisbe
	4.169–270 The Love Affairs of the Sun
	4.276–388 Salmacis and Hermaphroditus

---

42 Zeitlin (1990) 144.

4.416–562   *Ino and Athamas with Learchus and Melicertes*
4.563–603   *Cadmus & Harmonia: exile and transformation into snakes*

Met. 3.1–4.603 has been termed Ovid's *Thebaid*, insofar as it is the city of Thebes (and its environs) that provides a unifying thematic and topographical focus. Even when the narrative veers off — as in the case of Tiresias, Echo and Narcissus, and the daughters of Minyas (the 'Minyeides') — Thebes remains an important point of reference. So, for example, the Minyeides, who reside in the near-by city of Orchomenos, while in many ways forming a self-contained narrative unit within Ovid's *Thebaid*, are unable to escape the tragic forces that emanate from Thebes. Not unlike Pentheus, they fall victim to the powers of Bacchus, whom they unwisely choose to disregard.

Clearly, then, *Thebaid* is an appropriate label for *Met.* 3.1–4.603; no less appropriate, though, would be *Cadmeid* ('an epic poem about Cadmus and his offspring'), inasmuch as Ovid chronicles the fates of Cadmus and Harmonia, along with their four daughters and five grandsons:

Cadmus and Harmonia				
Daughters	Autonoe	Semele	Agave	Ino
Grandsons	Actaeon	Bacchus (father: Jupiter)	Pentheus (father: Echion)	Learchus and Melicertes (father: Athamas)

Twice Cadmus himself comes into focus: his heroics get the Theban narrative going at the beginning of Book 3; and his despairing exit from the city together with his wife and the transformation of the couple into snakes brings this particular narrative unit to a close. This 'frame' is worth a more detailed look since it defines the thematic terms for the episodes it encloses, including the set text.

The opening sequence treats events up to the foundation of the city: Cadmus' arrival in Boeotia, the slaughter of his companions by the dragon of Mars, Cadmus' revenge-killing of the beast, his sowing of its teeth at the behest of a divine voice, the rise of the Spartoi and their mutual slaughter, which leaves only a handful of survivors — Thebes' citizen population.[43] Ovid skips over the actual foundation (and the wedding of Cadmus and Harmonia), restricting himself to what amounts to a tragic prologue for the subsequent narrative:

> Iam stabant Thebae, poteras iam, Cadme, videri
> exilio felix: soceri tibi Marsque Venusque
> contigerant; huc adde genus de coniuge tanta,
> tot natos natasque et, pignora cara, nepotes,
> hos quoque iam iuvenes; sed scilicet ultima semper
> exspectanda dies hominis, dicique beatus
> ante obitum nemo supremaque funera debet.
> Prima nepos inter tot res tibi, Cadme, secundas
> causa fuit luctus ...
> (*Met.* 3.131–39)

> And now Thebes stood; now you could seem, Cadmus, a happy man even in exile. Mars and Venus had become your parents-in-law; add to this children of so distinguished a wife, so many sons and daughters and, pledges of your love, grandchildren, these too now at the brink of manhood. But of course man's last day must ever be awaited and no-one ought to be called happy before his death and funeral rites. Among such favourable circumstances, Cadmus, the first cause of grief was one of your grandsons ...

After recounting the wretched fates of Cadmus' children and grandchildren, Ovid returns to the royal couple: his Theban history ends with Cadmus and Harmonia heading off into self-imposed exile and eventually transforming into snakes (*Met.* 4.563–603). Cadmus himself prays for this metamorphosis as he recalls how it all began, thus bringing the narrative full circle:

> Nescit Agenorides natam parvumque nepotem
> aequoris esse deos; luctu serieque malorum
> victus et ostentis, quae plurima viderat, exit
> conditor urbe sua, tamquam fortuna locorum,
> non sua se premeret, longisque erroribus actus
> contigit Illyricos profuga cum coniuge fines.
> iamque malis annisque graves dum prima retractant

---

43 For details of these developments, see Comm. on 513–14.

fata domus releguntque suos sermone labores,
'num sacer ille mea traiectus cuspide serpens'
Cadmus ait 'fuerat, tum cum Sidone profectus
vipereos sparsi per humum, nova semina, dentes?
quem si cura deum tam certa vindicat ira,
ipse precor serpens in longam porrigar alvum'.
dixit, et ut serpens in longam tenditur alvum.
(*Met.* 4.563–76)

Cadmus was unaware that his daughter (Ino) and little grandson (Melicertes) had been changed to gods of the sea. Overcome with grief and the sequence of calamities and because of the many portents he had seen, the founding father left his city, as if the fortune of the site rather than his own were oppressing him. Driven on through long wanderings, at last the exile and his wife reached the borders of Illyria. At that point, heavy with woes and years, while they went over the early calamities of their house and their own troubles in conversation, Cadmus said: 'Was that a sacred serpent which my spear transfixed back when, recently departed from Sidon, I scattered his teeth, a novel type of seed, on to the earth? If the care of the gods is avenging him with such unerring wrath, I pray that I, too be stretched into snaky form as a serpent'. And as he spoke he was stretched into a snaky form as a serpent ...

A nexus of verbal correspondences correlates the beginning and end of Ovid's *Cadmeid*. At 3.131–42, Cadmus' apparent good fortune is quantified via his abundant progeny: he might seem enviable, the poet portentously observes, in view of his numerous daughters (*natas*), sons (*natos*), and grandchildren (*nepotes*). This initial plurality contrasts sharply with the singulars of the phrase *natam parvumque nepotem* at 4.563. The words refer to Cadmus' daughter Ino and grandson Melicertes, the only members of his family not yet visited by catastrophe — though Cadmus believes himself to have just witnessed their hellish destruction as well. For him they are the final link in the long chain of misfortunes which began with the gruesome demise of Actaeon (*prima ... causa fuit luctus*, 3.138–39), continued through Book 3 (including Pentheus) and came to its bitter end with the lethal madness of Ino and her husband, recounted at 4.481–542. It is precisely this long sequence of dreadful calamities (*luctu serieque malorum*, 4.564) which drives Cadmus from the city that he himself founded (*exit | conditor urbe sua*, 4.565–66).

We thus start and end with Cadmus in exile; but the two exiles could hardly be more different. At the beginning of Book 3 Cadmus is in his prime, about to perform the deeds which brought him heroic renown, i.e. the killing of the dragon of Mars and the founding of Thebes. In Book 4, by contrast, we encounter a man broken down by age and suffering who is desperately trying to come to terms with the series of misfortunes that has plagued his family. Ovid underscores the bleak transformation of Cadmus from the active protagonist of Book 3 into the despairing and gloomy figure we meet in Book 4 through pointed verbal play. Most strikingly, in assuming the shape of his erstwhile victim Cadmus fulfils the prophecy uttered immediately after his triumphant slaying of Mars' serpent:

> Dum spatium victor victi considerat hostis,
> vox subito audita est; neque erat cognoscere promptum,
> unde, sed audita est: 'quid, Agenore nate, peremptum
> serpentem spectas? et tu spectabere serpens'.
> (*Met.* 3.95–98)

> While the victor surveys the size of his vanquished foe, suddenly a voice is heard; it was impossible to recognize from where, but it was heard: 'Why, son of Agenor, do you gaze upon the serpent you killed? You too will be gazed upon as serpent'.

Through its startling prediction, the unattributed voice implicitly proclaims the dreadful law that in a tragic universe each source of good fortune contains the seeds of its own undoing. Like the serpent in this early scene, at 4.565 Cadmus is described as defeated (*victus*). In the later passage, moreover, Cadmus has, through bitter experience, come to understand the typically Theban proximity of victory and disaster at which Ovid already signalled, both overtly through the prophecy of Cadmus' ultimate transformation into the very shape of his conquered enemy, and more subtly through the collocation of *victor* and *victi* at 3.95. Cadmus' final realization that he killed a sacred beast closes down Ovid's Theban narrative by returning it to the point at which it all began. In a traumatic reversal, the very objects that once promised a prosperous future for Thebes, the teeth of the dragon — compare 3.103 *vipereos dentes, populi incrementa futuri* with 4.571–73, where Cadmus ponders the possibility that the *vipereos dentes* he used come from a sacred beast — in hindsight turn out to bear within them the burden of a curse that was bound to blight developments from the outset. Cadmus' wish to be transformed into a serpent arises from the painful realization that only a metamorphic 'return' to the origin of his city will put an end to his agony: it is a culminating illustration of the fact that Thebes is ever unable to differentiate itself from its troubled beginnings.[44]

In the course of the narrative arch that Ovid traces in his Theban history, we thus get a tragic conflation of human and beast and an equally tragic inversion of *victor* ('conqueror') and *victus* ('conquered') as Cadmus rises from a condition of exile to become king of his own city, and progenitor of a prosperous family, before being reduced again to his original status as a childless outcast. Yet the transformation of Cadmus into a snake might also elicit the cleansing laughter of a Satyr play after a day of tragic performances.[45] In this respect also it might be seen as a fitting Ovidian conclusion to the Theban saga. As Cadmus' wish to assume the shape of a dragon is incrementally realized, his horrified wife bemoans his vanishing human features and, more importantly, the unbearable zoomorphic divide that now sunders the couple (*Met.* 4.576–94). No sooner said than remedied: she promptly undergoes the same metamorphosis and joins her husband on the ground. While at the end of Euripides' *Bacchae*, the prophetic anticipation of Cadmus' transformation into a dragon sets up new horrors since he is to lead a foreign army against the Greeks (*Bacch.* 1330–43), Ovid's snakified Cadmus and Harmonia are truly peaceful creatures (cf. 4.602–03). In the *Metamorphoses* at least, the tragic energy of Thebes is spent.[46]

---

44 See again Zeitlin (1990) *passim*.
45 See Bömer (1976), 183 for the possibility that Ovid constructed the scene with actual Satyr plays in mind.
46 Cadmus' grandson Bacchus, however, provides the jumping-off point for the next mythic nucleus, centred on Perseus (4.604–10); and neither Bacchus nor 'Cadmean' Thebes will ever wholly recede from the background: they are on the map, permanent stock, and Ovid revisits Theban myths elsewhere in the *Metamorphoses*, notably in Book 6 (with the tale of Niobe and her sons and daughters), Book 9 (the Hercules saga) and in Book 13 with the daughter of Anius and the Theban cup that travels on to Rome. As John Henderson puts it, 'on the overarching grand scale, the *Metamorphoses* diagrams the formulaic triangulation of (tragically self-obliterating) Thebes vs. (tragically re-generating) Troy vs. (redemptively renaissant and self-perpetuating) ROME'.

5. The Set Text: Pentheus and Bacchus

It will be clear from our discussion so far that the Pentheus episode lies at the heart of Ovid's Theban narrative in a number of important respects. The setting for this episode is the city of Thebes, which, as we have seen, was founded by Cadmus, after his search for his abducted sister Europa proved fruitless.[47] Cadmus is now an old man, and has abdicated the throne of his city in favour of his grandson Pentheus. Early in the reign of the young king, a new religious cult sweeps in from the East, that of the god Bacchus (Greek Dionysus), son of the god Jupiter and the Theban princess Semele (their explosive affair and Bacchus' unusual birth were described earlier in Book 3, at 253–315). While nearly all Thebans welcome the new cult, Pentheus is obstinate in his scepticism and resistance, an attitude that leads to his doom.

5a. Sources and Intertexts

The story of Pentheus and Bacchus was well established long before Ovid's day. The myth was a popular subject with writers and artists alike, and is famously the subject of the *Bacchae*, a tragedy by the 5th-century BCE Athenian playwright Euripides. This tragedy was, as far as we can tell, Ovid's most important source and model.[48]

---

47 See Comm. on 513–14 for a fuller account of these preliminaries.
48 It needs to be borne in mind, though, that, as discussed earlier (§3a), the vicissitudes of textual survival do not allow absolute certainty on this point. Many other ancient tragedians, both Greek and Roman, wrote plays about the confrontation of Pentheus and Bacchus; but only Euripides' has survived in full.

Euripides begins his play with Bacchus' arrival at Thebes and a detailed exposition of his world, carefully elaborated in the prologue (1–63, spoken by the god himself) and the chorus upon their entry onto the stage (64–169, sung by Lydian women). The enthusiastic celebration of the Maenads in particular introduces the entire range of imagery and motifs commonly associated with Bacchic frenzy, highlighting notions of excess and boundary transgression.[49] In the subsequent scenes, Euripides proceeds to delineate the character of Pentheus, who flatly denies Bacchus' divinity and rejects his worship, and so resents all the more the enthusiastic reception of the god and his cult by the Theban populace. Euripides places particular emphasis on the Theban king's obsession with the sexual license he associates with the worship of Bacchus.[50] The story continues with Pentheus giving orders to his henchmen to capture Bacchus, who is presently brought on stage (*Bacch.* 432–42). In the initial interview Bacchus conceals his true identity, claiming merely to be one of the followers of the new deity, and he remains incognito until his final epiphany. His exchanges with Pentheus culminate in the key scene in which the god convinces Pentheus to cross-dress as a woman so he can spy on the Maenads on Mount Cithaeron — a grave offense given that their rites were both secret and an exclusively female matter. This leads to the grim denouement, in which Bacchus distorts the perception of Pentheus' mother Agave and her sisters, as well as the other Maenads, so that they misrecognize the disguised king as a wild beast which, in accordance with Bacchic rites, they proceed to tear limb from limb with their bare hands. Euripides' gruesome and haunting account of Pentheus' dismemberment comes in the form of a messenger's speech:

> 'Then were a thousand hands laid on the fir tree [sc. in which Pentheus was perched], and from the ground they tore it up, while he from his seat aloft came tumbling to the ground with lamentations long and loud; for well he knew his hour was come. His mother first, a priestess for the occasion, began the bloody deed and fell upon him; whereon he tore the snood from his hair, that hapless Agave might recognize and spare him, crying as he touched her cheek, "O mother! it is I, your own son Pentheus, the child you bore in Echion's halls; have pity on me, mother

---

49 See Otto (1933) on Dionysiac religion in general and Segal (1982) on Euripides' *Bacchae*.
50 Cf. Seidensticker (1972) 42.

5. The Set Text: Pentheus and Bacchus

dear! oh! do not for any sin of mine slay your own son". But she, the while, with foaming mouth and wildly rolling eyes, bereft of reason as she was, heeded him not; for the god possessed her. And she caught his left hand in her grip, and planting her foot upon her victim's trunk she tore the shoulder from its socket, not of her own strength, but the god made it an easy task to her hands; and Ino set to work upon the other side, rending the flesh with Autonoe and all the eager host of Bacchanals; and one united cry arose, the victim's groans while yet he breathed, and their triumphant shouts. One would make an arm her prey, another a foot with the sandal on it; and his ribs were stripped of flesh by their rending nails; and each one with blood-dabbled hands was tossing Pentheus' limbs about. Scattered lies his corpse, part beneath the rugged rocks, and part amid the deep dark woods, no easy task to find; but his mother has made his poor head her own, and fixing it upon the point of a thyrsus, as if it were a mountain lion's, she bears it through the midst of Cithaeron, having left her sisters with the Maenads at their rites. And she is entering these walls exulting in her hunting fraught with woe, acclaiming Bacchus her fellow-hunter who had helped her to triumph in a chase, where her only prize was tears'. (Eur. *Bacch.* 1109–47)

This is the 'classic' account of Pentheus' demise, but here as elsewhere, Ovid is in literary dialogue with multiple predecessors. In certain respects his version of the horrific event bears closer resemblance to that of a poem included (probably wrongly) in the Theocritean corpus as *Idyll* 26. This deals with the initiation of a young boy into the mysteries of Dionysus, with the father giving the following account of Pentheus' death and dismemberment:

[1] Ino, Autonoe and white-cheeked Agave, themselves three in number, led three groups of worshippers to the mountain. Some of them cut wild greenery from the densely growing oak trees, living ivy and asphodel that grows above ground, and made up twelve altars in a pure meadow, three to Semele and nine to Dionysus. Taking from their box the sacred objects made with care, they laid them reverently on the altars of freshly gathered foliage, just as Dionysus himself had taught them, and just as he preferred.

[10] Pentheus observed everything from a high rock, hidden in a mastic bush, a plant that grew in those parts. Autonoe, the first to see him, gave a dreadful yell and with a sudden movement kicked over the sacred objects of frenzied Bacchus, which the profane may not see. She became frenzied herself, and at once the others too became frenzied. Pentheus

fled in terror and they pursued him, hitching up their robes into their belts, knee-high. Pentheus spoke: 'What do you want, women?' Autonoe spoke: 'You will know soon enough, and before we tell you'. The mother gave a roar like a lioness with cubs as she carried off her son's head; Ino tore off his great shoulder, shoulder-blade and all, by setting her foot on his stomach; and Autonoe set to work in the same way. The other women butchered what was left and returned to Thebes all smeared with blood, bearing back from the mountain not Pentheus (Πενθῆα), but lamentation (πένθημα).

[27] This is no concern of mine, nor should anyone else care about an enemy of Dionysus, even if he suffered a worse fate than this, even if he were nine years old, or just embarking on his teeth. May I myself act piously, and may my actions please the pious. The eagle gained honour in this way from Zeus who bears the aegis. It is to children of the pious, not to those of the impious, that good things come.

[35] Farewell to mighty Dionysus, for whom on snowy Dracanus mighty Zeus opened up his own great thigh and placed him inside. Farewell, too, to beautiful Semele and her sisters, daughters of Cadmus, much admired by women of that time, who carried out this deed impelled by Dionysus, so that they are not to be blamed. Let no one criticize the actions of the gods. ([Theoc.] *Id.* 26)

All three texts share the same basic plot; but there are noteworthy variations on the level of detail. In Euripides and Ovid, for instance, Pentheus spies upon the maenads from a tree; in the Theocritean *Idyll*, by contrast, he is poised on a prominent rock. And whereas in Euripides Agave initiates the slaughter, in the *Idyll* and Ovid it is Agave's sister (and Pentheus' aunt) Autonoe. If Ovid conforms closely to Euripides' tragedy in narrative outline, then, there are clearly departures that look to other texts or versions.

Ovid's most striking innovation *vis-à-vis* Euripides has to do with the captive arrested by Pentheus' henchmen. This figure has a precedent in the *Bacchae*, but he is never explicitly identified as Bacchus-in-disguise, as he is in the earlier text. Indeed, he gives his name as Acoetes and provides a comparatively detailed autobiography that begins by describing his rise from the lowly profession of fisherman to that of helmsman (more on this in the following section). More crucially still, in explaining how he became a follower of the god, he tells the tale of how a group of wicked Tyrrhenian sailors, his erstwhile shipmates, were transformed into dolphins by Bacchus. This inset tale conveniently supplies the episode with the requisite metamorphosis (which was lacking in the narrative Ovid inherited from Euripides). It also constitutes a radical — and, it should be added, ingenious — departure from the tragic model.

Fig. 1 The Tyrrhenian Pirates change into dolphins (drawing after a black-figure vase, 6th/5th century BCE, Museum of Art, Toledo).

The inset narrative is, in essence, an extended version of a *Homeric Hymn to Dionysus*.[51] More specifically, it is a rendition of the longest of three hymns honouring Dionysus in a collection of some thirty such compositions, all anonymous, known as the *Homeric Hymns*. These Greek hexametric hymns vary in length from a handful of verses to several hundred lines. Each celebrates an individual deity. The collection's titular epithet *Homeric* is misleading, as the Hymns do not share authorship with the *Iliad* or *Odyssey* (nor, for that matter, with each other in most cases, for they are not the work of a single hand).[52] Here is the *Hymn* in question:

> [1] I will tell of Dionysus, the son of glorious Semele, how he appeared on a jutting headland by the shore of the fruitless sea, seeming like a stripling in the first flush of manhood: his rich, dark hair was waving about him, and on his strong shoulders he wore a purple robe. Presently there came swiftly over the sparkling sea Etruscan pirates on a well-decked ship — a miserable doom led them on. When they saw him they made signs to one another and sprang out quickly, and seizing him straightway, put him on board their ship exultingly; for they thought

---

51 Other versions or references to the tale include Apollod. 3.5.3; Prop. 3.17.25; Sen. *Oed*. 449.
52 The titular epithet arose from a misattribution by the Greek historian Thucydides (3.104), which has remained immune to correction through the ages.

him the son of heaven-nurtured kings. They sought to bound him with rude bonds, but these would not hold him, and the ropes fell far away from his hands and feet: and he sat with a smile in his dark eyes.

[15] Then the helmsman understood all and cried out at once to his fellows and said: 'Madmen! What god is this whom you have taken and bind, strong that he is? Not even the well-built ship can carry him. Surely this is either Zeus or Apollo who has the silver bow, or Poseidon, for he looks not like mortal men but like the gods who dwell on Olympus. Come, then, let us set him free upon the dark shore at once; do not lay hands on him, lest he grow angry and stir up dangerous winds and heavy squalls'.

[25] So said he, but the master chided him with taunting words: 'Madman, mark the wind and help hoist sail on the ship: catch all the sheets. As for this fellow we men will see to him; I reckon he is bound for Egypt or for Cyprus or to the Hyperboreans or further still. But in the end he will speak out and tell us his friends and all his wealth and his brothers, now that providence has thrown him in our way'.

[32] When he had said this, he had mast and sail hoisted on the ship, and the wind filled the sail and the crew hauled taut the sheets on either side. But soon strange things were seen among them. First of all, sweet, fragrant wine ran streaming throughout all the black ship and a heavenly smell arose, so that all the seamen were seized with amazement. And all at once a vine spread out both ways along the top of the sail with many clusters hanging down from it, and a dark ivy-plant twined about the mast, blossoming with flowers, and with rich berries growing on it; and all the thole pins were covered with garlands. When the pirates saw all this, then at last they bade the helmsman to put the ship to land. But the god changed into a dreadful lion there on the ship, on the bow, and roared loudly: amidships also he showed his wonders and created a shaggy bear which stood up ravening, while on the forepeak was the lion glaring fiercely with scowling brows. And so the sailors fled to the stern and crowded terrified about the right-minded helmsman, until suddenly the lion sprang upon the master and seized him; and when the sailors saw it they leapt out overboard one and all into the bright sea, escaping from a miserable fate, and were changed into dolphins. But on the helmsman Dionysus had mercy and held him back and made him altogether happy, saying to him: 'Take courage, good mariner; you have found favour with my heart. I am loud-crying Dionysus whom Cadmus' daughter Semele bore from union with Zeus'.

[58] Hail, child of fair-faced Semele! He who forgets you can in no wise order sweet song. (*Hymn. Hom.* 7)

Bringing the narrative matter of the *Hymn* in contact with Euripides' tragic plot is an inventive touch, and not just from the point of view of Ovid's metamorphic programme, as the tale told by Acoetes serves in addition as a cautionary tale for Pentheus.[53]

Fig. 2 'Vine Ship' with dolphins (drawing based on Attic black-figure *kylix* attributed to Exekias, c. 540–35 BCE, Staatliche Antikensammlungen, Munich).

5b. The Personnel of the Set Text

The set text abounds with colourful characters, many of whom make only fleeting appearances. There is the heterogeneous crowd of Thebans who, having fallen under the spell of Bacchus, rush to perform his rites (3.529–30): men (*viri*), married women (*matres*), unmarried women (*nurus*), common people (*vulgus*), aristocrats (*proceres*). There are Pentheus' relatives who vainly attempt to bring him to his senses, chief among them his grandfather Cadmus (*avus*) and his maternal uncle Athamas (3.564–65). There are the henchmen whom Pentheus sends out to capture Bacchus and who return, blood-spattered, with someone

---

53 John Henderson offers a valuable observation here: 'Setting a hymn in a narrative context, which is precisely lacking in the "prayerbook" Homeric Hymn collection, dramatizes the nature of hymns as motivated "in the moment" vehicles for rhetorical intervention. The same goes for all tales, not least mutant myths *about* mythmaking and mutation'.

identifying himself as Acoetes (3.572–76). Within Acoetes' inset narrative, we encounter a gang of wicked shipmates, many of whom are named (and some briefly delineated) with mock scrupulousness: Opheltes, Dictys, Libys, Melanthus, Alcimedon, Epopeus, Lycabas, Proreus, Aethalion, and Medon.[54] In the grim denouement on Mount Cithaeron, Pentheus' mother Agave and her sisters Autonoë and Ino, together with a miscellaneous crowd (*turba*) of fellow-maenads, lay violent hands on him. Ovid also reports in the episode's concluding verses that all the women of Thebes (designated *Ismenides*, after a local river) flock to Bacchus' altars to venerate his godhead (3.733–34). We may also add the old (*senes*) and young men (*iuvenes*) of Thebes whom Pentheus tries to rally against Bacchus (3.3.538–42), as well as a fleeting reference to the Bacchus-defiant Acrisius, king of Argos (3.559–60). Amidst this kaleidoscopic assortment of *dramatis personae*, four principal figures stand out: Tiresias, Pentheus, Bacchus, and Acoetes. Or perhaps we should say three, since the last two may in fact be one and the same figure.

(i) Tiresias

The prophet Tiresias is a quintessential Theban character found in numerous texts in both Greek and Latin literature. Thebes is his ancestral home: Tiresias' paternal grandfather, so tradition has it, was one of the five surviving Spartoi who comprised Cadmus' first citizen cohort, though Ovid, in line with his cursory treatment of the foundation sequence, omits details of his genealogy. He makes his earliest literary appearance in *Odyssey* 11, as the seer whom Odysseus seeks out in the Underworld in order to receive advice on his homecoming. But many of Tiresias' most memorable appearances are in Attic drama, where his special insight into the workings of the universe ensured him a stellar career. In four surviving scripts — Sophocles' *Oedipus the King* and *Antigone*, and Euripides' *Phoenician Women* and *Bacchae* — he unerringly predicts the tragic doom of his royal interlocutors (and perhaps even helps to move events along, since his predictions are typically met with suspicion, denial, or even wrath). If Homeric epic and Attic tragedy foreground his privileged access to divine knowledge late in life (or even

---

54 For discussion of this group, see Comm. on 605–07.

after death), other texts put the emphasis elsewhere, not least to explain how Tiresias acquired the gift of foresight in the first place. Here another aspect of his mythical CV comes to the fore: his unusual proclivity for sex changes. Tradition has it that the perambulating Tiresias once struck copulating snakes with his staff, whereupon he mysteriously morphed from male to female — only to return to his original sex when he did likewise several years later. Given his 'ambisextrous' past, one can see why Jupiter and Juno turned to him as uniquely qualified to settle their ambrosia-induced quarrel over which of the two sexes derives more pleasure from the act of love-making. Perhaps unsurprisingly, Jupiter insisted on women's greater sexual gratification, whereas Juno no less adamantly asserted the contrary. Upon being summoned, Tiresias adjudicated the dispute in Jupiter's favour, and was promptly struck blind by the infuriated Juno. Forbidden by cosmic law to undo the punishment inflicted by his wife, the well-pleased Jupiter granted Tiresias the gift of prophecy in recompense. Our earliest witness for this tale is pseudo-Hesiodic *Melampodia*, a fragmentary epic poem probably dating to the 6th century BCE.[55]

Ovid draws on this tradition and the more sober tragic antecedents in fleshing out Tiresias' biography in the *Metamorphoses*, thereby making of him 'an emblematic figure of both divine wisdom and sexual ambiguity'.[56] Tiresias initially floats into the narrative in his role as 'sexpert'. When first encountering him midway through Book 3, we get the tale of copulating snakes, sex changes, and erotic expertise, with the ensuing loss of sight and gain of fore-sight (*Met.* 3.316–38). Shortly thereafter, Tiresias proves his surpassing vatic ability by correctly, if riddlingly, foretelling the fate of Narcissus (an ingenious stand-in for Thebes' most famous son, Oedipus, who does not appear *in propria*

---

55 Hesiod's poem has not survived, but Apollod. 3.6.7 offers a summary of the tale (with attributions). Another tradition explains his loss of eyesight as the result of seeing the goddess Athena naked at her bath; infuriated, she struck him blind, but then felt remorse and granted him the gift of prophecy in recompense.

56 Michalopoulos (2012) 236, arguing earlier in the same work (p. 229) for an interrelation between Tiresias' sexual oscillations and his predictive powers: 'since prophetic knowledge stands on the verge between "here" and "there", between the human and the divine, we might argue as well that the seer's bisexuality becomes an emblem, or better, constitutes a metaphor for Tiresias' prophetic transcendence'. On the other hand, John Henderson cautions that 'even referring to Tiresias' "bisexuality" is already to fall into the trap set by the riddle of gendering sex!'

persona in Ovid's Theban History).⁵⁷ The seer warns Narcissus' mother Liriope that the beautiful boy will only reach old age 'if he does not come to know himself' (*si se non noverit*, 3.348). Ovid frames the episode of Narcissus — who *does* come to know himself — with two references (one proleptic, one retrospective) to Tiresias' unquestioned and well-deserved renown throughout Greece.⁵⁸ This quasi-universal acceptance of Tiresias as a prophetic authority serves as cue for the Pentheus-episode: the Theban king is the odd-man-out, whose ill-considered mockery of Tiresias sets the stage for his tragic downfall (*Met*. 3.511–25). Tiresias' vatic prognostications concerning Narcissus thus serve as pivot towards more 'weighty' narrative roles. In the Pentheus-episode, he appears in the guise of omniscient seer who confronts the reigning tyrant of Thebes — a scenario familiar from Sophocles' *Oedipus the King*. This is, however, a noteworthy departure from Euripides' *Bacchae*, in which, remarkably, the legendary seer utters no prophecies, but merely offers Pentheus advice, all the while acknowledging the scant hope that the young king will heed it (*Bacch*. 309–27). In this respect, then, by insisting on Tiresias' prophetic role — note the seer's explicit use of the verb *auguror* at 3.519 — Ovid 'corrects' the idiosyncratic choice of his primary model, and uses Tiresias' vatic utterances as a unifying motif in the elaboration of his Theban History.

Overall, then, in the *Metamorphoses*, as elsewhere, Tiresias presides over dramas of blindness (literal and mental) and insight, (royal) power and (divinely privileged) knowledge, concealing and revealing, riddling speech and hidden meanings (not least in contexts of sexual deviance).

(ii) Pentheus

Like Tiresias, Pentheus is descended from the Spartoi: he is the son of Agave, one of the four daughters of Cadmus and Harmonia, by Echion, one of the five survivors of the Sown-men's fratricidal slaughter, whose name means 'serpent' in ancient Greek.⁵⁹ 'Pentheus', too, is a speaking

---

57 For Narcissus as a substitute for Oedipus see Gildenhard and Zissos (2000a).
58 *Met*. 3.339–40; 3.511–12, i.e. the opening two lines of the set text. 'Typically, however, Ovid's Tiresias is first to tell Narcissus' tale, and to let our bard make Echo try to "get it together" with Narcissus in one impossible dis-joint tale of love scorned and twisted (see 386–87). New fame, then, for the old seer'. (John Henderson)
59 See Comm. on 513–14.

name, being connected etymologically to the Greek word πένθος ('grief, distress'), and so meaning something like 'man of sorrows'.[60] Given his gruesome demise, immortalized by Euripides in the *Bacchae*, the name can be considered an index of his destiny. To get a purchase on the figure of Pentheus in the *Metamorphoses*, it is useful to set Ovid's characterization of the young Theban king against his delineation in the *Bacchae*.[61]

As already noted, Euripides places special emphasis on Pentheus' obsession with the sexual license he associates with the worship of Bacchus. From his first reaction to the exodus of Theban women, who quit their homes for the mountains in order to take part in Bacchic rites, to his later rather puerile desire illicitly to catch a glimpse of these same rites, the issues of sexual transgression and the concomitant violation of household stability dominate Pentheus' imagination.[62] In the *Metamorphoses* Pentheus' character is delineated rather differently. As in the *Bacchae*, the Theban king deeply resents Bacchus' takeover of his city; but Ovid's Pentheus conceives of the god's advent in martial terms, tantamount to a military assault upon his city, which he, as king, is called upon to repel. He is dismayed by the inability of the citizenry to stand up to what he regards as a feeble and unworthy foe. The very idea that a group of revellers known for orgiastic noise, magical tricks, female ululations, alcoholic excess, and sexual license can overpower the population of a city descended from a dragon of Mars offends his martial pride (3.531–37). In his vain exhortation to his fellow Thebans he goes so far as to adduce the dragon of Mars, which his grandfather Cadmus slew, as a paragon of virtue that bravely gave its life in defence of its lair, fighting valiantly against overwhelming odds (3.543–46). Imagery of the battlefield dominates both Pentheus' rhetoric and Ovid's presentation of Pentheus to us in the narrative. So, for example, the response of Pentheus to the caterwauling of the Maenads on Mount Cithaeron is likened to that of a warhorse hearing the trumpeter of an army giving the signal to fight (3.701–07).

---

60 See Eur. *Bacch.* 367 with Dodds (1960) *ad loc.* Note also the etymological figure on 'Pentheus' (Πενθῆα) and 'lamentation' (πένθημα) at [Theoc.] *Id.* 26.26 (the poem is quoted in full above, §5a): πένθημα καὶ οὐ Πενθῆα φέροισαι.

61 That Pentheus has come to the throne at a very young age is evident in Ovid's as in Euripides' account: see Comm. on 540–42.

62 Cf. e.g. *Bacch.* 233–38, 260–62, 352–54, 453–59, 487, 957–58.

The shift away from the Euripidean preoccupation with sexual license (as well as Pentheus' own subliminal erotic desires) is achieved in part through intertextual engagement with Ovid's great Roman epic predecessor, Virgil.[63] The Ovidian Pentheus enriches his rallying cry to the citizens of Thebes with allusions to the *Aeneid*:

> vosne, senes, mirer, qui longa per aequora vecti
> hac Tyron, hac profugos posuistis sede penates,
> nunc sinitis sine Marte capi?
> (*Met.* 3.538–40)

> 'Should I wonder about you, old men, who, having crossed boundless seas, re-founded Tyre in this place, re-established your exiled household gods in this place, that you now allow yourselves to be captured without armed resistance?'

The obvious parallels to the Aeneas-story are all the more striking for being in overt contradiction with the earlier narrative, where it was reported that Cadmus' Phoenician companions were slain to a man by the dragon prior to the foundation of Thebes. But Pentheus here fashions Cadmus himself as an Aeneas *avant la lettre*, a leader of an exiled people, *profugi* from the East, who traversed the sea to settle his people and their *penates* in a new homeland. The Romanizing touches continue with the characterization of Thebans as a *proles Mavortia* (3.531).[64] Somewhat later in his speech, Pentheus again uses language reminiscent of the *Aeneid* in chastising his derelict citizen body, deploring what he sees as its unconditional surrender to Bacchus, derisively styled as an unarmed and utterly unwarlike boy:

> at nunc a puero Thebae capientur inermi,
> quem neque bella iuvant nec tela nec usus equorum,
> sed madidus murra crinis mollesque coronae
> purpuraque et pictis intextum vestibus aurum.
> (*Met.* 3.553–56)

---

63 The lives of Virgil (70–19 BCE) and Ovid (43 BCE–17 CE) overlap, but only during the latter's youth. In any event, Virgil's *Aeneid* became an instant 'classic' and is treated as such in the *Metamorphoses* — that is to say, it is frequently the focus of Ovid's intertextual engagement.

64 A point emphasized by Hardie (1990) 229. Ovid similarly characterizes Romulus and Remus, the founders of Rome, as *Martia proles* at *Fast.* 3.59.

'But now an unarmed boy will conquer Thebes, whom neither weapons, wars nor horses delight, but hair drenched in myrrh, soft garlands, purple and gold woven into embroidered robes'.

Pentheus' language here recalls that of the pugnacious African king Iarbas, who in a prayer to Jupiter denounces Aeneas when the latter has forgotten his epic calling and degenerated, together with Dido, into the world of illicit love (*Aen.* 4.215–18).

Ovid follows Euripides in having Pentheus issue orders for Bacchus' arrest, and in both texts his henchmen return with one of the god's followers instead (*Bacch.* 432–42; *Met.* 3.564–76) — though in the Greek drama this is in fact the god in disguise, and, as discussed below, the same may hold in the *Metamorphoses*. In the *Bacchae*, Pentheus' interrogation of the prisoner leads to the latter convincing him to don female attire in order illicitly to witness the proceedings on Mount Cithaeron. This scene, with its emphasis on theatrical cross-dressing and gender-bending is crucial and emblematic for Euripides.[65] It is thus significant that Ovid omits it from his account as not pertinent to his delineation of Pentheus. Instead, after the lengthy inset narrative of the prisoner Acoetes, the narrative focus returns to Pentheus, now more bellicose than ever. The defining emotion is wrath (*ira*). Without further ado, he storms to his doom. Ovid's Pentheus, then, unlike his Euripidean counterpart, never succumbs to the temptation of gender-bending or any other 'Bacchic' impulses. Rather, the emphasis on the king's martial disposition coupled with allusions to the *Aeneid* serve to recast the Euripidean tragedy in a more Roman and a more epic key.[66]

Why does Pentheus resist Bacchus so vehemently? As ruler of Thebes, he identifies himself with his city; he is convinced that he is acting in the interest of the civic community (as the lone representative of law and order), entertains feelings of moral and intellectual superiority, and is beholden to the pursuit of power and honour. Although, as we have seen, Ovid chose not to develop some of Pentheus' 'Euripidean' character traits, he retains other qualities, in

---

65 Cf. Zeitlin (1990) 74–75.
66 At the same time, as John Henderson points out, 'Ovid's merging of Thebes and Troy threatens the "triangulation" formula for ROME (see above, n. 46) — while picking up on the way Virgil has merged his "Thebes" (tragic Carthage) with Troy to-be-reborn-as-ROME'.

particular those that speak to a somewhat tyrannical disposition, so that E. R. Dodds' assessment of the Pentheus of the *Bacchae* holds true for his counterpart in the *Metamorphoses*: the Theban king exhibits an 'absence of self-control, ... willingness to believe the worst on hearsay evidence ... or on none whatsoever, ... brutality towards the helpless ...; and a stupid reliance on physical force as a means of settling spiritual problems'.[67] In a detailed study of Euripides' Pentheus, Bernd Seidensticker characterizes the Theban king not just as a tyrant, but an 'authoritarian personality'.[68] A number of the traits adduced by Seidensticker recur in Ovid's Pentheus, and contribute to his undoing in the confrontation with Bacchus:[69]

(a) Ethnocentrism, i.e. the belief in the superiority of one's own nation or community, which coincides with fear of 'the other' and the irrational belief that contact with the foreign contaminates the self or the society one lives in. In both Euripides and Ovid, this is a key theme, as Pentheus endeavours to repulse Bacchus and his cult as something alien, Eastern, and corrosive of the norms and values he holds dear.[70] He exhibits a xenophobia that manifests itself in the chauvinistic rejection of the non-Greek as inferior and decadent.

(b) Aggressiveness bordering on brutality to protect the self against others, i.e. ethnocentrism coupled with a tendency towards violence. While Euripides' Pentheus takes a 'camp' turn into cross-dressing, Ovid's figure remains a robust, masculine, independent individual who sticks to his views and escalates violence when met with resistance.[71]

(c) Belief that men are superior to women, who are conceived of as passive and as tied to traditional roles of wife and mother. In Euripides, female (sexual) license is a major concern for Pentheus, and whereas Ovid plays down

---

67 Dodds (1960) xliii and *ad* 214.
68 Seidensticker (1972) 57.
69 The following is based on Seidensticker (1972) 57–61.
70 See e.g. 3.555–56 with Comm.
71 Pentheus' lack of self-control is apparent throughout the episode, and in particular at 3.566–67 (with following simile), 578–79, 692–95, 704–07. For Euripides' treatment, see e.g. *Bacch*. 214 with Dodds (1960) *ad loc.*

the importance of gender, his Pentheus too is beholden to a narrow set of martial and masculine values.⁷²

(*d*) *Conventionalism, conformity, commitment to conservative values, which often goes along with thinking in prejudices and stereotypes, the tendency to generalize, the use of clichés, and a limited degree of creativity and flexibility.* In both Euripides' play and Ovid's epic, Pentheus is committed to preserving the status quo and unable to adjust to new situations.⁷³ He does not listen to his advisers and the warnings of his kin and proves incapable of viewing the world from another perspective. Confronted with the arrival of a new god, he mounts a stubborn resistance that includes the rhetorical denigration of his perceived adversary via a familiar set of prejudices about Easterners.

All in all, then, Pentheus is particularly lacking in the flexible intelligence that enables a person to respond in a healthy and balanced manner to the kind of divinity that is Bacchus — polymorphous, subversive of norms, destructive of boundaries, challenging the conventional order of things, and defying orthodoxy — in particular in the realm of gender-relations. Instead of pursuing a path of accommodation, Pentheus fatally opts for confrontation; instead of embracing his divine kin (Bacchus, after all, is his cousin — Semele and Agave are sisters), he chooses blanket rejection, turning himself into a blasphemous *theomachos* ('someone who assaults the gods') — and ultimately a victim of divine wrath.

(iii) Bacchus

Bacchus/Dionysus, god of wine, mystic ecstasy and theatre, is one of the oldest Greek divinities to leave a trace in our literary record: his name (*di-wo-nu-so*) features on linear-B tablets from Pylos and Crete, datable to c. 1250 BCE.⁷⁴ Homer, too, knows of Dionysus, mentioning his female entourage (*Il.* 6.133), and alluding to his birth (*Il.* 14.325). Hesiod, in his *Theogony* (940–42), likewise recounts the birth of Dionysus, highlighting

---

72 See Comm. on 531–63, 532–37 and 536–67.
73 See Comm. on 520.
74 *Der Neue Pauly* III (1997) 651–52 (Schlesier).

that a mortal woman gave birth to an immortal child. This is one of many remarkable aspects of the god: product of the sexual union of Jupiter with the Theban princess Semele, his foetus is in fact brought to term in his father's thigh after his mother dies in pregnancy.[75] Following a period of infancy, the god wanders the earth seeking recognition of his divinity. Unlike other Olympian deities, he encounters human defiance, deriving in large part from scepticism as to his godhood. Given his parentage, this is not altogether surprising: as the offspring of a mortal mother and a divine father, he might well have been expected to belong to the class of semi-divine 'heroes'.[76] There are many individuals with similar parentage who fall short of divine status, even though they may receive worship after death in the form of hero-cult.

With respect to the broader mythological background, modern philology has shown that Greek mythology is at least to some degree inherited from a set of stories that were originally common to all Indo-European cultures. The name of the supreme Olympian deity, the sky god and father 'Zeus' has cognates in other Indo-European languages.[77] Many of the other divinities worshipped by the Greeks seem to have been imported from other cultures. Those of importance tended to be placed in some kind of familial relation to the sky father Zeus/Jupiter. The last major such addition to the pantheon was the god Dionysus/Bacchus, who became one of many of Zeus' children born outside of the supreme god's marriage with Hera/Juno. A good deal of Greek mythology tells of the struggles of Zeus' progeny born, as it were, out of wedlock to gain recognition and assert their rights and status on either the divine or the human level; the story of Bacchus and Pentheus is a cautionary tale dealing with the latter.

---

[75] Ovid provides a decidedly salacious version of this birth story earlier in Book 3 at 253–315.

[76] There was, in fact, a tradition that presented Dionysus/Bacchus as a vigorous demigod who won a place in heaven through military conquest and the bestowal of benefits upon humankind (e.g. Cic. *Leg.* 2.19, Virg. *Aen.* 6.804–05; Hor. *Carm.* 3.3.13–15, Val. Fl. 1.566–67). A legendary cycle (gradually assimilated to the career of Alexander the Great) featuring eastern expeditions and, above all, conquests in India, rose to prominence in the Hellenistic period and passed into popular art, as well as the iconography of various Hellenistic kings and Roman generals: see further Zissos (2008) 325.

[77] Compare 'Zeus pater' and 'Jupiter', whom the Romans also called 'Diespiter' and understood as 'Dies pater', i.e. 'father of the day' or 'sky father'.

Bacchus is then, despite the antiquity of his cult, a belated addition to the pantheon, a notorious latecomer, or 'new arrival' from the East. Ovid calls him *advena*, and the attributes *novus* ('new') and *ignotus* ('unknown') are programmatic.[78]

One of the unusual aspects of Bacchus' cult is that he had predominantly female attendants and devotees ('maenads') to perform his rites, contrary to the overarching principle that women were restricted to the active worship of female deities. His physical representation is also noteworthy for its variation: early artistic depictions of Dionysus/Bacchus show him as a fully developed man, complete with beard, but already by the 5th century BCE it had become the norm for writers, painters and sculptors to depict him as a more boyish figure, beardless, and with a softer, almost feminine, physique — which is how he is described in Ovid's Pentheus episode.[79] That this trend continued beyond antiquity can be seen in, for example, Michelangelo's sculpture 'Bacchus' (fig. 3) and the painting of the same name (fig. 4) by Caravaggio.

Fig. 3 'Bacchus' by Michelangelo (1496–97). https://commons.wikimedia.org/wiki/File:Bacchus,_Michelangelo,_1496-97,_Bargello_Florenz-04.jpg

---

[78] Cf. Pentheus' sneering reference to τὸν νεωστὶ δαίμονα | Διόνυσον ['the new god Dionysus'] at Eur. *Bacch.* 219–20; on the god's newness and strangeness, see also Comm. on 520.

[79] See Comm. on 607 *virginea ... forma*.

Fig. 4 'Bacchus' by Caravaggio (1593–94). https://commons.wikimedia.org/wiki/File:Michelangelo_Caravaggio_007.jpg

The god's proverbial androgyny and his entourage of maenads defy entrenched gender stereotypes and were thus bound to occasion anxiety in a patriarchal world. As such, writers and artists found Bacchus to be an ideal figure for the interrogation of notions of masculinity and related cultural norms. It has already been noted that Euripides makes fear of female sexual license, perceived as a threat to the patriarchal order of the city-state, one of the primary motivations for Pentheus' resistance to the new cult. As we have seen, this aspect is toned down in the *Metamorphoses*, but it is not altogether effaced. Thus, even in Ovid's version there are glimmers of the cult's utopian appeal arising from the collapse of the distinctions that define the socio-political order.[80] In the worship of Bacchus the indiscriminate mixing of categories means that age, gender, socio-economic class, and legal status become irrelevant. Ovid highlights this principle at the very beginning of the Pentheus episode:

---

[80] This utopian appeal works in tandem with various Golden Age motifs, such as life without toil, that were associated with the god.

5. The Set Text: Pentheus and Bacchus

> Liber <u>adest</u>, festisque fremunt <u>ululatibus</u> agri:
> <u>turba ruit</u>, mixtaeque viris matresque nurusque
> vulgusque proceresque ignota ad sacra feruntur.
> (*Met.* 3.528–30)

Ovid recalls this joyful beginning at the grisly end when Agave summons her maddened sisters: *'o geminae'* clamavit *'*<u>adeste</u> sorores!'* (3.713) and shortly thereafter lets rip with ritual shrieking (<u>ululavit</u> Agave, 3.725). The indiscriminate crowd that initially rushed to worship Bacchus has become a band of Maenads rushing upon Pentheus: <u>ruit</u> *omnis in unum* | <u>turba</u> *furens* (3.715–16). Pentheus is singled out here, just as at the outset, when he was the lone individual (*ex omnibus unus*, 3.513) who refused to believe Tiresias' prophecy about Bacchus. Such emphatic ring composition highlights the inherent duality of Bacchus' nature, which combines carefree revelling with baneful doom, and once more exemplifies the 'conversion of Dionysiac celebration into madness, death, and destruction'[81] that is repeatedly fated to occur at Thebes. In his train, Bacchus brings hallucination and paranoia — surreal dissolution of identity, collapsing and re-doubling roles at will — and the story of Pentheus is a classic and exemplary case. The set text acts out one of the starkest instances in literature of consciousness made prey to delirium unknowingly beside itself.

Bacchus' overt narrative presence is much reduced in the Ovidian episode *vis-à-vis* the Euripidean model. Ovid offers a brief notice of the god's arrival at Thebes, simply declaring that the god has come (*Liber adest*, 3.528) and received a warm welcome as a new divinity that reaches across boundaries of class and gender (cf. 3.528–30). But we do not get the god himself as a speaking character — at least not at the outset. Indeed, a suggestive feature of the set text is that Bacchus, arguably the episode's most important character, has no explicit narrative presence. Acoetes' embedded narrative is the only place in the entire episode where the god appears in person. Bacchus nevertheless looms over narrative events as an 'absent presence'. Given this curious state of affairs, Acoetes' account of the god's transformation of Etruscan pirates into dolphins takes on added significance. As we have seen,

---

[81] Zeitlin (1993) 158.

the embedded narrative is based on the account in the longest *Homeric Hymn to Dionysus*.

(iv) Acoetes

The internal narrator Acoetes is the last major character of the set text. In the *Homeric Hymn to Dionysus*, the helmsman, the one member of the crew not transformed into a dolphin, remains anonymous and devoid of background. Ovid's internal narrator, the figure captured by Pentheus' henchmen, claims to be this helmsman; he goes on to identify himself as a certain Acoetes from Lydia (3.582–83), an acolyte of the god (*accessi sacris Baccheaque sacra frequento*, 3.691). He provides a fairly detailed autobiography, culminating in the narrative of the *Hymn*. He claims to be of very humble origins, with a father so poor that he bequeathed to his son nothing beyond the art of fishing. Not wishing to win his livelihood in this humble manner, Acoetes learns the helmsman's art and plies his trade on the sea until his encounter with Bacchus, which leads to him joining the god's entourage. The encounter takes place when, *en route* to Delos, the ship puts in on the island of Chios. There, members of Acoetes' crew kidnap a beautiful young boy who, according to Acoetes, turned out to be Bacchus (*tum denique Bacchus | (Bacchus enim fuerat)* ..., 3.629–30). As in the *Hymn*, Acoetes is the lone member of his ship's crew to recognize the divinity of the captive and, having been spared the metamorphic fate of his comrades, proceeds to join Bacchus' entourage. The question arises: is Acoetes really who he claims to be? There is much to suggest otherwise.

The first point to observe is that, as noted in the previous section, Pentheus' capture of Acoetes in Ovid has a precedent in Euripides' play, where the stranger who is brought before Pentheus is undoubtedly Dionysus himself, though disguised as one of his followers. Euripides prepares this scene in which the god of the theatre dons a mask (as it were) from the outset.[82] To ensure that the audience is able to follow along, the god broadcasts his subterfuge in the prologue speech:

---

82 Acting a part is of course appropriate to the god's identity as divine patron of the theatre. Cf. Cole (2007) 234: 'Dionysus is a god who plays many roles, and he can change his appearance at will. As god of the theatre, he is associated with the process of transition actors undergo when taking on a new role, because the actor puts on a new identity with each new mask'.

μορφὴν δ᾽ ἀμείψας ἐκ θεοῦ βροτησίαν
πάρειμι ...
(Eur. *Bacch.* 4–5)

And having taken a mortal form instead of a god's, I am here ...

Towards the end of the same monologue, the deity reiterates the point, to make quite sure that everyone in his audience has grasped what he is up to:

ὧν οὕνεκ᾽ εἶδος θνητὸν ἀλλάξας ἔχω
μορφήν τ᾽ ἐμὴν μετέβαλον εἰς ἀνδρὸς φύσιν.
(Eur. *Bacch.* 53–54)

On which account I have changed my form to a mortal one and altered my shape into that of a man.

When later on in the play Pentheus' henchmen bring the anonymous stranger on stage (*Bacch.* 434–519), even the least attentive audience member will have been able to identify the stranger as Dionysus.

In a poignant exchange later in the tragedy, Pentheus asks the stranger, who claims to have seen Dionysus, of what nature he was (477). The disguised god's response, 'whatever person he wished' (ὁποῖος ἤθελ᾽, Eur. *Bacch.* 478), archly evokes his own protean nature. If Euripides' god is explicitly a master of disguise and deception, Ovid's would appear to be so by implication — and with the effect, by a characteristic stroke of metapoetic ingenuity, projected beyond the narrative frame. In the Greek tragedy the riddle of Bacchus' identity remains confined to characters *within* the play (in particular, of course, Pentheus) and does *not* concern the audience, for whom, as we have just seen, Euripides clarifies the situation before the action begins. In the *Metamorphoses*, by contrast, the god remains an enigmatic and elusive figure for *us*, the readers.[83] Ovid provides nothing equivalent to the prologue scene in Euripides that would give the game away, but rather tantalizes us with the possibility that Bacchus does appear in the narrative in disguised form. This possibility is raised when Pentheus' henchmen, having been ordered to arrest Bacchus, return instead with a captured stranger who, as we have just seen, identifies himself

---

83 The point is made by Feldherr (1997) 29: 'the audience of this narrative ... faces the same challenge as the characters within it'.

as Acoetes. But the fact that Acoetes has the same narrative function as the disguised Euripidean god strongly suggests, by intertextual parallelism, that Acoetes is indeed Bacchus.[84] Further support for this view can be found in his statement of Lydian origins (3.582–83) and the miraculous circumstances of his liberation (3.699–700). But while this identification seems *probable* for various reasons, the fact remains that Acoetes is never *explicitly* equated with the god anywhere in the text. Indeed, apart from the narrator's general pronouncement that Bacchus has reached Thebes (*Liber adest*, 3.528), the only moment in which we encounter the god in person in the entire episode occurs during the *inset* narrative about the Tyrrhenian sailors told by Acoetes. Paradoxically, if we accept that Acoetes is indeed the god in disguise, then the veracity of his inset narrative — which again features a deceptive and dissembling Bacchus — would be thrown into doubt, inasmuch as it would then be nothing more than the autobiography of a mortal persona assumed by the deity.

The plot thickens further if we take into account a piece of information preserved in Servius' ancient commentary on the *Aeneid*. The crucial titbit concerns a Virgilian simile featuring Pentheus as 'vehicle':

> ... Eumenidum veluti demens videt agmina Pentheus
> et solem geminum et duplicis se ostendere Thebas ...
> (*Aen.* 4.469–70)
>
> ... even as raving Pentheus sees the bands of the Furies, and a double sun and twofold Thebes rise to view ...

In his annotation to this simile, Servius reports that Virgil derived this image from the (now lost) tragedy *Pentheus* by the early Roman playwright Pacuvius, arguably modelled on Euripides' *Bacchae*. The commentator goes on to mention that in Pacuvius' play the name of the stranger who was brought on stage by the henchmen happened to be Acoetes:[85]

---

84 Note that in Euripides' play Bacchus/Dionysus states that he hails from Lydia both in his own form (*Bacch.* 38–39) and when disguised (*Bacch.* 464): see further Comm. on 582–83.

85 The issues surrounding this *testimonium* are complex (some scholars have even suggested that Servius Auctus draws on Ovid for his summary of Pacuvius' play!); Schierl (2006) 418–22 offers a survey of the secondary literature on Pacuvius' *Pentheus* (*vel Bacchae*).

Pentheum autem furuisse traditur secundum Pacuvii tragoediam. de quo fabula talis est: Pentheus, Echionis et Agaves filius, Thebanorum rex, cum indignaretur ex matertera sua Semele genitum Liberum patrem coli tamquam deum, ut primum comperit eum in Cithaerone monte esse, misit satellites, qui eum (i.e. Bacchum) vinctum ad se perducerent. qui cum ipsum non invenissent, unum ex comitibus eius Acoeten captum ad Pentheum perduxerunt. is, cum de eo graviorem poenam constitueret, iussit eum interim claudi vinctum; cumque sponte sua et carceris fores apertae essent et vincula Acoeti excidissent, miratus Pentheus, spectaturus sacra Liberi patris Cithaerona petit ... (Serv. on *Aen.* 4.469)

Pentheus' madness is drawn from a tragedy by Pacuvius. The plot of which is as follows: Pentheus, son of Echion and Agave, king of Thebes, resented that Father Liber, born from his aunt Semele, was worshipped as a god; as soon as he heard that Liber was on Mount Cithaeron, he sent servants to bring Liber bound to him. When they did not find Liber himself, they captured Acoetes, one of his comrades, and brought him to Pentheus. While Pentheus pondered a worse punishment for him, he ordered him to be locked away in the meantime, bound as he was, when out of their own accord the doors of the prison flew open and the bonds fell off Acoetes. Pentheus was astonished and set out for Mount Cithaeron to spy on the rites of Father Liber ...

This annotation, while not solving the riddle of Acoetes' identity in the *Metamorphoses* account, offers some interesting insights into the metaliterary game of hide-and-seek being played here. In essence, Ovid endows his Acoetes with a triple intertextual identity, insofar as he recalls three literary figures at once: (i) the helmsman of the *Homeric Hymn to Dionysus* (who, in the hymn, remains anonymous); (ii) the disguised god Dionysus of Euripides' *Bacchae* (who operates in human guise but doesn't assume a pseudonym); and (iii) the homonymous character from Pacuvius' tragedy *Pentheus* (since the play has survived only in pitiful fragments, it is impossible for us to know whether Acoetes in Pacuvius was Bacchus in disguise).

Faced with this intertextual jigsaw puzzle, some scholars consider the solution to be obvious: 'Ovid does not identify Acoetes with the god, but clearly expects his readers to do so'.[86] Others feel that Ovid has constructed his text in such a way that an unequivocal resolution of the riddle remains deliberately beyond our reach:

---

86 Kenney (1986) 394.

The narrative parallels to Euripides' play strongly suggest that we take Acoetes to be the god in disguise, but he is never identified as such directly. There are hints in this direction, but by leaving out an epiphany and keeping his god firmly offstage, Ovid ensures that we recognize Bacchus only when he appears as what he is not, as a character who recedes ever further back into the realm of miraculous narrative.[87]

Taking Acoetes to be Bacchus results in some delicious ironies, while offering degrees of metaliterary enrichment. To begin with, as Acoetes, Bacchus would perform an ingenious generic encroachment by incorporating into the central part of his own tragedy (Euripides' *Bacchae*) the very *Hymn* in which his transformative powers are celebrated — a shift in emphasis very much in line with the thematic outlook of the *Metamorphoses*, i.e. the text in which he is currently operating. While the author of the *Hymn to Dionysus* disposed of the transformation of the crew into dolphins in two and a half words (δελφῖνες δ᾽ ἐγένοντο, 'they became dolphins' *Hymn. Hom.* 7.53), Acoetes gives one of the most striking descriptions of transformation in Ovid's entire epic (3.671–82).

Concerning the hymn narrative, Philip Hardie well observes that 'as a god whose identity is founded on doubling, Bacchus has the space within himself to address a successful hymn to himself … ("Acoetes" speaks)'.[88] If Bacchus hymns himself, as it were, then several places in the hymnic narrative, in which he refers to himself, sparkle with Dionysiac wit. For example, 'Acoetes' reports that the first time he set eyes on the drunken Bacchus he immediately recognized his (own) divine essence:

> ille mero somnoque gravis titubare videtur
> vixque sequi; specto cultum faciemque gradumque:
> nil ibi, quod credi posset mortale, videbam.
> (*Met.* 3.608–10)

Somewhat later, 'Acoetes' sounds another arch note in professing the veracity of his account:[89]

---

87 Feldherr (2010) 187.
88 Hardie (2002a) 170.
89 Cf. Eur. *Bacch.* 500 (Dionysus speaking about himself): καὶ νῦν ἃ πάσχω πλησίον παρὼν ὁρᾷ ('Even now he is near and sees what I am experiencing').

> per tibi nunc ipsum (nec enim praesentior illo
> est deus) adiuro, tam me tibi vera referre
> quam veri maiora fide ...
> (*Met.* 3.658–60)

If Acoetes is indeed Bacchus, then there is an amusing double-entendre in his parenthetical remark that 'no god is closer than he' (*nec enim praesentior illo | est deus*), appended to an appeal to his own godhead for the veracity of his tale. At the same time, the duplicitous nature of Acoetes-as-Bacchus gives the overall utterance a rather ominous force. Within Ovid's Pentheus episode, the story of the Tyrrhenian sailors functions anyway as a speech-genre the Greeks called *ainos* (the English 'enigma' and 'enigmatic' derive from it), i.e. 'an allusive tale containing an ulterior purpose'.[90] The understanding or misunderstanding of the *ainigma* ('riddle') in the *ainos* ('riddling tale') can serve as a kind of ethical litmus test, dividing people into 'better' and 'worse' categories. By not understanding the message implicit in the embedded narrative, namely that Bacchus is a god who demands recognition and respect, Pentheus proves that he belongs among the latter. It is undoubtedly significant that he never considers the possibility that there may be more to the stranger than meets the eye, thus committing an offense with fatal consequences in classical literature, from Homer to tragedy and beyond.[91]

While the hymnic material displaces the tragic from the narrative center of the episode, Ovid, by creating an intertextual 'mask' with metapoetic significance for Bacchus, nevertheless manages to rehearse crucial preoccupations of the Euripidean play. The god's status as author figure who coordinates the generic terms of his narrative existence closely resembles the 'metadramatic' powers Vernant ascribes to the god in Euripides' *Bacchae*: 'It is as if, throughout the spectacle, even as he appears on stage beside the other characters in the play, Dionysus

---

90 Verdenius (1962) 389, cited by Nagy (1979) 237 in his discussion of the term.
91 Cf. Murnaghan (1987) 68: 'Both in the Homeric epics and in the Homeric Hymns, failure to recognize a disguised god often brings mortals to disaster, and this disaster is frequently accompanied by a display of divine anger, as in the case of the sailors in the *Hymn to Dionysus* or of Metaneira in the *Hymn to Demeter*'.

was also operating at another level, behind the scene, putting the plot together and directing it towards its *denouement*'.[92]

The ambiguities of identity surrounding Acoetes-Bacchus are also emblematic of Bacchus' presence in Ovid's Theban History more generally:

> Bacchus' presence is problematic: it is not always easy to tell when he is present, or in what shape or form, and a suspicion arises that he has been present in Thebes from the beginning. We know already of his earlier intermittent presence in the city, at first in Semele's womb before the embryo was snatched up to heaven to gestate in Jupiter's thigh, and then again briefly as the nursling of Ino, before being whisked off to India for the rest of his infancy (310–15). But as the god of drama, he has been present from the first act of the Theban story, the birth of the Sown Men, compared in a simile as they rise from the earth to the figures appearing on a theatre curtain as it is raised (3.111–14). Like the famous simile at *Aeneid* 4.469–73 comparing Dido in her frenzy to mythological characters on stage, Ovid's simile alerts us to a generic switch within a hexameter epic into a dramatic mode.[93]

By not featuring Bacchus (explicitly) as a protagonist in the Pentheus-episode, Ovid captures something important about the god: 'Dionysus wants to be seen to be a god, to be manifest to mortals as a god, to make himself known, to reveal himself, to be known, recognized, understood ... But Dionysus reveals himself by concealing himself, makes himself manifest by hiding himself from the eyes of all those who believe only in what they see'.[94] In Ovid's narrative, Bacchus' presence is thus pervasive yet elusive: he (as it were) invites *you* to spot and capture the god in his text! And this is not a challenge to be undertaken lightly — or in the ham-fisted fashion of a Pentheus.

---

92   Vernant (1988) 381–82.
93   Hardie (2002a) 166–67.
94   Vernant (1988) 391.

6. The Bacchanalia and Roman Culture

The story of Pentheus and Bacchus comes out of Greek myth and is situated in a Greek milieu. But we have already seen (above, §3a) that Ovid's treatment of these tales is often refracted through Roman cultural experience. In the case of the set text, one such influence, which does not register explicitly in the narrative but is judged to be of some importance by commentators, is a senatorial intervention against the cult of Bacchus in 186 BCE (i.e. nearly two centuries before Ovid composed the *Metamorphoses*), as well as its repercussions in literary texts — dramatic plays initially (tragedies and comedies that have unfortunately only survived in fragments) and then also in Livy's monumental history of Rome, which Ovid would have known. The distinction between the (religious) politics of 2nd century BCE Rome, specifically the measures taken against followers of the Bacchic cult in 186 BCE and the literary account of Livy, written in the Augustan period, is, of course, important to keep in mind.

Mid-Republican Rome experienced something quite similar to Ovid's Thebes: the arrival of a cult of Bacchus, which merged with Italy's cult of Liber, most likely sometime towards the end of the 3rd century BCE.[95] Not much is known about the so-called Bacchanalia: as with all mystery religions, the doings of the worshippers have remained mysterious. But it is clear that, after an initial period of toleration, which allowed the rites to spread throughout Italy, the Roman senate

---

95   For the native Italian deity Liber, see also Comm. on 520.

concluded that certain boundaries of law and order had been breached by cult members and issued a decree against the Bacchic associations responsible for organizing the worship. A copy of this decree has survived, and offers precious insight into the affair.[96] To begin with, it is clear that the senatorial intervention was not directed against Bacchus as a foreign divinity. Rather, the senate seems to have been 'acting in particular against the behaviour of cult members in relation to each other, and not in relation to the god: Rome wished, therefore, to preclude the possibility that cults could serve as vehicles for achieving local solidarity'.[97] The prohibitions of the decree suggest that the target was less the religious practice as such than the possibility of political fraternization afforded by a cult community.[98] Indeed, 'the decree makes no effort to ban the worship of Bacchus entirely, only to specify the conditions of worship'.[99] What Roman officials seem to have feared was the possibility that, unless brought under senatorial control, the cult might serve as a vehicle for anti-Roman political associations and activities. Arguably, the shift from Euripides' emphasis on illicit sex to Ovid's focus on power politics (mirrored in the way their respective figures of Pentheus react to the arrival of Bacchus) reflects this concern.

The account of the historian Livy is also extant (Liv. 39.8–19), offering the modern reader a vivid and salacious chronicle of the affair, in which sex, intrigue, and xenophobia register insistently. It is, in fact, shot through with Augustan anachronisms; whether consciously or not, Livy has inflected his treatment with contemporary concerns (such as Augustus' moral legislation). The idiom in which he describes the activities of those involved in the worship of Bacchus has interesting

---

[96] The *senatus consultum de Bacchanalibus* ('senatorial decree concerning the Bacchanalia'), *CIL* 12.581.

[97] Ando (2007) 437.

[98] The pertinent section of the senatorial decree stipulates: 'None of them shall seek to have money in common. No one shall seek to appoint either man or woman as master or acting master, or seek henceforth to exchange mutual oaths, vows, pledges or promises, nor shall anyone seek to create mutual guarantees. No one shall seek to perform rites in secret, nor shall anyone seek to perform rites in public or private or outside the city, unless he has approached the urban *praetor* and is given permission with a senatorial decree … No one shall seek to perform rites when more than five men and women are gathered together, nor shall more than two men or more than three women seek to be present there, except by permission of the urban *praetor* and the senate …' (trans. Beard, North and Price).

[99] Orlin (2010) 64.

parallels with Pentheus' characterization of Bacchants and their rites in Ovid's account. The theme of sexual license registers with particular emphasis:

> 'When wine had inflamed their minds, and night and the mingling of males with females and young with old, had destroyed all sense of modesty, every variety of debauchery began to be practiced, since each one had to hand the form of pleasure to which his nature was most inclined. (Liv. 39.8)

Later in the account, Livy has one of the consuls inveigh against the veneration of 'those gods who would drive our minds, enthralled by vile and alien rites (*pravis et externis religionibus*), to every crime and every lust' (39.15). The denigration continues with accusations of trickery and fraud (cf. Pentheus' imputation of *magicae fraudes* at *Met.* 3.534), political conspiracy and even ritual murder (followed by the sacrilegious disposal of the victims' bodies). Livy's rhetoric against this 'evil' finds an analogy in Pentheus' outrage against Bacchus and his followers in Ovid; both conceive of the cult's propagation in terms of territorial encroachment, though Pentheus' metaphor of choice is military conquest, whereas Livy's is a spreading pestilence: 'the destructive force of this wickedness spread from Etruria to Rome like a contagion' (*huius mali labes ex Etruria Romam veluti contagione morbi penetravit*, Liv. 39.9).

TEXT

3.511–18

cognita res meritam vati per Achaidas urbes
attulerat famam, nomenque erat auguris ingens;
spernit Echionides tamen hunc ex omnibus unus
contemptor superum Pentheus praesagaque ridet
verba senis tenebrasque et cladem lucis ademptae   515
obicit. ille movens albentia tempora canis
'quam felix esses, si tu quoque luminis huius
orbus' ait 'fieres, ne Bacchica sacra videres!

Study Questions

- What is the *res* mentioned in 511?
- What noun does the adjective *meritam* (511) agree with? What is name for this kind of separation of attribute and noun? What is the effect of its use here?
- Parse *vati*.
- Parse *attulerat*.
- What is the subject of *spernit* (513)?
- Identify the respective accusative object(s) of *spernit* (513), *ridet* (514), and *obicit* (516).
- Parse *superum*.
- What does the *-que* after *praesaga* (514) link? The *-que* after *tenebras* (515)? The *et* in 515?
- Parse *senis*.
- Parse *canis* — how does it fit into the sentence?
- What type of conditional clause does *si* (517) introduce? What is its protasis?
- Parse *fieres*.
- How does Ovid bring the theme of 'blindness and insight' into play here?

Stylistic Appreciation

Analyze the rhetorical design of *spernit Echionides tamen hunc ex omnibus unus | contemptor superum Pentheus praesagaque ridet | verba senis tenebrasque et cladem lucis ademptae | obicit* (513–16), paying attention not least to Ovid's placement of words in the nominative, accusative objects, and verbs.

Discussion Points

How does Ovid characterize Pentheus and Tiresias here? What type of power do these figures represent, respectively? Can you think of similar conflicts elsewhere in classical (and contemporary) literature and culture?

cognosco, -oscere, -ovi, -itum	to get to know in the perfect often = to know
vates/ vatis, -is, m./f.	prophet, seer; poet
Achais, -idos, f. adj.	Greek
augur, -uris, m.	prophet, seer; augur
Echionides	(patronymic) 'son of Echion'
praesagus, -a, -um	portending, ominous
superi, -orum (or *superum*)	those who dwell above; gods
adimo, -imere, -emi, -emptum	to remove by physical force, take away
obicio, -icere, -ieci, -iectum	to throw in the way/ in one's teeth
albeo, -ere	to be white (with), appear white
tempus, -oris, n.	the side of the forehead, temple (a less common sense of the Latin word for 'time')
cani, -orum, m. pl. [= *cani capilli*]	grey hairs (not to be confused with *canis, -is*, m./f., 'dog')
orbus, -a, -um	deprived (of), bereaved, orphaned

3.519–26

namque dies aderit, quam non procul auguror esse,
qua novus huc veniat, proles Semeleia, Liber, 520
quem nisi templorum fueris dignatus honore,
mille lacer spargere locis et sanguine silvas
foedabis matremque tuam matrisque sorores.
eveniet! neque enim dignabere numen honore,
meque sub his tenebris nimium vidisse quereris'. 525
talia dicentem proturbat Echione natus.

Study Questions

- Explain the syntax of *quam non procul auguror esse* (519).
- How does *Semeleia* (520) scan — and why?
- Why type of condition does *nisi* (521) introduce?
- On what noun does the genitive *templorum* (521) depend?
- What word does *mille* (522) modify?
- How does *lacer* fit into the syntax of the sentence?
- Parse *spargere* (522).
- What does the *-que* after *matrem* (523) link? And what the *-que* after *matris* (523)?
- Parse and scan *eveniet* (524)
- Parse *dignabere* (524).
- What does the *-que* after *me* (525) link?
- Explain the syntax of *me* (525).
- Parse *dicentem*.
- What kind of ablative is *Echione* (526)?

Stylistic Appreciation

Discuss Ovid's use of tense (present; future; future perfect) and repetition (e.g. *fueris dignatus ~ dignabere*) in this segment. How does it enhance the authority of Tiresias?

Discussion Points

Tiresias here announces that what soon will go down in the text is the epic equivalent of a modern splatter-movie: horror is in store, as well as the graphic portrayal of gore and violence (see esp. 522–23: *mille lacer spargere locis et sanguine silvas | foedabis matremque tuam matrisque sorores*). Do you *really* want to read on? And if so, why?

auguro, -are, -avi, -atum or (as here) as deponent: *auguror, -ari, -atus*	to foretell by augury, predict, prophesy
procul (adv.)	some way off, (far) away
proles, -is, f.	offspring
digno, -are, -avi, -atum or (as here) as deponent: *dignor, -ari, -atus*	to consider worthy
lacer, -era, -um	mutilated, mangled; torn, rent
spargo, -gere, -si, -sum	to scatter, sprinkle, strew, disperse
foedo, -are, -avi, -atum	to make filthy/unclean, soil, stain, befoul
numen, -inis, n.	divine power, divinity
proturbo, -are, -avi, -atum	to drive forth, push out of the way

3.527–37

dicta fides sequitur, responsaque vatis aguntur.
Liber adest, festisque fremunt ululatibus agri:
turba ruit, mixtaeque viris matresque nurusque
vulgusque proceresque ignota ad sacra feruntur. 530
'Quis furor, anguigenae, proles Mavortia, vestras
attonuit mentes?' Pentheus ait; 'aerane tantum
aere repulsa valent et adunco tibia cornu
et magicae fraudes, ut, quos non bellicus ensis,
non tuba terruerit, non strictis agmina telis, 535
femineae voces et mota insania vino
obscenique greges et inania tympana vincant?

Study Questions
- Parse *dicta*.
- Who is Liber?
- What is the subject of *fremunt* (528)? What is the effect of its placement in the sentence?
- Sort out what each of the five -*que* in 529–30 (*festisque, mixtaeque, matresque, nurusque, vulgusque, proceresque*) links. Which one is technically speaking superfluous? Why does Ovid use it nevertheless?
- What is the case of *anguigenae* and *proles Mavortia* (531)?
- Identify the three subjects of *valent* (the main verb of the sentence) (533).
- What type of clause does *ut* (534) introduce?
- What is the antecedent of the relative pronoun *quos*?
- Identify the three subjects of *terruerit* (the verb of the relative clause introduced by *quos*) (535).
- Identify the four subjects of *vincant* (the verb of the *ut*-clause) (537).

Stylistic Appreciation
- How does Ovid bring out stylistically the Dionysiac spirit that has gripped the inhabitants of Thebes in 527–30? (Include consideration of the use of the connective -*que*.)
- Analyze the overall design of Pentheus' rhetorical question *aerane ... vincant?* (532–37).

Discussion Points
- Why is Pentheus so upset about the behaviour of his subjects? To what does he object specifically?
- Discuss the role of gender in Pentheus' rhetoric.
- What 'character type' does Pentheus conform to? Can you think of contemporary public figures who exhibit similar traits?

Liber, -eri, m.	Bacchus
festus, -a, -um	festive, merry
(cf. *dies festus*	a holiday observed in honour of a god)
fremo, -ere, -ui, -itum	to rumble, roar, hum, buzz
ululatus, -us, m.	drawn-out cries, howling, yelling
ruo, -ere, -i	to rush
misceo, -ere, -ui, mixtum	to mix, blend, mingle, confound
nurus, -us, f.	daughter-in-law
(here: in poetry, usually in plural)	young (married) woman
proceres, -um, m. pl.	the leading men of a country
anguigena, -ae, m. [*anguis* + *genus*]	offspring of a serpent or dragon
Mavortius, -a, -um	of or belonging to Mars, warlike
attono, -are, -ui, -itum	to strike with lightening, drive crazy
aes, aeris, n.	copper, bronze, brass (musical) instrument made thereof
tantum (adverbial use of the acc. of *tantus*)	to such an extent/ degree
repello, -ere, reppuli, repulsum	to drive back, repel, repulse
aduncus, -a, -um	hooked, curved
tibia, -ae, f.	pipe
(cf. *tibia curva*	a pipe with a curved end, associated with Eastern religious rites)
cornu, -us, n.	horn
fraus, -dis, f.	mischief, crime, deceit, trickery
ensis, -is, m.	sword
stringo, -ngere, -nxi, -ctum	to bind fast, secure; draw tight; scratch (here) to bare, unsheathe
insania, -ae, f.	madness, frenzy, folly
obscenus, -a, -um	disgusting, filthy, loathsome, lewd
grex, -egis m.	flock, herd, band, troop
inanis, -is, -e	empty, hollow
tympanum, -i, n.	percussive instrument, drum

3.538–50

vosne, senes, mirer, qui longa per aequora vecti
hac Tyron, hac profugos posuistis sede penates,
nunc sinitis sine Marte capi? vosne, acrior aetas, 540
o iuvenes, propiorque meae, quos arma tenere,
non thyrsos, galeaque tegi, non fronde decebat?
este, precor, memores, qua sitis stirpe creati,
illiusque animos, qui multos perdidit unus,
sumite serpentis! pro fontibus ille lacuque 545
interiit: at vos pro fama vincite vestra!
ille dedit leto fortes: vos pellite molles
et patrium retinete decus! si fata vetabant
stare diu Thebas, utinam tormenta virique
moenia diruerent, ferrumque ignisque sonarent! 550

Study Questions
- What case is *senes* (538)?
- Identify and explain the mood of *mirer* (538).
- What noun do the demonstrative adjectives *hac — hac* (539) modify?
- What construction does *sinitis* (540) introduce and what part of it has been omitted (and needs to be supplied mentally)?
- Explain the case of *meae*. What noun has to be supplied mentally after *meae*?
- What is the antecedent of *quos* (541)? Why is *quos* in the accusative?
- Parse *este* (543).
- Identify and explain the mood of *sitis ... creati* (543).
- What noun does *illius* (544) modify?
- What does the *-que* after *illius* (544) link?
- On what noun does the genitive *serpentis* (545) depend?
- What does the *-que* after *lacu* (545) link?
- Parse *vos* (546).
- What kind of conditional sequence does *si* (548) introduce? (Note: the combination imperfect indicative (*vetabant*) in the protasis + imperfect subjunctive (*diruerent, sonarent*) in the apodosis does not easily match onto any type you will find in grammars.)
- Explain the form of *Thebas* (549).

veho, -here, -xi, -ctum here passive in middle sense	to convey, carry to travel, sail, ride
Tyros, i, f.	Tyre (a city on the Phoenician coast)
profugus, -a, -um	fugitive, exiled
penates, -ium, m. pl.	tutelary divinities of the household
acer, acris, acre	sharp, fierce, vigorous, energetic
thyrsus, -i, m.	a wand crowned with ivy used in the worship of Bacchus
galea, -ae, f.	a soldier's helmet
frons, frondis, f.	foliage, leafy boughs, garlands
memor, -oris (adjective)	mindful
fons, -ntis, m.	spring, well, fountain
lacus, -us, m.	lake, pond, pool
intereo, -ire, -ii, -itum	to die, perish
decus, -oris, n.	high esteem, honour, glory
patrius, -a, -um	of/ belonging to a father, ancestral, native
Thebae, -arum, f. pl.	Thebes
tormentum, -i, n.	rope, catapult; torture, agony
diruo, -ere, -i, -tum	to demolish, wreck

Stylistic Appreciation

Analyze the rhetorical techniques Pentheus uses in his appeal to the Thebans. Are they effective?

Discussion Points

- What other epic famously features exiles who sailed across the sea with their tutelary household divinities? Are the parallels significant?
- What do you make of the fact that Pentheus upholds the murderous dragon of Mars who killed off most of the companions of his grandfather Cadmus upon his arrival at the future site of Thebes (see *Met.* 3.1–49) as a positive role-model?

3.551–61

essemus miseri sine crimine, sorsque querenda,
non celanda foret, lacrimaeque pudore carerent;
at nunc a puero Thebae capientur inermi,
quem neque bella iuvant nec tela nec usus equorum,
sed madidus murra crinis mollesque coronae   555
purpuraque et pictis intextum vestibus aurum,
quem quidem ego actutum (modo vos absistite) cogam
adsumptumque patrem commentaque sacra fateri.
an satis Acrisio est animi, contemnere vanum
numen et Argolicas venienti claudere portas: 560
Penthea terrebit cum totis advena Thebis?

Study Questions

- Identify and explain the tense and mood of *essemus*, *querenda + celanda foret*, and *carerent* (551–52)
- What kind of ablative is *pudore* (552)?
- What is the subject of *capientur* (553)?
- Identify the seven (!) subjects (three negatives, four positives) that go with *iuvant* (554–56).
- Explain the grammar and discuss the meaning and design of *pictis intextum vestibus aurum* (556).
- Explain how the infinitive *fateri* (558) fits into the sentence. What kind of construction does it introduce?
- What kind of genitive is *animi* (559)? On what word does it depend?
- Parse *venienti*. How does it fit into the sentence?
- Parse *Penthea* (561).

Stylistic Appreciation

- What formal devices does Pentheus use to reinforce his mockery of Bacchus?
- Looking back over the speech, analyze its overall design with particular attention to Pentheus' (changing) interaction with his audience.

Discussion Points

- In his portrayal of Bacchus, Pentheus uses several stereotypes to characterize him as strange and foreign — a technique called 'othering' (to make someone look different from oneself). What are these stereotypes? Do they still have currency in contemporary culture? If so, where?
- Bacchus demands infraction and suspension of the norms and expectations that bind (a) society. Tabulate these as Pentheus' speech captures them.

sors, -tis, f.	lot, fortune, destiny
queror, -ri, -stus	to regret, complain, protest
celo, -are, -avi, -atum	to conceal from view, hide
pudor, -oris, m.	feeling of shame; dishonour
inermis, -is, -e	unarmed, lacking military power
murra, -ae, f.	myrrh
crinis, -is, m.	hair
purpura, -ae, f.	shellfish yielding purple dye; purple dye; purple-dyed cloth
pingo, -ere, pinxi, pictum	to adorn with colour, paint, embroider
intexo, -ere, -ui, -tum	to weave into, embroider on
actutum (adverb)	forthwith, immediately
assumo, -ere, -psi, -ptum	to insert, add; choose for oneself, adopt here: to lay claim to (wrongly)
comminiscor, -inisci, -entus	to think up, contrive, invent, fabricate
advena, ae, m./f.	new arrival, foreigner, stranger

3.562–71

ite citi' (famulis hoc imperat), 'ite ducemque
attrahite huc vinctum! iussis mora segnis abesto!'
hunc avus, hunc Athamas, hunc cetera turba suorum
corripiunt dictis frustraque inhibere laborant.   565
acrior admonitu est inritaturque retenta
et crescit rabies moderaminaque ipsa nocebant:
sic ego torrentem, qua nil obstabat eunti,
lenius et modico strepitu decurrere vidi;
at quacumque trabes obstructaque saxa tenebant,   570
spumeus et fervens et ab obice saevior ibat.

Study Questions
- Parse *ite* (562). What is the rhetorical effect of its repetition (*ite — ite*)?
- What is the rhetorical effect of the parenthesis *famulis hoc imperat*?
- Parse *vinctum* (563).
- What noun does the adjective *segnis* (563) modify?
- Parse *abesto* (563).
- Ponder Ovid's use of tense in 564–67: *corripiunt — laborant — est —inritatur — crescit — nocebant*.
- What noun do the attributes *acrior* and *retenta* (566) modify? What is the rhetorical effect of this kind of placement?
- Parse *eunti* (568). What noun does it modify?
- Parse *lenius* (569).
- What is the subject of *ibat* (571)?

Stylistic Appreciation
- What is the technical term for the repetition of *hunc* (564)? What is its rhetorical effect here?
- Discuss Ovid's use of the simile in lines 568–71: how do the components of the simile match up to the surrounding narrative? How does Ovid draw on nature to illustrate an emotional condition?
- Who makes the claim of autopsy (*ego ... vidi*) and what effect does this have?

Discussion Points
Does the phenomenon Ovid here describes, i.e. that attempts at diffusing Pentheus' anger actually worsen his condition, ring psychologically true? Why would that be the case? Can you think of other literary figures (or real-life persons) who manifest similar tendencies?

famulus, -i, m.	servant, attendant
attraho, -here, -xi, -ctum	to draw with force, drag in
vincio, -cire, vinxi, vinctum	to tie up, bind
[cf. *vinco, -ere, vici, victum*	to win, conquer]
mora, -ae, f.	delay
segnis, -is, -e	slothful, inactive, sluggish
avus, -i, m.	grandfather
corripio, -ipere, -ipui, -eptum	to seize, grasp to censure, rebuke, find fault with
inrito, -are, -avi, -atum	to move to anger, provoke, annoy
retineo, -ere, -ui, retentum	to hold fast, detain; delay, check
moderamen, -inis, n.	control
torrens, -ntis, m.	rushing stream, torrent
strepitus, -us, m.	noise, clamour, uproar, din, turmoil
trabs, -bis, f.	tree-trunk, beam
obstruo, -xi, -ctum	to build before or against; to impede, obstruct, barricade
saxa obstructa	stones placed in the way
obex, -icis, m./f.	bar, bolt; barrier, obstacle

3.572–81

ecce cruentati redeunt et, Bacchus ubi esset,
quaerenti domino Bacchum vidisse negarunt;
'hunc' dixere 'tamen comitem famulumque sacrorum
cepimus' et tradunt manibus post terga ligatis   575
sacra dei quendam Tyrrhena gente secutum.
adspicit hunc Pentheus oculis, quos ira tremendos
fecerat, et quamquam poenae vix tempora differt,
'o periture tuaque aliis documenta dature
morte', ait, 'ede tuum nomen nomenque parentum   580
et patriam, morisque novi cur sacra frequentes!'

Study Questions
- Identify and explain the tense and mood of *esset* (572).
- Parse *quaerenti* (573).
- Parse *negarunt* (573). What construction does it introduce?
- Parse *dixere* (574).
- What is the accusative object of *tradunt* (575)? And what is the accusative object of the participle *secutum* (576)?
- What construction is *manibus post terga legatis*?
- What kind of ablative is *Tyrrhena gente* (576)?
- What does the *et* between *fecerat* and *quamquam* link (578)?
- Parse *periture* and *dature* (579).
- Scan lines 579–80. What noun does the attribute *tua* modify?
- Parse *parentum* (580).
- What does the *-que* after *moris* link?
- Identify and explain the mood of *frequentes* (581).

Stylistic Appreciation
Discuss the dramatic force of the geminations *Bacchus* (573) ~ *Bacchum* (574) and *tuum nomen nomenque parentum* (580), and of the polyptoton *sacrorum* (574), *sacra dei* (576), *sacra* (581).

Discussion Points
Comment on how Ovid handles the theme of sight in these lines. You may wish to focus on lexical items to do with seeing (*ecce, vidisse, adspicit, oculis*) and words that evoke graphic images (*cruentati, tremendos*). Who sees what?

ecce (interjection)	See! Behold! Look! Lo and behold!
cruento, -are, -avi, -atus	to stain with blood; to pollute with blood-guiltiness
comes, -itis, m. (f.)	companion
ligo, -are, -avi, -atum	to fasten, bind, attach
quidam, quaedam, quiddam	a certain (unspecified) person, someone
Tyrrhenus, -a, -um	Tuscan, Etruscan
gens, -tis, f.	race, nation, people; a (Roman) clan
tremendus, -a, -um	such as to cause dread, awe-inspiring
differo, -rre, distuli, dilatum	to scatter; to postpone, defer, put off
documentum, -i, n.	an example (serving as a precedent, warning, instruction)
edo, -ere, -idi, -itum	to emit; bring forth; utter; declare to make known in words, disclose, tell
mos, moris, m.	established practice, custom
frequento, -are, -avi, -atum	to populate, make crowded to visit or attend (a person) constantly to celebrate, observe

3.582–91

ille metu vacuus 'nomen mihi' dixit 'Acoetes,
patria Maeonia est, humili de plebe parentes.
non mihi quae duri colerent pater arva iuvenci,
lanigerosve greges, non ulla armenta reliquit;   585
pauper et ipse fuit linoque solebat et hamis
decipere et calamo salientis ducere pisces.
ars illi sua census erat; cum traderet artem,
'accipe, quas habeo, studii successor et heres',
dixit 'opes', moriensque mihi nihil ille reliquit   590
praeter aquas: unum hoc possum appellare paternum.

Study Questions

- What kind of ablative is *metu* (582)?
- Lines 584–85 jumble a main clause and a relative clause: rewrite in standard prose order.
- What is the antecedent of the relative pronoun *quae* (584)?
- Identify the subject and the object of *colerent* (584)
- What is the mood of *colerent* (584) and why?
- Identify the subject and the (three) accusative objects of *reliquit* (585).
- What is the direct object of *decipere* (587)?
- Parse *salientis* (587). What noun does it agree with?
- What kind of dative is *illi* (588)?
- What is the accusative object of *accipe* and the antecedent of *quas* (589)?

Stylistic Appreciation

Discuss the devices by which Acoetes manages to take nine lines to say 'my parents were poor and I inherited nothing'. Can you detect touches of irony, more specifically formulations reminiscent of elevated epic style that are here used to express the unremarkable and the everyday?

Discussion Points

- What do you make of the presence of words such as *plebs* (583) and *census* (588) that evoke the political culture of republican and early imperial Rome?
- What might make you wonder if this sounds like Bacchus, god and metonymy of wine, talking?

Maeonia, -ae, f.	Lydia Etruria (because the Etruscans were said to be descended from the Lydians)
humilis, -is, -e	low, base, humble, obscure, poor
plebs, -bis, f.	the common people, lower class
iuvencus, -i, m.	a young bullock
laniger, -gera, -gerum	wool-bearing, fleecy
grex, gregis, m.	flock, herd; troop, band
armentum, -i, n.	cattle for ploughing
pauper, paupera, pauperum	poor
linum, -i, n.	thread, rope, cable; net
hamus, -i, m.	hook
decipio, -ere, -cepi, -ceptum	to catch, ensnare, entrap, beguile
calamus, -i, m.	reed; object made thereof, such as: fishing-rod
salio, -ire, salui	to leap, spring, bound
piscis, -is, m.	fish
census, -us, m.	a registering and rating of Roman citizens or property hence: wealth, riches, property
trado, -ere, tradidi, traditum	to hand over, transmit, betray, surrender
heres, heredis	heir, heiress
ops, opis, f.	power, might; property, wealth; help
appello, -are, -avi, -atum	to drive toward, accost to address, speak to, call upon *to call, term, entitle, declare
paternus, -a, -um	belonging to a father, paternal

3.592–99

mox ego, ne scopulis haererem semper in isdem,
addidici regimen dextra moderante carinae
flectere et Oleniae sidus pluviale Capellae
Taygetenque Hyadasque oculis Arctonque notavi   595
ventorumque domos et portus puppibus aptos.
forte petens Delon Chiae telluris ad oras
applicor et dextris adducor litora remis
doque levis saltus udaeque inmittor harenae:

Study Questions
- What type of subordinate clause does *ne* (592) introduce?
- What is the force of *ad-* in *addidici* (593)?
- What kind of construction is *dextra moderante* (593)?
- On what noun does the genitive *carinae* (593) depend?
- What is the accusative object of *flectere* (594)?
- Identify the six accusative objects of *notavi* (595).
- Scan line 599 — how does the scanning help in figuring out grammar and meaning?
- Identify and explain the voice of *applicor* (598), *adducor* (598) and *immittor* (599).

Stylistic Appreciation
Acoetes continues to take long to say little. Discuss the techniques by which he beefs up 'I learned to be a helmsman and happened to land on Chios'.

Discussion Points
Can you identify the stars and constellations Ovid mentions here on a star-chart? Why has he chosen those and not others? Do they add up to a coherent picture?

scopulus, -i, m.	rock, cliff, crag
haereo, -ere, haesi, haesum	to hang, stick, cleave, cling, sit fast
addisco, -scere, -dici (here + inf.)	to learn in addition, learn further
moderor, -ari, -atus	to moderate, temper; guide, govern
regimen, -inis, n.	here: 'steering-oar'
Olenius, -a, -um [= Gk Ôlenios]	Olenian, poetic for Achaian
pluvialis, -is, -e	rainy
capella, -ae, f.	she-goat; star in the constellation Auriga
Taygete, -es, f.	a daughter of Atlas and Pleione, one of the Pleiades
Hyades, -um, f.	the Hyades (a group of seven stars) daughters of Atlas, sisters of the Pleiades
Arctos, -i, f.	Great and Lesser Bear, North Pole
puppis, -is, f.	stern; ship
forte (adverb; from *fors*)	perchance
Chius, -a, -um	of the island Chios, Chian
applico, -are, -avi, -atum (*ad*) here middle/passive:	to bring into contact, put in (at) (of persons): to land (at)
adduco, -cere, -xi, -ctum here middle/passive:	to lead or bring (of persons): to sail (a ship) to
levis, -is, -e	light (with short -e-) [contrast *lêvis* = smooth]
saltus, -us, m.	a jump, leap
udus, -a, -um	wet, moist, damp, humid
immitto, -ittere, -isi, -issum middle/passive (+ dat.):	to cause to go, send to throw oneself, leap (on or into)

3.600–10

nox ibi consumpta est; aurora rubescere primo   600
coeperat: exsurgo laticesque inferre recentis
admoneo monstroque viam, quae ducat ad undas;
ipse quid aura mihi tumulo promittat ab alto
prospicio comitesque voco repetoque carinam.
"adsumus en" inquit sociorum primus Opheltes,   605
utque putat, praedam deserto nactus in agro,
virginea puerum ducit per litora forma.
ille mero somnoque gravis titubare videtur
vixque sequi; specto cultum faciemque gradumque:
nil ibi, quod credi posset mortale, videbam.   610

Study Questions
- Identify and explain the mood of *ducat* (602).
- Identify and explain the mood of *promittat* (603).
- What kind of clause does *ut* (606) introduce? (Consider the mood of *putat*.)
- What does the *-que* after *ut* (606) link?
- What kind of ablative is *virginea ... forma*?
- What kind of ablatives are *mero* and *somno*?
- Parse *credi* (610).
- Identify and explain the mood of *posset* (610).

Stylistic Appreciation
- Analyze the rhetorical design of 601 (*exsurgo...*) — 604 (*...carinam*), paying particular attention to symmetry and order.
- Analyze the design of 607 and the gender-issues it raises.

Discussion Points
- Why does Opheltes believe that a beautiful, intoxicated young boy they chanced upon in an empty field makes for a suitable victim of kidnapping? What kind of character/ society does his reaction evoke?
- How does Acoetes identify Bacchus?

consumo, -ere, -sumpsi, -sumptum	to take up, consume; *of time*: to spend, pass
rubesco, -ere, rubui	to grow red, turn red, redden
exsurgo, -ere, surrexi	to rise up, get up
latex, -icis, m.	liquid, fluid, water
recens, -entis	fresh, young, recent
promitto, -ere, -misi, -missum	to send/ put forth to forebode, foretell, predict to promise, hold out, cause to expect
prospicio, -ere, -exi, -ectum	to look forward/ into the distance to look out, exercise foresight, discern
en (interjection)	lo! behold! see! see there!
nanciscor, -i, nactus/ nanctus	to get, obtain; meet with, stumble on
virgineus, -a, -um	maidenly, virginal
merum, -i, n.	pure, unmixed wine
titubo, -are, -avi, -atum	to stagger, totter, reel
cultus, -us, m.	care, cultivation, refinement, style style of dress, external appearance, garb
gradus, -us, m.	step, pace

3.611–20

et sensi et dixi sociis: "quod numen in isto
corpore sit, dubito; sed corpore numen in isto est!
quisquis es, o faveas nostrisque laboribus adsis;
his quoque des veniam!" "pro nobis mitte precari!"
Dictys ait, quo non alius conscendere summas   615
ocior antemnas prensoque rudente relabi.
hoc Libys, hoc flavus, prorae tutela, Melanthus,
hoc probat Alcimedon et, qui requiemque modumque
voce dabat remis, animorum hortator, Epopeus,
hoc omnes alii: praedae tam caeca cupido est.   620

Study Questions
- Explain why *sit* (612) is in the subjunctive.
- Explain why *faveas, adsis* (613), and *des* (614) are in the subjunctive.
- Parse *mitte* (614).
- What kind of ablative is the relative pronoun *quo* (615)?
- What is the verb of the relative clause introduced by *quo* (615–16)?
- How do the infinitives *conscendere* (615) and *relabi* (616) fit into the syntax of the sentence?
- What kind of construction is *prenso rudente* (616)?
- What does the *-que* after *prenso* (616) link?
- Explain the syntax of *prorae tutela* (617) and *animorum hortator* (619).
- Identify the five subjects (and four accusative objects) of *probat* (618).
- What is the antecedent of *qui* (618)?
- What type of genitive is *praedae* (620)?

dubito, -are, -avi, -atum	to be uncertain, be in doubt, waver
faveo, -ere, favi, fautum	to be favourable, be well disposed
venia, -ae, f.	indulgence, kindness; permission; forbearance, pardon, forgiveness
conscendere, -ere, -i, -nsum	to mount, ascend; to embark
antemna, -ae, f.	a sail yard
prendo, -ere, -di, -sum	to lay hold of, grasp, snatch, seize
rudens, -entis, m.	rope, line, cord
relabor, -bi, -lapsus	to slide or glide back; slide down
flavus, -a, -um	golden-yellow, blond
prora, -ae, f.	forepart of a ship, prow
tutela, -ae, f.	charge, care, safeguard; guardianship keeper, warder, guardian
remus, -i, m.	oar

Stylistic Appreciation

- What is the term for the stylistic device that Ovid uses in 611–12 *quod numen in isto corpore sit, dubito; sed corpore numen in isto est*! What is its effect here?
- What is the technical term for, and the rhetorical effect of, the fourfold repetition of *hoc* in 617–20?
- How does Ovid generate interest in the catalogue of the members of the crew?
- Why is *flavus ... Melanthus* (617) funny?
- What kind of figure is *prorae tutela* (617)?
- How does Ovid use style to reinforce the contrast between Acoetes and his crew?

Discussion Points

Discuss the psychology/motivation behind the positions of Acoetes and the rest of crew. Consider the social dynamics that unfold here, with one lone voice taking a principled if seemingly hopeless stance against the rest. Where else in ancient and modern literature do we find this situation?

3.621–33

"non tamen hanc sacro violari pondere pinum
perpetiar" dixi; "pars hic mihi maxima iuris"
inque aditu obsisto: furit audacissimus omni
de numero Lycabas, qui Tusca pulsus ab urbe
exilium dira poenam pro caede luebat;   625
is mihi, dum resto, iuvenali guttura pugno
rupit et excussum misisset in aequora, si non
haesissem, quamvis amens, in fune retentus.
inpia turba probat factum; tum denique Bacchus
(Bacchus enim fuerat), veluti clamore solutus   630
sit sopor aque mero redeant in pectora sensus,
"quid facitis? quis clamor?" ait "qua, dicite, nautae,
huc ope perveni? quo me deferre paratis?"

Study Questions
- What noun does the demonstrative adjective *hanc* (621) modify?
- Parse *perpetiar* (622).
- What is the verb in the clause *pars hic mihi maxima iuris* (622)?
- Identify and explain the case of *mihi* (622).
- What kind of genitive is *iuris* (622)? On what noun does it depend?
- What kind of ablative is *iuvenali ... pugno* (626)?
- What kind of condition does *si non* (627) introduce? What is the apodosis?
- What is the main verb of the sentence that starts with *tum denique Bacchus* (629)?
- What kind of ablative is *clamore* (630)?
- What does the *-que* after the preposition *a* (631) link?
- What noun does the interrogative adjective *qua* (632) modify?

Stylistic Appreciation
- Discuss how the Latin re-enacts the way Bacchus gradually emerges out of his drunken stupor.
- Is there a point to the *s*-alliteration *solutus | sit sopor ... sensus*?

Discussion Points
Why do things turn violent?

pinus, -us (and *-i*), f.	pine, pine-tree; anything made of pine-wood; ship
perpetior, -ti, -ssus	to suffer to the full; tolerate, put up with
aditus, -us, m.	approach, entry, entrance
obsisto, -ere, -stiti, -stitum	to set oneself before; to oppose, resist
pello, -ere, -pepuli, pulsus	to strike; here: to drive into exile, banish
Tuscus, -a, -um	of Etruria or its inhabitants, Etruscan
luo, -ere, lui	to pay a debt or penalty
luere poenam/ poenas	to suffer/ undergo as punishment
resto, -are, restiti	to stop behind; to withstand, resist, oppose
iuvenalis, -is, -e	youthful
guttur, -uris, n.	gullet, throat
pugnus, -i, m.	fist
rumpo, -ere, rupi, ruptum	to break, burst, tear, rend, rupture
excutio, -tere, -ssi, -ssum	to shake off, throw
funis, -is, m.	rope, cord
quamvis	(*adv.*) ever so much, exceedingly; (*conj.*) although, albeit
retineo, -ere, -ui, -tentum	to hold/ keep back, not let go, hold fast
solvo, -ere, solvi, solutum	to free, set free, release
sopor, -oris, m.	sleep; drowsiness
defero, -ferre, -tuli, -latum	to bear or bring away; impeach, accuse

3.634–43

"pone metum" Proreus, "et quos contingere portus
 ede velis!" dixit; "terra sistere petita".   635
"Naxon" ait Liber "cursus advertite vestros!
 illa mihi domus est, vobis erit hospita tellus".
per mare fallaces perque omnia numina iurant
 sic fore meque iubent pictae dare vela carinae.
dextera Naxos erat: dextra mihi lintea danti   640
"quid facis, o demens? quis te furor", inquit "Acoete",
pro se quisque, "tenet? laevam pete!" maxima nutu
pars mihi significat, pars quid velit ore susurro.

Study Questions
- Parse *pone* (634) and *ede* (635).
- What does the *et* in line 634 link?
- What kind of subordinate clause does *quos* introduce? What noun does it modify? What are the subject and the verb of the subordinate clause?
- Parse *velis* (635).
- Scan line 635 and parse *terra* and *sistere*.
- What kind of accusative is *Naxon*?
- What kinds of dative are *mihi* and *vobis* (637)?
- What kind of clause does *iurant* (638) introduce?
- Parse *fore* (639).
- What kind of clause does *iubent* (639) introduce?
- Parse *danti* (640).
- What case is *demens* (641) in?
- Why is *velit* (643) in the subjunctive?

contingo, -ere, -tigi, -tactum	to touch, take hold of, seize to reach, come to, arrive at, meet with
hospes, -itis, m./ *hospita, -ae*, f.	host; guest used adjectively: hospitable
fallax, -acis	deceitful, deceptive
pingo, -ere, pinxi, pictum	to adorn with colour, paint, embroider
linteum, -i, n.	linen cloth; sail
nutus, -us, m.	a nod
significo, -are, -avi, -atum	to show (by signs), point out, intimate
os, oris, n.	mouth
susurrus, -a, -um	muttering, whispering

Stylistic Appreciation

This is a highly 'dramatic' sequence, with a lot of direct speech (including imperatives and vocatives) along with whispering and accompanying gestures and movements. One way to appreciate the theatrical quality is to reconceive the passage as a script with stage directions:

> *Proreus (fallaciter)*: 'pone metum et ede quos portus contingere velis! terra petita sistere'.
>
> *Liber*: 'Cursus vestros Naxon advertite! illa mihi domus est, tellus vobis hospita erit'.
>
> *Omnes (fallaciter)*: 'per mare et per omnia numina sic fore iuramus. Acoete, vela da ventis!'
>
> *Pro se quisque (pars nutu, pars ore susurro)*: 'quid facis, o demens? quis te furor, Acoete, tenet? laevam pete!'

Discussion Points

The action that unfolds here resembles a farce, mime, or comedy — that is, dramatic genres of slapstick-entertainment value that are far less elevated than epic or tragedy. Why do you think Ovid lets rip like this in terms of his generic registers?

3.644–55

obstipui "capiat"que "aliquis moderamina!" dixi
meque ministerio scelerisque artisque removi. 645
increpor a cunctis, totumque inmurmurat agmen;
e quibus Aethalion "te scilicet omnis in uno
nostra salus posita est!" ait et subit ipse meumque
explet opus Naxoque petit diversa relicta.
tum deus inludens, tamquam modo denique fraudem 650
senserit, e puppi pontum prospectat adunca
et flenti similis "non haec mihi litora, nautae,
promisistis" ait, "non haec mihi terra rogata est!
quo merui poenam facto? quae gloria vestra est,
si puerum iuvenes, si multi fallitis unum?" 655

Study Questions
- What does the *que* after *capiat* (644) link? What the *-que* after *me* (645)?
- Parse *te* (647).
- What is the rhetorical force of *scilicet* (647)?
- What kind of construction is *Naxo ... relicta* (649)?
- What is the main verb of the sentence that begins with *tum deus* (650)?
- Parse *senserit* (651) and explain the mood.
- What does the *et* at the beginning of line 652 link?
- What noun does the attribute *adunca* (651) modify?
- Parse *flenti* (652).
- What kinds (plural!) of dative are *mihi* in 652 and *mihi* in 653?
- What noun does the interrogative adjective *quo* modify (654)? What case is it in?

Stylistic Appreciation
Discuss the rhetorical devices Bacchus uses to express his outrage at the crew's treachery, with particular attention to the design of 655.

Discussion Points
Can you think of other moments in literature (or other media, such as cinema) in which an all-powerful character initially 'plays possum' or feigns naïveté when set upon by a gang of toughs, only to emerge victoriously? What makes this scenario so attractive?

obstipesco, -ere, obstipui	to be stupefied; be amazed; struck dumb
moderamen, -inis, n.	means of managing; rudder, helm
ministerium, -ii, n.	office, function, service; administration
increpo, -are, increpui, increpitum	to make a noise; to upbraid loudly, chide
immurmuro, -are, -avi, -atum	to murmur in, at, or against
agmen, -inis, n.	multitude (in motion), group, band, army
scilicet (adverb)	it is evident, clear, plain, manifest of course, naturally, undoubtedly *ironically*: of course, doubtless, forsooth
subeo, -ire, -ii, -itum	to come or go under; to take the place of
expleo, -ere, -evi, -etum	to fill up; to complete, finish
diversus, -a, -um	different, opposite, contrary, conflicting
inludo, -ere, -si, -sum	to mock, ridicule; to play at
tamquam	as if
fraus, fraudis, f.	deceit, fraud, deception; offence, crime
puppis, -is, f.	the hinder part of the ship, stern
pontus, -i, m.	the sea
aduncus, -a, -um	hooked; curved
fleo, -ere, flevi, fletum	to weep, cry, shed tears
similis, -e (with gen. or, as here, dat.)	like, resembling, similar
mereo, -ere, -ui, -itum	to deserve, merit, be entitled to; earn
fallo, -ere, fefelli, falsum	to deceive, trick, dupe, cheat

3.656–65

iamdudum flebam: lacrimas manus inpia nostras
ridet et inpellit properantibus aequora remis.
per tibi nunc ipsum (nec enim praesentior illo
est deus) adiuro, tam me tibi vera referre
quam veri maiora fide: stetit aequore puppis   660
haud aliter quam si siccum navale teneret.
illi admirantes remorum in verbere perstant
velaque deducunt geminaque ope currere temptant:
inpediunt hederae remos nexuque recurvo
serpunt et gravidis distinguunt vela corymbis.   665

Study Questions

- Explain the tense of *flebam*.
- What kind of construction is *properantibus … remis* (657)?
- What word does the preposition *per* (658) govern?
- What kind of ablative is *illo* (658)?
- What is the subject accusative, what the infinitive of the indirect statement introduced by *adiuro* (659)?
- What are the two accusative objects of *referre* (659)?
- What kind of ablative is *fide* (660)?
- Explain the mood of *teneret* (661).
- On what noun does the genitive *remorum* (662) depend?
- What is the subject of *inpediunt* (664), *serpunt* (665) and *distinguunt* (665)?

Stylistic appreciation

- Analyze the rhetorical design of lines 662–65, with special attention to stylistic symmetries.
- Scan line 662 and explore possible links between metre and sense.

Discussion Points

What are the rhetorical strategies Acoetes employs to render the incredible truthful? Compare them to those found in other texts (such as the Bible) that are invested in portraying divine interventions in human life that defy empirical plausibility as historical facts.

iamdudum	long since, a long time ago
fleo, -ere, flevi, fletum	to weep, cry, shed tears; bewail, lament
propero, -are, -avi, -atum	to hasten, quicken; make haste
adiuro, -are, -avi, -atum	to swear to, confirm by oath
verum, -i, n.	what is true or real; the truth, reality, fact
fides, -ei, f.	faith, confidence, credence, belief trustworthiness, faithfulness, credibility
siccus, -a, -um	dry
navale, -is, n.	dock, dockyard
verber, -eris, n.	lash, whip, scourge, rod; stroke, blow
persto, -are, -stiti	to stand firm, continue; persist
deduco, -ere, -xi, -ctum	to lead, fetch, bring down
geminus, -a, -um	born at the same time, twin-born paired, double, both, two
impedio, -ire, -ivi, -itum	to entangle, ensnare, shackle, hamper to hold fast, detain, obstruct
hedera, -ae, f.	ivy
recurvus, -a, -um	bent back on itself, bent round
serpo, -ere, -si	to crawl [cf. *serpens, -ntis*: snake]
gravidus, -a, -um	pregnant; laden, filled, full
distinguo, -guere, -xi, -ctum	to divide off, mark out; embellish, adorn
corymbus, -i, m.	a cluster of ivy-berries

3.666–75

ipse racemiferis frontem circumdatus uvis
pampineis agitat velatam frondibus hastam;
quem circa tigres simulacraque inania lyncum
pictarumque iacent fera corpora pantherarum.
exsiluere viri, sive hoc insania fecit 670
sive timor, primusque Medon nigrescere coepit
corpore et expresso spinae curvamine flecti.
incipit huic Lycabas "in quae miracula" dixit
"verteris?" et lati rictus et panda loquenti
naris erat, squamamque cutis durata trahebat. 675

Study Questions
- What kind of accusative is *frontem* (666)?
- What noun does *racemiferis* modify?
- Identify the accusative object of *agitat* (667).
- Scan line 669: what is unusual about its metrical design?
- Parse *exsiluere* (670).
- What does the *et* after *corpore* (672) link?
- What kind of construction is *expresso … curvamine* (672)?
- Parse *verteris* (674).
- What is the verb of the clause starting with *lati rictus* (674)?
- Parse *loquenti* (674).
- What does the *-que* after *squamam* (675) link?

Stylistic Appreciation
How does Ovid render Bacchus' epiphany graphic and effective? (Be sure to include comments on its impact on the audience in the text.) How does he manage to visualize the phenomenon of transformation?

Discussion Points
This block of text brings together gods, humans, and beasts (including the transformation of humans into beasts). Discuss how ancient (and modern) cultures configure these three 'life-forms' and their interrelation.

racemifer, -era, -erum	bearing clusters [of grapes]
uva, -ae, f.	grape
pampineus, -a, -um	full of tendrils or vine-leaves
velo, -are, -avi, -atum	to cover (up), wrap, envelop, veil
hasta, -ae, f.	lance, spear
circa (adverb)	around, round about, all around
simulacrum, -i, n.	likeness, image, form, figure
inanis, -is, -e	empty, void; lifeless, dead
lynx, lyncis, f.	a lynx
panthera, -ae, f.	a panther
exsilio, -ire, -ui	to spring out, bound forth, leap up
nigresco, -ere, -grui	to become black, grow dark
exprimo, -ere, -pressi, -pressum	to press or squeeze out, force out
curvamen, -inis, n.	curvature; curved form; arc
verto, -ere, -ti, -sum	to turn; to change, alter, transform; to translate; to overturn, overthrow
latus, -a, -um	broad, wide, extended
rictus, -us, m.	the mouth wide-open; gaping jaws
pandus, -a, -um	bent, crooked, curved
naris, -is, f.	nose
squama, -ae, f.	a scale
cutis, -is, f.	skin

3.676–86

at Libys obstantis dum vult obvertere remos,
in spatium resilire manus breve vidit et illas
iam non posse manus, iam pinnas posse vocari.
alter ad intortos cupiens dare bracchia funes
bracchia non habuit truncoque repandus in undas   680
corpore desiluit: falcata novissima cauda est,
qualia dividuae sinuantur cornua lunae.
undique dant saltus multaque adspergine rorant
emerguntque iterum redeuntque sub aequora rursus
inque chori ludunt speciem lascivaque iactant   685
corpora et acceptum patulis mare naribus efflant.

Study Questions
- Parse and scan *obstantis* (676). What noun does it modify? How does metre reinforce meaning?
- Parse *manus* (677) and explain its syntactical function in the sentence.
- What noun does the attribute *breve* (677) agree with?
- What construction does *vidit* (677) introduce?
- What noun does the attribute *dividuae* (682) modify?
- Parse *saltus* (683).
- On what noun does the genitive *chori* (685) depend?

Stylistic Appreciation
- Discuss the ways in which Ovid represents the disappearance of human anatomy — and the appearance of dolphinesque features.
- How do lines 683–86 enact the frolicking of dolphins in the sea?

Discussion Points
Has the transformation into dolphins also altered the character of the sailors?

obverto, -ere, -ti, -sum	to turn towards/ against; direct towards
resilio, -ire, -ui (-ii)	to jump back, rebound, shrink
penna, ae f. / *pinna, ae* f.	feather, wing; fin
intorqueo, -ere, -torsi, -tortum	to twist, turn round; brandish, hurl
intortus, -a, -um	twisted (made by twisting) involved, entwined
bracchium, -ii, n.	arm, forearm (from hand to elbow)
funis, -is, m.	rope
truncus, -a, -um	maimed, mutilated, disfigured
repandus, -a, -um	bent backwards, turned up
falcatus, -a, -um [from *falx*: sickle]	armed with scythes; sickle-shaped, curved
cauda, -ae, f.	tail
dividuus, -a, -um	divided, separated; with *luna*: half-moon
sinuo, -are, -avi, -atum	to bend, wind, curve
roro, -are, -avi, -atum [*ros + o*]	(intr.) to shed moisture, to drizzle
aspergo, -ginis f.	action of sprinkling; what is sprinkled *here*: spraying
rursus (adverb)	back again, again
chorus, -i, m.	dance; chorus
species, -ei, f.	sight, appearance
in speciem	so as to give an appearance/ impression
lascivus, -a, -um	playful, frisky, frolicsome; mischievous
patulus, -a, -um	wide-open, gaping
accipio, -ere, accepi, acceptum	to take, receive
efflo, -are, -avi, -atum	to blow out, breathe out

3.687–95

de modo viginti (tot enim ratis illa ferebat)
restabam solus: pavidum gelidoque trementem
corpore vixque meo firmat deus "excute" dicens
"corde metum Dianque tene!" delatus in illam   690
accessi sacris Baccheaque sacra frequento'.
'Praebuimus longis' Pentheus 'ambagibus aures',
inquit 'ut ira mora vires absumere posset.
praecipitem, famuli, rapite hunc cruciataque diris
corpora tormentis Stygiae demittite nocti!'   695

Study Questions
- What is the accusative object of *ferebat* (687)?
- What kind of ablative is *corde* (690)?
- What words does the *-que* after *Diam* link?
- Parse *tene* (690).
- Scan line 691. Why does the *-e-* in *Bacchea* scan long?
- Scan line 693. What case is *ira*, what case *mora*?
- What case is *famuli* (694)?
- What does the *-que* after *cruciata* link?

Stylistic Appreciation
How does Ovid bring out Pentheus' pent-up anger?

Discussion Points
Does Pentheus have a point when he calls Acoetes' story 'a long-winded runaround' (cf. *longis … ambagibus*)?

viginti (numeral adjective, indeclinable)	twenty
modo (adverb)	only, merely; of time just passed: a moment ago
ratis, -is, f.	a wooden vessel, raft, boat
tremo, -ere, -ui	to shake, quake, quiver, tremble
firmo, -are, -avi, -atum	to strengthen, fortify, support, encourage
excutio, -ere, -cussi, -cussum	to shake out or off; remove, banish
cor, cordis, n.	heart
Dia, -ae, f.	an old name for the island of Naxos
defero, -ferre, -tuli, -latum	to bear, carry, bring; transfer, deliver
accedo, -ere, -essi, -cessum	to go/ come near, approach; enter upon
Baccheus, -a, -um	of Bacchus, Bacchic
praebeo, -ere, -ui, -itum	to hold forth, reach out; give, furnish
ambages, -is, f.	a going around, roundabout way circumlocution, evasion, riddle
auris, -is, f.	ear [not to be confused with *aura, -ae,* f. = breeze]
absumo, -ere, -psi, -ptum	to use up, consume, exhaust
praeceps, -ipitis	headlong, impetuous
crucio, -are, -avi, -atum	to put to the rack, torture, torment
dirus, -a, -um	fearful, awful; ill-omened, ominous
Stygius, -a, -um	Stygian, hellish, infernal
demitto, -ittere, -isi, -issum	to let fall, make descend, send down

3.696–707

protinus abstractus solidis Tyrrhenus Acoetes
clauditur in tectis; et dum crudelia iussae
instrumenta necis ferrumque ignesque parantur,
sponte sua patuisse fores lapsasque lacertis
sponte sua fama est nullo solvente catenas. 700
perstat Echionides, nec iam iubet ire, sed ipse
vadit ubi electus facienda ad sacra Cithaeron
cantibus et clara bacchantum voce sonabat.
ut fremit acer equus, cum bellicus aere canoro
signa dedit tubicen pugnaeque adsumit amorem, 705
Penthea sic ictus longis ululatibus aether
movit, et audito clamore recanduit ira.

Study Questions
- What noun does the attribute *solidis* (696) modify? How does the word order enact meaning?
- Parse *iussae* (697). What noun does it agree with?
- What type of ablative is *lacertis* (699)?
- What does the *-que* after *lapsas* (699) link?
- Identify the two subject accusatives and the two infinitives of the indirect statement introduced by *fama est* (700).
- What construction is *nullo solvente* (700)?
- Parse *bacchantum* (703).
- What noun does the attribute *bellicus* (704) modify?
- What kind of genitive is *pugnae* (705)?
- Parse *ictus* (706). What noun does it agree with?
- What type of ablative is *longis ululatibus* (706)?
- What kind of construction is *audito clamore* (707)?

Stylistic Appreciation
- How does Ovid generate a sense of marvel at the liberation of Acoetes?
- Discuss the illustrative value of the simile in lines 704–05.

Discussion Points
Profile Pentheus' state of mind. Why does he remain unimpressed by the miraculous liberation of Acoetes? What makes him rush to his doom on Mount Cithaeron?

protinus	right on, straightaway, immediately
abstraho, -here, -xi, -ctum	to drag away, remove forcibly
sponte sua	of itself, spontaneously
foris, -is, mainly in plural: *fores, -um*, f.	door, gate
labor, -bi, -psus	to move, glide; to slip, fall
lacertus, -i, m.	upper arm (from shoulder to elbow)
catena, -ae, f.	fetter, shackle, chain
persto, -are, -stiti	to stand firmly, remain steadfast, persist
vado, -ere	to go, walk, rush
Cithairon/ Cithaeron, -onis, m.	Cithaeron (mountain in Boeotia)
eligo, -igere, -egi, -ectum	to select, choose, pick out
bacchor, -ari, -atus	to celebrate the rites of Bacchus, to act like a Bacchante, rave, rage
fremo, -ere, -ui, -itum	to roar, resound, growl, grumble
canorus, -a, -um	melodious, euphonious
tubicen, -cinis, m.	a trumpeter
icio, -ere, -i, -tum	to strike, smite
recandesco, -ere, -dui	to grow white/ hot (again), glow

3.708–18

monte fere medio est, cingentibus ultima silvis,
purus ab arboribus, spectabilis undique, campus:
hic oculis illum cernentem sacra profanis   710
prima videt, prima est insano concita cursu,
prima suum misso violavit Penthea thyrso
mater et 'o geminae' clamavit 'adeste sorores!
ille aper, in nostris errat qui maximus agris,
ille mihi feriendus aper'. ruit omnis in unum   715
turba furens; cunctae coeunt trepidumque sequuntur,
iam trepidum, iam verba minus violenta loquentem,
iam se damnantem, iam se peccasse fatentem.

Study Questions
- What is the subject of the sentence starting *monte fere medio est...* (708–09)?
- What kind of construction is *cingentibus ultima silvis* (708)? How does *ultima* fit in?
- What is the subject of the sentence starting *hic oculis...* (710–13)?
- What kind of construction does *videt* (711) govern?
- What kind of construction is *misso ... thyrso* (712)?
- What type of dative is *mihi* (715)?
- What construction does *fatentem* introduce (718)?

Stylistic Appreciation
How does Ovid rhetorically embellish the final show down between Pentheus and his mother (as well as the rest of the Maenads)?

Discussion Points
Discuss the drama of sight that plays itself out in these lines: who sees whom seeing what from where? Should the transformative visions induced by madness and hallucination count as types of metamorphosis?

mons, -ntis, m.	mountain
cingo, -ere, -xi, -nctum	to circle, surround, encompass
purus, -a, -um	clean, free, clear; undefiled, unstained
spectabilis, -is, -e	that may be seen; visible
undique (adverb)	from all parts, on all sides
hîc (adverb of place)	in this place, here
concieo, -ciere, -civi, -citum	to urge, bring or assemble together to move violently, shake, stir up, rouse
thyrsus, -i, m.	Bacchic staff, thyrsus
geminus, -a, -um	born at the same time, twin-born paired, double, both, *two
aper, -pri, m.	boar
ferio, -ire	to knock, strike; to slay, kill
pecco, -are, -avi, -atum	to transgress, commit a fault, offend
fateor, -eri, fassus	to confess, own, grant

3.719–28

saucius ille tamen 'fer opem, matertera' dixit
'Autonoe! moveant animos Actaeonis umbrae!' 720
illa, quis Actaeon, nescit dextramque precantis
abstulit, Inoo lacerata est altera raptu.
non habet infelix quae matri bracchia tendat,
trunca sed ostendens dereptis vulnera membris
'adspice, mater!' ait. visis ululavit Agave 725
collaque iactavit movitque per aera crinem
avulsumque caput digitis conplexa cruentis
clamat: 'io comites, opus hoc victoria nostra est!'

Study Questions
- Parse *fer* (719).
- Explain the tense and mood of *moveant* (720). What is its subject?
- What verb needs to be supplied with *quis Actaeon* (721)?
- Parse *precantis* (721).
- What noun does the adjective *Inoo* (722) modify?
- What noun has to be supplied mentally after *altera* (722)?
- What is the accusative object of *habet* and antecedent of *quae* (723)?
- What noun does *trunca* (724) modify?
- What construction is *dereptis … membris* (724)?
- What kind of ablative is *visis*?

Stylistic Appreciation
Compare Ovid's techniques in describing the dismemberment of Pentheus with those used in contemporary splatter-movies.

Discussion Points
What are the ethics of depicting extreme forms of violence? Is there an aesthetics of the gruesome? Is Ovid's description of Pentheus' dismemberment entertaining — or even witty? Or rather grotesque and revolting?

saucius, -a, -um	wounded, hurt, injured
matertera, ae, f.	aunt (a mother's sister)
Actaeon, -onis, m.	Actaeon
umbra, -ae, f.	shade, shadow; shade, ghost
aufero, auferre, abstuli, ablatum	to take off, carry off, remove, snatch off
Inous, -a, -um	of or belonging to Ino
lacero, -are, -avi, -atum	to tear to pieces, mangle, rend, mutilate
raptus, -us, m.	a carrying off by force; violent rending
truncus, -a, -um	maimed, mutilated, mangled, disfigured
deripio, -ere, -ripui, -reptum	to tear off, tear away, remove violently
visum, i, n. (ppp of *video*)	something seen, sight, appearance, vision
collum, -i, n.	neck
iacto, -are, -avi, -atum	to throw, scatter; to toss, shake
avello, -ere, -velli, -vulsum	to pull off/ away, to rend off, tear away
digitus, -i, m.	finger
cruentus, -a, -um	stained with blood, bloody
complector, complecti, complexus	to entwine; to clasp, embrace

3.729–33

non citius frondes autumni frigore tactas
iamque male haerentes alta rapit arbore ventus,   730
quam sunt membra viri manibus direpta nefandis.
talibus exemplis monitae nova sacra frequentant
turaque dant sanctasque colunt Ismenides aras.

Study Questions

- Parse *citius* (729).
- What are the subject and the verb of the sentence starting with *non citius...* (729–30)?
- What kind of ablative is *alta ... arbore* (730)?
- What kind of ablative is *manibus ... nefandis* (731)?
- What is the subject of the sentence starting with *talibus exemplis...* (732–33)?

Stylistic Appreciation

Assess the explanatory value and the appropriateness of the simile Ovid uses to illustrate Pentheus' dismemberment.

Discussion Points

Why does Ovid turn the doom of Pentheus into an *exemplum* that stimulates religious worship — despite the fact that he stated earlier that the Theban king was the only one in Thebes who refused to honour Bacchus with cultic veneration? (Note that Ovid specifies the Theban *women* as the ones taught Bacchus' lesson.) What do you make of a religion/ divinity who practises this sort of didacticism? Are there hints in the text that Ovid disapproves of Pentheus' punishment?

autumnus, -i, m.	autumn
frigor, -oris, m.	cold
tango, -ere, tetigi, tactum	to touch, take hold of
diripio, -ere, -pui, direptum	to tear asunder/ in pieces, lay waste
moneo, -ere, -ui, monitum	to remind; to admonish, advice, warn; to instruct, teach
tus, turis, n.	incense, frankincense
Ismenis, -idis, f.	a Theban woman [from *Ismenus*, a river of Boeotia near Thebes]

COMMENTARY

© Ingo Gildenhard and Andrew Zissos, CC BY 4.0   http://dx.doi.org/10.11647/OBP.0073.03

The setting for this episode is the Greek city of Thebes, founded by Cadmus (513–14 n.). Cadmus is by now an old man, and has abdicated the throne of his city in favour of his grandson Pentheus. Early in the reign of the young king, a wild new religious cult sweeps in from the East, that of the god Bacchus, son of the supreme god Jupiter and the Theban princess Semele. While all other Thebans welcome the new cult, Pentheus proves to be sceptical and resistant, an attitude that leads to his doom. (For further discussion of setting and mythological background, see Intro. §4). The set text can be divided into the following sections: (i) Tiresias' Warning to Pentheus (511–26); (ii) Pentheus' Rejection of Bacchus (527–71); (iii) The Captive Acoetes and His Tale (572–691); (iv) Pentheus' Gruesome Demise (692–733).

511–26
Tiresias' Warning to Pentheus

This brief but complex section includes: (i) transition from the previous story, the tale of Narcissus, whose fate the seer Tiresias unerringly foretold; (ii) introduction of the next character destined for doom on Thebes' killing fields: the young king Pentheus, the only one left to scorn Tiresias; (iii) Tiresias' anticipation of events to come: the clash between Pentheus and Bacchus (in essence also an encapsulation of Euripides' tragedy *Bacchae*).

The narrative speeds along here: Tiresias' prediction of Bacchus' arrival and its fulfilment come in quick succession. This initial briskness stands in contrast to the elements of 'slow-mo' that Ovid will soon introduce (and which make up the lion's share of the set text): the speeches of Pentheus and of Acoetes. In Euripides' *Bacchae*, the verbal clash between Pentheus and Tiresias does not occur until some way into the drama.

511–12 cognita … ingens. These two lines form the pivot from the tale of Narcissus (just concluded) to the story of Pentheus (about to start). Ovid opts for straightforward syntax: we get two main verbs, *attulerat* and *erat*, linked by the *-que* attached to *nomen*. The design, revolving around the synonyms *famam ~ nomen* and *vati ~ auguris* (on which more below), is intricate: *meritam … famam* ‹› *nomen … ingens* form a *chiasmus; and *vati attulerat* ‹› *erat auguris* are also arranged chiastically.

A regular Latin idiom is the use of the perfect passive participle to modify a (concrete) noun where English would have, in place of the participle, an abstract noun and the preposition 'of'. Examples include *post transactam fabulam* ('after the play having been performed' = 'after the performance of the play', Plaut. *Cas.* 84), and *nuntiata clades* ('the disaster having been reported' = 'the news of the disaster', Liv. 10.4). In similar fashion here the qualification of the noun *res* by **cognita** (perf. pass. part. of *cognoscere*, 'get to know' or, in the perfect, simply 'know') yields the sense 'knowledge of the matter'.

The 'matter' referred to is the story of Narcissus and, more specifically, the fulfilment of Tiresias' prophecy concerning the boy's fate. As such it harks back to the beginning of that episode: *enixa est utero pulcherrima pleno | infantem nymphe, iam tunc qui posset amari, | Narcissumque vocat. de quo consultus, an esset | tempora maturae visurus longa senectae, | fatidicus vates 'si se non noverit' inquit. | vana diu visa est vox auguris: exitus illam | resque probat letique genus novitasque furoris.* ('The beautiful nymph [sc. Liriope, mother of Narcissus] brought forth from her full womb an infant loveable even then [sc. at its birth] and named him Narcissus. When consulted about him, as to whether he would live a long time and see a ripe old age, the fate-speaking prophet [sc. Tiresias] replied: "If he shall not know himself". For a long time the prophet's utterance seemed an empty one, but the boy's demise proved it true — the event, the manner of his death, the strangeness of his passion', 3.344–50). Ovid's linking of the two episodes in this manner raises an interesting question: 'Will knowing *about* (Tiresias knowing about) Narcissus help anyone else (know themselves)? We read on (but will it help ... *anyone?*)'. (John Henderson).

meritam ... famam (notice the 'framing' arrangement) is the direct object of *attulerat*; the indirect object is **vati**, a 3rd declension noun, referring to Tiresias. A *vates* was originally a divinely inspired prophet (the meaning to the fore here); but the word also came to be used in the Augustan period as the designation of choice for poets (as opposed to the Greek loanword *poeta*), thereby enhancing the intrinsic metapoetic potential of prophet figures in epic narrative.

John Henderson points to an interesting twist here: 'with *famam* Ovid uses this bridge between narrative layers and segments to sound the grand theme that epic poetry confers renown (see Hardie 2012) — usually, upon characters, who make a name for themselves simply by being named in their epic, but here (by surprise: Echo and Narcissus have been headlining, but they just leave backing *vox* and flower, disembodying into white leaves) instead upon the role of the teller in the story he foretold, and as well upon his role as stand-in mouthpiece for the bard Ovid. By implication, scorning Pentheus is scorning not just Bacchus but the power of epic, and blindly slighting the shape-shifting ... Ovid. And reading (this) epic is to enter the laboratory of storytelling'.

The poetic adjective *Achais -idos* (f.), meaning 'Greek', is a Greek loan word (Ἀχαΐς -ΐδος). It is found in Greek poetry from Homeric epic (*Il.* 1.254 etc.) onwards, but does not occur in extant Latin literature before Ovid (who has it again at *Met.* 5.306 and 15.293). *Achais* imparts a more elevated — and more epic — tone than would a more conventional adjective (such as *Graecus, -a, -um*). 'Achaia' (the Latin spelling, or *version*, through linguistic metamorphosis) was strictly speaking a region of the Peloponnese, but such synecdochical usage (one region of Greece stands for the whole) is widespread in epic poetry. In Ovid's day, moreover, 'Achaia' had currency as the name of the Roman province that encompassed all of southern Greece (including the entire Peloponnese and regions immediately to the north of the Gulf of Corinth; the remaining areas comprised the province 'Macedonia'). Such play on linguistic and geopolitical registers occurs throughout the poem and feeds into Ovid's trans-cultural and imperialist poetics: overall, the *Metamorphoses* traces the transition of history and empire from Greece to Rome, with Rome (and its empire) hyperbolically conceived as tantamount to the world (see Intro. §3c). Here the geographical specification simultaneously enhances and delimits Tiresias' fame: it knew no bounds ... among the cities of *Greece*. The phrase **per Achaidas urbes** should probably be taken *apo koinou with (i) *cognita res*, (ii) *famam ... attulerat*, and (iii) *nomen erat ... ingens*. It also harks back to the opening of the Narcissus episode: *Ille [sc. Tiresias]* per Aonias *fama celeberrimus* urbes | *inreprehensa dabat populo responsa petenti* ['He, renowned throughout the cities of Boeotia, gave faultless prophecies to those seeking them', 3.339–40]. Put differently, Tiresias' fame grows as Ovid's narrative unfolds: whereas it was limited to Boeotia at the beginning of the Narcissus episode, at the beginning of the Pentheus episode it has reached all of Greece.

nomen has the pregnant sense of 'famous name', 'renown', 'celebrity'; **ingens** makes clear that Tiresias has become the Ovidian equivalent of a Hollywood A-lister thanks to his unerring soothsaying. The genitive *auguris*, which depends on *nomen*, is used loosely as a synonym for *vates* in the previous verse. In republican and early-imperial Rome, an *augur* was a special type of religious functionary. Unlike the *vates* who relied on divine inspiration, an augur divined divine will (and especially their plans for the future) from signs observed in nature, often the flight- and eating-patterns of birds. But poets often used such terms more or less interchangeably in the general sense of 'soothsayer' (L-S s.v. *augur* ii), as here. Technically speaking, *vates* is the more appropriate label: the blind Tiresias could hardly base his predictions on the inspection of *empirical* signs; his access to the divine sphere — and hence inspired knowledge of the future, a prerogative of the gods — operates via a *metaphysical* connection. But with *augur* Ovid, in addition to introducing variety into his religious nomenclature, invokes a specific priesthood of Roman civic religion. By such subtle effects, Rome's presence is felt throughout the *Metamorphoses*, even though the city itself will not materialize until Book 14.

513–16 spernit ... obicit. The new story starts rancorously, with the verbs *spernit*, *ridet* and *obicit* sounding a derisive note. The shared subject of these verbs needs to be assembled from bits and pieces littered across lines 513–14: *Echionides*, (*ex omnibus*) *unus*, *contemptor superum*, and *Pentheus*. Our understanding of the syntax evolves as we read along. The patronymic *Echionides* ('son of Echion') could be a viable subject and seems to suffice until we reach *ex omnibus unus*, at which point it becomes preferable to take *Echionides* as standing in apposition ('a single individual, the son of Echion ...'). Two more appositional expressions follow in the subsequent line: the general attribution *contemptor superum* and the proper name *Pentheus*. Ovid thus introduces his new protagonist, the young king of Thebes, through a complex sequence of designations: we first get his lineage (he is the son of Echion), then learn that he stands apart from everyone concerning Tiresias (*ex omnibus unus*) and that he is a blasphemer (*contemptor superum*); and finally we get the actual name (*Pentheus*). Reshuffled, we get: 'A single individual, Pentheus, the son of Echion, a blasphemer of the gods, still holds him in contempt ...' This build-up has an ominous effect, not merely introducing Pentheus as the principal character (the next to stamp his name on epic, to star in Ovid), but also adumbrating his downfall (the flipside of the *fama* factory; but infamy's still a form of fame). Those who challenge the gods tend to meet a sticky end in the *Metamorphoses* (513–14 n.); the 'piecemeal' fashion in which Ovid introduces Pentheus here may subtly anticipate his physical disintegration at the end, where he gets torn limb from limb.

Note the placement of the verbs within a *tricolon arrangement: *spernit* comes at the beginning of line and clause; *ridet* comes at the end of line and in the middle of its clause; *obicit* comes at the beginning of the line and the end of the clause — and is further set off by enjambment and the abrupt *diaeresis after the first foot. The effect is to maintain focus upon Pentheus' actions with deliberate variation. It should be noted that Narcissus too 'scorned' (Echo: 393 *spreta*) — but Pentheus ups the ante, to make a complete hatchet job of it, and of himself.

513–14 spernit ... Pentheus. The conjunction **tamen** gives the preceding two lines a concessive force ('Even though the story of Narcissus ... Pentheus nevertheless ...'). **Echionides** is a patronymic, which identifies an individual by a male ancestor (often his father). The patronymic is characteristic of ancient epic language, both Greek and Latin (which borrowed it from Greek). It is found from the very first line of Western literature (Hom. *Il.* 1.1 'Sing, Muse, of the wrath of *Peleus' son* [Πηληϊάδεω] Achilles ...') onwards. Here the patronymic identifies Pentheus as son of Echion, one of the surviving Spartoi (Σπαρτοί, the 'Sown-men'); his mother was Agave, one of the four daughters of Cadmus and Harmonia (see Intro. §4). The reference to Echion points back to the beginning of Book 3, where Ovid tells the story of the foundation of Thebes. Cadmus had been ordered by his father Agenor, king of Phoenicia, to search for his sister Europa (who had been abducted by Jupiter in the form of a bull). Since finding Europa proved impossible, and Agenor had forbidden his son to return without her, Cadmus was in effect forced into exile. He thus resolved to found a new city, and at length arrived at the location in Boeotia where the Delphic oracle had indicated he should do so. Thereupon he sent his comrades to fetch water, only to have them slaughtered by the dragon who dwelt in the nearby spring. Cadmus took his revenge by slaying the beast and was thereupon instructed by an anonymous voice from the sky to sow its teeth into the ground. The Spartoi soon rose from the earth in great number, but promptly began to slay each other through bloody fratricide, until only five remained. Cadmus went on to found Thebes with these five survivors, of whom Echion alone is mentioned by name (3.126 *quorum fuit unus Echion* — 'one of them was Echion'). With these balancing references to Echion, Ovid imparts a sense of continuity and cohesion, while affirming the importance of lineage and Thebes' (partial) autochthonous origins for his Theban narrative. At the same time, such references keep in view the peculiar 'Theban condition' — its inhabitants' seemingly genetic predisposition to familial strife, which repeatedly brings the city to disaster. Pentheus will make much of the city's serpentine ancestry in his upcoming speech. Indeed, 'Echion' derives from *echis* (ἔχις), the Greek term for 'viper', so Pentheus is quite literally 'serpent spawn' or, taking more liberties, 'viper-king' — which goes some way to explaining his bizarre praise of the serpent of Mars later on in the tale (543–48).

In ***ex omnibus unus*** the preposition is used partitively: out of all those who heard of Tiresias' correct prediction of Narcissus' fate only a single individual (still) holds him in contempt. Speaking more broadly, the play of 'one versus many' (and related motifs) recurs throughout the episode: 544 (Pentheus on the dragon of Mars) … *qui multos perdidit unus* …; 564–65 (Pentheus' family trying to dissuade him from fighting Bacchus) *hunc avus, hunc Athamas, hunc cetera turba suorum | corripiunt dictis frustraque inhibere laborant*; 617–20 (Acoetes shouted down by his crew) *hoc [probant] omnes alii* …; 646 (Acoetes being beset by his crew) *increpor a cunctis* …; 647–48 (Aethalion mocking Acoetes after his refusal to stay at the helm) *'te scilicet omnis in uno | nostra salus posita est'*; 654–55 (Bacchus in disguise pleading with the sailors) *quae gloria vestra est, | si puerum iuvenes, si multi fallitis unum?*; 687–88 (Acoetes being the sole member of the crew not turned into a dolphin) *de modo viginti … | solus restabam* …; 715–16 (the throng of Bacchants attacking Pentheus) *ruit omnis in unum | turba furens* … The respective merits of the stances of individual and crowd fluctuate over the course of the narrative. At the outset, the individual (Pentheus) is misguided — both in scorning Tiresias and in refusing to permit the worship of Bacchus. In Acoetes' tale, the opposite case arises: the ship's crew is manifestly criminal and sacrilegious (an *impia turba*, 629) in its showdown with Acoetes, who alone manifests religious scruples. The final scene involves a more ambiguous situation: Pentheus, facing imminent dismemberment, at last sees the error of his ways — but too late: the divinely deranged crowd tears him into pieces, though with 'blasphemous hands' (*manibus … nefandis*, 731). John Henderson adds that 'Ovid, in typical fashion, will show just how wooden his build-up for Pentheus is when he nevertheless adds (i) further unbelievers (batty Theban *women*, 4.1–4), and then (ii) the "sole" surviving Cadmeid to reject Bacchus' godhood (Acrisius of Argos, 4.607–10), which kick-starts the next saga via the breathtakingly *fake* "bridge", as Acrisius doesn't believe in Perseus' claim to be son of Jupiter *either*…! (see 559–61 n.)'.

The form **superum** is syncopated gen. pl. of *superi*, 'the gods above'; it is an objective genitive, dependent on **contemptor**. The expression calls to mind the description of Mezentius as *contemptor divum* at *Aen.* 7.648, and further reminiscences of this Virgilian figure occur later in the set text (582–83, 623–25 nn.). Speaking more broadly, mortals defying gods is a prominent theme in the early books of the *Metamorphoses*, where an entire human race with blasphemous proclivities comes into being from the blood of giants slain while hubristically attacking the seat of the gods on Mount Olympus (*Met.* 1.157–62). The first representative of this particular race treated in the narrative is the vicious tyrant Lycaon, who tests Jupiter's divinity by serving him a meal of human flesh and then attempting to murder him; it is this conduct that convinces Jupiter to eradicate the entire race of human beings (save the pious couple Deucalion and Pyrrha) in a flood of biblical proportions. It is, moreover, hardly coincidental that the giants, the human race fashioned by the Earth out of their blood, and Pentheus (via his descent from Echion) are all autochthonous, i.e. 'born from the earth': they are genetically predisposed (as it were) to challenge the *superi* ('gods above'). Indeed, in the choral ode at Eur. *Bacch.* 538–44, Echion is actually said to be one of the giants who opposed the gods and Pentheus, his son, quite literally 'born from a dragon'. In any event, *contemptores superum* almost invariably come to a bad end, so the phrase imparts a sense of foreboding: Pentheus' fate, it is safe to assume, won't be a happy one. The fact that Pentheus is a king — and as such acts as a privileged representative of Theban society towards the divine sphere — exacerbates his transgression, while creating a civic crisis (see Additional Information after 531–63 n.); but on the whole, Ovid follows Euripides in presenting Pentheus' tale as a personal and familial tragedy rather than one of Theban society at large.

514–15 praesagaque … senis. The *-que* after *praesaga* links *spernit* and *ridet*. **senis** (gen. sing. of *senex*, 'old man') focalises Tiresias *both* as

Pentheus mis-sees him as an 'old woffler doom-monger' *and* as we are to recognize him, as 'wizened voice of authority' (see 516–18 n.). Yes, it's the old old story, of tradition — don't fight it! *praesaga ... verba* speaks both to his prophecy regarding Narcissus and to his prophetic powers more generally (on which see Intro. §5b-i).

515–16 tenebrasque ... obicit. The *-que* after *tenebras* links *ridet* and *obicit*, the *et* links *tenebras* and *cladem*. Notice that *tenebras* and *cladem lucis ademptae* are virtually synonymous, both referring (in poetic language) to Tiresias' blindness, and so producing a 'theme-and-variation' effect (cf. 646 with n.), which adds emphasis. We also have a mild instance of **hysteron proteron* insofar as *tenebras* indicates the condition or effect, whereas *cladem lucis ademptae* refers to the moment of deprivation or cause. The circumstances of the blinding were recounted at 3.316–38 (see Intro. §5b-i; the key lines are also cited below). *lucis ademptae* is genitive of apposition (AG §343d) with **cladem**: *lucis* speaks to vision (*OLD* s.v. 8), *ademptae* (perf. pass. part. of *adimo*) to its loss. **obicit**, here in the sense of 'to cite (before an opponent as a ground for condemnation)' (*OLD* s.v. 10), presupposes an indirect object in the dative such as *ei*, which is easily supplied, and implies that Tiresias is in the physical presence of Pentheus. This is indeed the case, as the following makes clear, but constitutes a rather sudden and unmediated narrative turn.

516–18 ille ... videres. The main clause of this segment outside the direct speech consists of *ille* (subject) and *ait* (verb), with *movens* being a circumstantial participle agreeing with *ille* and governing the accusative object *albentia tempora* (Tiresias is shaking his head indignantly as he speaks). **albentia** is present participle of *albeo*, modifying *tempora*, to which it stands in predicative position: 'the temples white with ...' rather than 'the white temples'. This distinction is important, as otherwise you'll be hard put to fit in **canis**, an instrumental ablative governed by *albentia*; it comes from *cani, -orum* (m. pl.), strictly meaning 'grey hair', but here used metonymically in the sense 'old age'. Tiresias' visible signs of old age call to mind the reverence due to the elderly (in ancient as in modern thought), thereby underscoring Pentheus' rude conduct. The seer ingeniously reacts to Pentheus' contempt by reversing the terms of the latter's mockery. As with his foretelling of Narcissus' fate (see 511–12 n.), so here Tiresias utters a *prima facie* counterintuitive statement that reconceives an apparent misfortune (the loss of sight) as a blessing. The sense is that Pentheus would be better off if he too were blind because his decision to spy on the Bacchic rites will prove fatal. In broader thematic terms, Ovid subtly announces here another (fatal) case of illicit gazing, reprising the motif from the tale of Actaeon earlier in Book 3. Naturally the whole passage re-echoes with Narcissus' brand of dysopia too — and his failure to *listen*.

Both *esses* and *fieres* are 2nd pers. sing. imperfect subjunctives (from *sum* and *fio*, respectively), forming a riddling present counterfactual condition (AG §517). We first get the apodosis (the exclamatory *quam felix esses*), then the protasis (*si ... fieres*). Why Pentheus would be exceedingly fortunate (*quam felix*) if he, too, were blind is explained above.

The adjective **orbus** can take either an ablative or a genitive, as here with **luminis huius**, to indicate the thing of which one is deprived or bereft (cf. AG §349a). In post-classical Latin *orbus* by itself (i.e. without the genitive attribute *luminis* vel sim.) came to mean 'blind': see *OLD* s.v. 6, with reference to Apul. *Met*. 5.9, where *Fortuna* is called *orba et saeva et iniqua* ('blind, savage, and unjust'). *lumen* signifies 'eyesight' here; it has the same sense in the prelude at 3.336–38 *at pater omnipotens ... pro lumine adempto | scire futura dedit poenamque levavit honore* ('But the all-powerful father granted [Tiresias] knowledge of things to come in compensation for his loss of sight and lessened [Juno's] punishment by this honour'). In essence, we have an exchange of one type of vision ('eye-sight') for another ('fore-sight'), which explains Tiresias' use of the demonstrative pronoun *huius*. He may have lost one particular type of *lumen* (the use of his eyes), but he has gained another kind in recompense, i.e. mental il-*lumin*-ation/ understanding. See?

Tiresias completes the counterfactual condition with a negative result clause, **ne Bacchica sacra videres**. The adjective *Bacchicus* is one of several name-based adjectives derived from *Bacchus*; others include *Baccheus, Bacchius,* and *Bacheius*. The form *Bacchicus* is found only three times before Ovid in extant Latin, with the first two occurrences coming from fragments of early tragedies (Naevius' *Lycurgus* and Ennius' *Athamas*). Though a small sample size, this suggests that Ovid may have employed it here as having tragic affiliations. *Bacchica sacra* refers to rites performed by (usually frenzied and/ or inebriated) worshippers in honour of Bacchus; the particular allusion here is to the *trieterica orgia*, nocturnal rites held by the Thebans every third year on Mount Cithaeron. The adjective *sacer* ('consecrated to a deity', 'divine') and the associated noun *sacra* ('religious rites') are key terms that recur throughout the set text: 530 *ignota ad <u>sacra</u>*; 558 (Pentheus speaking) *commenta ... <u>sacra</u>*; 574 *famulum ... <u>sacrorum</u>*; 580–81 (Pentheus addressing Acoetes) *ede ... | morisque novi cur <u>sacra</u> frequentes*; 621–22 (Acoetes with reference to Bacchus) *non tamen hanc <u>sacro</u> violari pondere pinum | perpetiar*; 690–91 (the end of Acoetes' tale) *delatus in illam | accessi <u>sacris</u> Baccheaque <u>sacra</u> frequento*; 702 *electus facienda ad <u>sacra</u> Cithaeron*; 710–11 *hic oculis illum cernentem <u>sacra</u> profanis | prima videt ...*; 732–33 *talibus exemplis monitae nova <u>sacra</u> frequentant | turaque dant sanctasque colunt Ismenides aras*. The emphasis is on the recognition of the new rites as authentic, on recognizing a divinity in human guise, and on joining up when Bacchus comes along.

> Additional Information: Feldherr (1997, 47) points out that the theme of sacrifice pervades Book 3 and links the story of Pentheus with the foundation of the city at the book's opening: 'Images of sacrifice feature in the book's first and last episodes and so provide a thematic frame uniting the death of Pentheus with the foundation of Thebes. After the miraculous cow has led the followers of Cadmus to the site of Thebes, the first act of the settlers is to prepare a sacrifice. It is while collecting water for libations that the colonists encounter the dragon who kills them ... At the book's conclusion not only can the dismemberment of Pentheus be compared to a Bacchic *sparagmos*, but the poem's final couplet treats his death as a warning to convince the women of Thebes "to attend the new *sacra*, to give incense, and to cultivate the sacred altars". In both cases the sacrifice unites its participants as members of a new community whose existence the rites themselves confirm. Thus the initial sacrifice can be clearly connected with the rituals of founding the city of Thebes itself, while the final lines make clear that it is as members of the Theban state (*Ismenides*) that the women will participate in Bacchic rites'. Feldherr goes on to link this concern with sacrifice in Ovid's Theban history to the theories of the French cultural historian René Girard, who sees as the primary purpose of sacrifice not so much, or not only, communication with the gods, as the regulation of cyclical violence arising within any community as a result of competition. Naturally, any variety of human, and therefore corrupted, sacrifice must *also* taint the foundation it may bless — with tragedy (Zeitlin 1965).

519–23 namque ... sorores. Tiresias anticipates the arrival of Bacchus in 519–20 and then goes on to spell out with a conditional sequence what will happen to Pentheus if he fails to honour the new god. The two parts of the sentence are loosely linked by the connecting relative *quem* (= *et eum*) at the beginning of line 521. The main verb of the first half is *aderit*; the main verbs of the second half are *spargere* and *foedabis*.

519. The archetype of *namque dies aderit* is the famous Homeric expression ἔσσεται ἦμαρ ὅτ' ἄν ... ('the day shall come when ...', Hom. *Il.* 4.164). *namque* ('for indeed', 'for truly') is 'an emphatic confirmative particle, a strengthened *nam*, closely resembling that particle in its uses, but introducing the reason or explanation with more assurance' (L-S s.v.). The antecedent of the relative pronoun **quam** is **dies**, whose gender can be either masculine or feminine: when used of a fixed or appointed day, as here, it is feminine (AG §97a). In terms of syntax, *quam* functions both as the accusative object of *auguror* and as the subject accusative of the indirect statement introduced by *auguror* (the infinitive being *esse*). The verb **auguror** is a deponent version of the more usual *auguro*, with no difference in sense. The adverb *procul* is the predicate of *quam*: '... which, I foretell, is not far off'.

520 qua ... Liber. The antecedent of *qua* (an ablative of time) is again *dies*. Tiresias' use of the subjunctive **veniat** could be a modest touch reflecting the seer's religious scruples (i.e. he opts for a potential subjunctive rather than future indicative), but that would be hard to square with the forcefulness of the preceding *namque dies aderit*. It may rather be that the present subjunctive (which in any case carries an intrinsic future force) was regular to express a solid future assumption in a temporal clause determining an antecedent, as here: cf. Liv. 8.7.7 *dum dies ista venit qua ... exercitus moveatis* ('until that day comes on which you move the army'). Some scholars have argued for the existence of a 'prospective' or 'anticipatory' subjunctive in Latin (as in Greek), though the small number of examples adduced, and the fact that they are restricted to subordinate clauses, leaves the matter uncertain.

The god Bacchus (Greek Dionysus) is variously referred to in Latin epic: *Liber* is one of his several poetic designations. Originally an Italian fertility god, Liber (the name signifies 'free') came to be associated with Bacchus despite the apparent lack of any original association with wine (see Bömer on Ov. *Fast.* 3.512). ***novus*** can mean 'new', but also 'strange' (*OLD* s.v. 2). With respect to the former sense, Liber/ Bacchus is the most recent addition to the divine pantheon (see Intro. §5b-iii), as well as 'the big new thing' in Book 3. With respect to the latter sense, he is a god with an unusual pedigree: while partially of Theban origin — a little earlier in the poem Ovid recounts his sensational double birth arising from the union of Jupiter and Cadmus' daughter Semele (3.310–15; see Intro. §5b-iii) — he returns to his native city from the East as a 'newcomer'. The themes of unfamiliarity, newness, and arrival from foreign parts recur throughout the episode, as Bacchus establishes his new cult against the resistance of his cousin Pentheus (the son of Cadmus' daughter Agave): 530 *ignota ... sacra*; 558 *commentaque sacra*; 561 *advena*; 581 *moris ... novi ... sacra*; 732 *nova sacra*. Speaking more broadly, the adjective *novus* is a keynote of the whole poem, which begins with *in nova fert animus mutatas dicere formas | corpora* ('my mind carries me to tell of forms changed into new bodies, 1.1–2); newness is of course intrinsic to metamorphosis, and there is a strong hint of literary novelty in this declaration as well. In Roman culture more generally, though, 'newness' was often seen as threatening venerated tradition, so that the connotations of *novus* were decidedly ambivalent. *res novae* meant 'revolution', and this is precisely what Ovid's Pentheus fears (as indeed does Euripides' Pentheus, who speaks of νεοχμὰ ... κακά [literally 'new evils', often translated 'revolution'] at *Bacch.* 216).

The name-based adjective *Semeleius, -a, -um* is derived from *Semele* (Σεμέλη), the mother of Bacchus. The use of a name-based adjective in agreement with its noun rather than noun + genitive, which we would expect in prose, is typical of epic language; the usage with *proles* is formulaic: earlier in the poem, Ovid has *Clymeneia proles* (of Phaethon, son of Clymene, 2.19) and *proles Stheneleia* (of Cycnus, son of Sthenelus, 2.367); later in the set text we will see *proles Mavortia* (of the Spartoi, 3.531). Note that *Semeleia* scans ⏑ ⏑ — ⏑ ⏑, with the third 'e' long as representing the long Greek vowel 'êta' (η).

521–23 quem ... sorores. The relative pronoun ***quem*** (referring back to *Liber*, the last word of the previous line) is a 'connecting relative' (equivalent to *et eum*; cf. AG §303) and accusative object of the verb of the *nisi*-clause, i.e. *fueris dignatus*. Tiresias here uses a 'future more vivid' conditional sequence (AG §516.1), with future perfect in the protasis (*fueris dignatus*) and future in the apodosis: *spargêre* (= *spargêris*, i.e. 2nd pers. sing. fut. indic. pass.: 'you will be scattered') and *foedabis*.

The protasis of the condition, i.e. the *nisi*-clause, is less complicated than it might seem at first glance. Its verb is the future perfect periphrastic ***fueris dignatus***, from the deponent *dignor*. (The regular form for the future perfect as given in grammars would be *dignatus eris*, i.e. perf. pass. part. + a future form of *sum*; alternatively, Latin writers could use the future *perfect* form of *sum*, as Ovid does here). *dignor*, a transitive verb, is constructed with its own object in the accusative and an objective ablative (connected with the adjective *dignus* that the verb implies): 'to deem *x* (acc.) worthy of *y* (abl.)'. ***templorum*** is a genitive of definition with ***honore***: 'the honour of temples' is concrete advice; Tiresias is suggesting the building of such to honour Bacchus.

The indeclinable ***mille*** modifies ***locis*** (ablative of place). ***lacer***, which prefigures 722: *lacerata est* [sc. *manus*], stands in predicative position to the subject of the sentence (i.e. you): 'torn to pieces, you will be scattered ...' Several stylistic touches turn this into a particularly macabre visualization of Pentheus' gruesome end. The *hyperbaton *mille ... locis* underscores the shocking hyperbole of *mille*, which anticipates the 'vehicle' of the simile used by Ovid to cap the account of Pentheus being ripped to pieces: a tree shedding its leaves in autumn (729–31). As Keith (2002, 267) points out, the sound of the Latin *spargere* recalls the Greek technical term for ritual dismemberment of the Bacchic kind, i.e. *sparagmos*. Listen. Can you already hear the serpent spawn (513–14 n.) being torn to bits and sprayed across *mille locis s-anguine s-ilvas*?

Gore (***sanguine***) is a recurrent motif of the Pentheus episode. In fact, the set text is among the most 'gore-nographic' portions of the *Metamorphoses*, offering the ancient epic equivalent of a Hollywood splatter-film. The verb ***foedabis*** ('you shall defile/ pollute'), made conspicuous by enjambment, contributes to the effect: it rhetorically turns the victim of dismemberment into the perpetrator of a religious offence, a prospect that Tiresias seems to dwell on with a measure of spondaic foreboding (*foedabis* scans – – –). After ***silvas***, we get two more alarming accusative objects of *foedabis*: his mother Agave (***matrem***) and maternal aunts Autonoe and Ino (***matris sorores***), who, as the unwitting perpetrators of his dismemberment, will be splattered with their *proles*' blood; his grim death will thus not only befoul the natural world, it will also pollute — both metaphorically and literally — kinship relations. The recurrence of the same word in different cases (here *mater*, which occurs first in the accusative, *matrem*, then the genitive, *matris*) is called *polyptoton. Here it underscores the primal horror of Pentheus' fate: he is going to be torn apart by relatives normally associated with love, tenderness and nurturing: his mother and maternal aunts.

Note that, in addition to polyptoton, *matrem* and *matris sorores* are linked by correlating *-que ... -que*. This correlating usage (in which the first *-que* is, strictly speaking, redundant) is a mannerism of elevated epic language that is not found in normal prose usage. It is generally used to connect a pair of words or expressions that are parallel in form and/ or sense, often terms designating family relations, as here. The device goes back to Ennius, who probably introduced *-que ... -que* in imitation of Homeric τε ... τε. It is metrically convenient, since the particle *-que* scans short (AG §604a.1), and so is particularly frequent at the close of the verse. Further occurrences of correlating *-que ... -que* in the set text can be found at 529, 550, 558, 609, 618, 645.

524. Tiresias' solemn one-word declaration **eveniet** ('It shall come to pass!') is abrupt and unequivocal, dispensing with the conditionality of his earlier formulation. Metre underscores the dramatic exclamation: *eveniet* scans as a choriamb (— ⌣ ⌣ —), and is marked off by a sharp trithemimeral *caesura, which pause enables the force of the utterance fully to sink in. *eveniet* is followed by additional future indicatives (*dignabere, quereris*) that reinforce the sense of certainty.

Hard on the heels of *spargere* (522), we have another alternative 2nd pers. sing. fut. indic. pass. form in **dignabere** (i.e. equivalent to *dignaberis*). The word **numen** is etymologically connected to *nuto* ('nod'), and speaks to divine will (so, for example Cicero speaks of *numen et vim deorum*, 'the will and power of the gods', *Nat. D.* 2.95). Over time, however, it came to be used as a virtual synonym of *deus* ('god'), and that is the sense of the term here, as again at 560.

525. The verb **quereris** (2nd pers. sing. fut. indic. pass. of the deponent *queror*, 'to lament') governs an indirect statement with **me** as subject accusative and **vidisse** as infinitive. With **sub his tenebris** ('in this darkness', referring to blindness), Tiresias picks up (echoes) the idiom of Pentheus' taunt in 515–16 (<u>tenebras</u>que *et cladem lucis ademptae | obicit*):

the deictic adjective *his* is an explicit gesture back to it. The ability to see (*vidisse*) that Tiresias mentions here is his prophetic vision: he ominously declares that Pentheus will lament that he, the seer, has seen 'only too well' (*nimium*, literally 'excessively, too much').

526 talia ... natus. The subject of the clause is Pentheus, designated **Echione natus**, a poeticism combining the past participle of *nascor* and an ablative of origin without a preposition (AG §403a): 'born of (i.e. son of) Echion'. It is equivalent to the patronymic *Echionides* used earlier (513 with n.). The two references to Pentheus by way of his father's name (and hence his chthonic origins as a descendant of the serpent of Mars) provide a fitting frame for the opening encounter between the prophet and the king.

The present tense of the circumstantial participle **dicentem**, which modifies an implied *eum* (sc. Tiresias), indicates that the action of the participle and the main verb **proturbat** are contemporaneous. Put differently, Pentheus rudely pushes Tiresias away while he is still speaking, thereby supplementing the verbal taunts of 514–16 with physical abuse.

> Additional Information: Ovid uses the verb *proturbat* only twice in the entire poem, here and at 3.80 with reference to the dragon of Mars (*obstantis proturbat pectore silvas*, 'he sweeps down with his breast the trees in his path'). This is part of a broader strategy of using lexical and thematic reminiscences, along with other effects, subtly to remind the reader of Pentheus' serpentine lineage. You might look for sibilant hissing in his diction (e.g. 543–45 with n.); an inclination towards meteoric anger (cf. 3.72 where <u>solitas</u> ... *iras* identifies anger as a hallmark of the dragon's mental disposition); fearful, flashing eyes that express that anger (577–78 with n.). More subtly, Ovid unleashes a pair of similes in which the serpent and Pentheus are likened to rivers (568–71 n.).

527–71
Pentheus' Rejection of Bacchus

527–30 dicta … feruntur. After the opening confrontation between Pentheus and Tiresias, designed to set the scene, these four transitional verses are all action. The syntax is paratactic throughout, with barely a whiff of subordination: *sequitur, aguntur, adest, fremunt, ruit, feruntur* — all are (indicative) verbs of main clauses; the whiff is the participle *mixtae*. Ovid manages to generate a sense of the spirit of the Bacchic revelry he is depicting by such touches as the polysyndetic profusion of *-que* and the matching choriambic openings of 528 (*Liber adest*) and 529 (*turba ruit*).

527. The initial *dicta fides sequitur* is a variation on *verba fides sequitur* at *Fast.* 1.359. In both cases *fides* means 'proof, confirmation' (*OLD* s.v. 4a). *dicta* is n. pl. acc. of the perf. pass. part. of *dicere*: 'the things that have been said', or 'the pronouncement' (the English noun 'dictum' has the same derivation). Note the playful word order: from a formal point of view, *fides* does what Ovid says it does: it 'follows' *dicta* in the verse. Derived from the perfect participle of *respondere* ('answer'), the noun *responsum* can, as here, have the technical sense of 'an answer given by an oracle or soothsayer' (*OLD* s.v. 2a). Allow yourself a little leeway in translating *aguntur*: 'actually happen' or even 'come true'.

As at 511, the diction echoes the beginning of the Narcissus episode: *Ille [sc. Tiresias] per Aonias fama celeberrimus urbes | inreprehensa dabat populo responsa petenti; | prima fide vocisque ratae temptamina sumpsit | caerula Liriope* ('he, of stellar renown through all the Boeotian towns, gave unerring responses to the people who sought them; the first to put his trustworthiness and truthful utterance to the test was the river-nymph Liriope', 3.339–42). Tiresias, then, has an impressive 'track record' in prophecy. Ovid is telling you, he should be listened to.

How much time has elapsed from Pentheus thrusting away of the prophesying Tiresias in 526 and the realization of the latter's prophecy as announced in the following verse? Not much, judging from the present tense of *sequitur* and *aguntur*. Likewise, the emphatic *Liber adest* in 528 suggests the arrival of Bacchus is almost instantaneous, as sudden as an epiphany. The 'prologue' has come to an end; hey presto! The action starts.

528. The compact declaration ***Liber adest*** scans as a choriamb (— ᴗ ᴗ —), thus corresponding metrically to and recalling (as well, of course, as beginning to fulfil) the pithy opening of 524 *eveniet*! For *Liber*, designating Bacchus, see 520 n.

The *-que* displaced onto *festis* links the verbs *adest* and *fremunt*. *festis* speaks to the festive, even joyful, atmosphere of the proceedings at this point. Onomatopoeic ***ululatibus*** is used here of ritual howling: when on earth, the god Bacchus was said to be accompanied by bands of women called Maenads (Greek μαινάδες or 'raving ones') who danced riotously and emitted frenzied cries (*ululatus*) in his honour. Add to this the clashing of cymbals and the beating of drums (532–34 n.), and it is safe to say that the region is abuzz with the arrival of Bacchus and his raucous entourage. The *alliteration *festis... fremunt* (continued by *feruntur* in 530) nicely reinforces this impression. As Weber (2002, 329) points out, the 'verb *fremere* is something of a *vox propria* for the Bacchic roar; [it] is probably cognate with Greek βρέμειν and, hence, with Dionysus' epithet *Bromius*'. Note that ***agri*** is meant 'locally' here, i.e. the land in the vicinity of Thebes (as opposed to the city itself), but also more broadly the countryside as the characteristic location of Bacchic revelry and the scene for the showdown smithereens.

529 turba ruit. The Theban population rushes out of the city *en masse*, to welcome the new deity and join in the riotous cult activity. Note that the mood-setting verse opening is again choriambic (— ᴗ ᴗ —), rhythmically echoing the start of the previous line and reinforcing the relationship of cause (*Liber adest*) and effect (*turba ruit*). John Henderson adds: 'Ovid adapts the epic hexameter to mood-set "release inhibitions" — and join (have us one and all join in with) the Bacchic choir (530). Pentheus is to become a text for worshippers to hymn the power of their awesome god for ever after, amen'.

529–30 mixtaeque ... feruntur. The *-que* after *mixtae* links *ruit* and *feruntur*. Ovid creates something of a polysyndetic onslaught here, with the following two instances of correlating *-que ... -que* linking, in the first instance, **matres** and **nurus** ('mothers and young married women' or, more specifically, 'mothers and daughters-in-law' being a poetic combination, tantamount to specifying 'women') and, in the second, **vulgus** and **proceres**. The keynote of the sentence is **mixtae**: under the influence of Bacchus social distinctions collapse. Ovid first focuses on gender (*viris, matres, nurus*), then on socio-economic status (*vulgus, proceres*). Note that the *-que* after *vulgus* scans long by position before the two consonants of the following word.

The life- and culture-changing arrival of the new god inaugurates a hitherto unknown cult, whence the **ignota ... sacra** to which the Thebans flock (in this sense, *ignota* harks back to 520 and Bacchus/Liber's attribute *novus*). Passive forms of *fero* frequently have the 'middle' sense 'carry oneself on' (i.e. 'proceed'), as here with **feruntur**; but there is often a hint of an external as well as internal impetus. Hence, in contrast to the active *ruit* of the previous line, the passive form suggests that the revellers are carried along in their ecstasy, i.e. have shed part of their rational agency. This is a subtle reminder that Bacchus, like few other divinities, will infiltrate the mind and induce altered states of consciousness — a quasi-metamorphic point that bears on the grim conclusion of the episode.

531–63
Pentheus' Speech

Pentheus attempts to stem the Bacchic 'invasion' of his city — or, rather, the mass exodus of the Theban citizenry to the countryside to partake in the new rites. He launches into a passionate speech that rings the changes on various rhetorical registers. It falls into five parts: (i) Three rhetorical questions, addressed to the citizens of Thebes (531–32 *Quis furor, anguigenae ... attonuit mentes?*; 532–37 *aerane tantum ... tympana vincant?*; 538–42 *vosne, senes, mirer ... vosne, acrior aetas ...?*); (ii) Promotion of the dragon of Mars as *exemplum*, interspersed with imperatives (543 *este, precor, memores*; 545 *sumite*; 546 *vincite*; 547–48 *pellite ... et ... retinete*); (iii) A series of conditions, (counterfactual) wishes, (self-)exhortations, and normative statements (548 *si ... vetabant*; 549–50 *utinam ... diruerent ... sonarent*; 551–52 *essemus ... querenda, non celanda foret, ... carerent*); (iv) Anticipation of the events to come in the indicative, with reference to Bacchus and himself, with a parenthetical imperative dismissing his audience (553 *a puero Thebae capientur inermi ...*; 557 *quem ... ego ... (modo vos absistite) cogam*); (v) A final rhetorical question, which Pentheus addresses to himself, in the 3rd person, above all (561 *Penthea terrebit cum totis advena Thebis?*).

Within the literary universe of the *Metamorphoses* the speech clearly fails to achieve its objective. The parenthetical imperative in 557 (*modo vos absistite*) all but admits defeat, as Pentheus has started to realize that he will be in this fight more or less on his own. The speech, then, indirectly chronicles Pentheus' growing isolation from the rest of the citizen body and his desperate and delusional identification with Thebes, culminating in the final Caesarian gesture of speaking of himself in the 3rd person. Not only does Pentheus fail to win over his internal audience, but members of the latter actually endeavour to dissuade him from his intended course of action (as indicated at 564–65). The speech is thus not directly pertinent to the action; Ovid uses it rather to elucidate aspects of Pentheus' character. The literary inspiration for the speech comes from the opening of Euripides' *Bacchae*, in which Pentheus, likewise without success, rebukes Cadmus (accompanied by Tiresias) as he leaves the city to join in the Bacchic rites (everyone else has evidently already left): 'I see ... my own grandfather — what a ridiculous sight! — playing the Bacchant, complete with wand! Sir, I am embarrassed by the very sight of you — you old fool. Shake off that ivy! Rid your hands of the thyrsus, grandfather!' (Eur. *Bacch.* 248–54).

Ovid's Pentheus addresses a much larger group: the male citizens of Thebes. The exclusion of women from this expanded group is noteworthy, for two reasons. As Ovid has just pointed out, the followers of Bacchus flooding out of the city are an indiscriminate mixture of all age groups and of both genders, across class boundaries (529–30); if anything, the spotlight is on the women. And in Euripides' *Bacchae*, though the women have already left the city, Pentheus singles out the female population of his city for special attention (215–32, 260–63). As McNamara (2010, 180) notes, the switch in focus contributes to Ovid's re-characterization of Pentheus and introduces a whiff of tragic irony: 'Pentheus' disregard of the female members of his audience parallels his argument ... which urges the men to reject femininity in favour of masculinity. He dismisses women at his peril, of course; it is at their hands that he will meet his death (3.708–31)'.

> Additional Information: To understand the extent of the civic crisis created by Pentheus' rift with his fellow Thebans, we must bear in mind that the human world described by Ovid at this point (and found in ancient myth more broadly) consisted of independent city-states, such as Thebes, whose members were bound by shared laws and religious practices. Individual religious activity and differentiated belief were less significant than they are today: it was primarily collectively, as a socio-political unit, that members of city-states interacted with the divine sphere, with leading figures often 'performing' the interaction through collective ritual acts. Hence a major rift between a ruler and the broader citizen body in this domain would constitute a grievous problem — none more grave.

531–32 Quis ... mentes? As an interrogative *quis* is usually substantival, but is sometimes found as a m. adjective, as here and again at 632 (*quis clamor?*). So *quis* modifies *furor* (on which more below), the subject of the sentence (cf. 3.641). The verb **attonuit** is present perfect ('has thunderstruck' your minds) rather than simple past ('did thunderstrike'): the inhabitants are in the thrall of Bacchic possession while Pentheus attempts to reason with them. *quis furor* is a question that, as Hardie (1990, 225) points out, Pentheus 'might with more propriety address to himself' (cf. 577–78 with n.). The dramatic query has an epic antecedent at Virg. *Aen.* 5.670, where the young prince Ascanius addresses the flipped-out Trojan women who are trying to set fire to their own fleet with *quis furor iste novus?* ('What strange madness is this?').

References to madness or insanity recur throughout the Pentheus episode, as here with *furor* (again at 641). Other signifiers belonging to the semantic field of madness include *amens* (628), *demens* (641), *furor/ furens* (623, 716), and *insania/ insanus* (536, 670, 711). The various attributions, however, show that madness is in the eyes of the beholder: the terms are applied indiscriminately by Pentheus to describe the conduct of the Maenads (as here), and by the narrator to describe Pentheus. The same is true of the inset tale that follows: the crew accuses Acoetes of madness (641–42), Acoetes the crew. This split reality poses a challenge for readers: we have to make up our own minds as to which of these attributions to accept. Ovid uses additional means to suggest that a given individual is out of his or her mind. In Pentheus' case, he highlights the fact that the Theban king is in thrall to violent emotions, in particular anger (*ira*: 577, 693, 707; *rabies*: 567). In terms of genre, *furor* originally belongs to the world of tragedy — there is no equivalent to the 'constitutional insanity' so characteristic of the tragic stage in the Homeric epics (though Homeric heroes are of course emotionally incontinent, especially when their honour is at stake, and do 'lose it' at times). From 5th-century Athenian tragedy, the phenomenon or theme of 'madness' migrated into epic, not least *Aeneid* 4, which features the tragedy of Dido deranged.

The two vocatives belong to lofty epic diction: **anguigenae** is a compound adjective (a composite of *anguis*, 'snake' and *-gena*, 'born from') and **proles Mavortia** a poetic formula (520 n.). Taken together they make for a highly evocative address to the citizenry, and one that recalls its legendary origins. The compound *anguigenae* refers back to the dragon of Mars that dwelled at the site of the future city, and speaks to the birth of the Thebans from the serpent's teeth (513–14 n.); an equally appropriate compound is *terrigenae*, 'earth-born' (a composite of *terra*, 'earth' and *-gena*, 'born from'), which Ovid uses at 3.118, when he recounts the birth of the Spartoi. As for *proles Mavortia*, it should probably be taken as roughly synonymous with *anguigenae* ('the offspring of [the dragon of] Mars'), particularly as earlier accounts have Mars sire the dragon: Ovid would then be alluding to such traditions in the manner of a *doctus poeta* ('learned poet'). An alternative might be to understand a reference to the fact that Cadmus, the founder of Thebes, married Harmonia, the daughter of Mars and Venus (*Met*. 3.132–33). For a Roman reader, such references to 'Martian' lineage would call to mind other founding figures who descended from Mars (and, not unlike the Spartoi, also perpetrated fratricide in the course of laying the foundation of a new city): the twins Romulus and Remus, with the former founding Rome after slaying the latter. According to hoary legend, their sire was Mars, who impregnated the Vestal Virgin Ilia. If it is hard to repress Roman analogies here, it will soon become well-nigh impossible (538–40 n.).

532–37 aerane ... vincant? Pentheus here launches into a long rhetorical question to rally his Thebans. The main verb is *valent*, which takes three subjects: *aera* (in the participial phrase *aere repulsa*), *tibia* (with the further specification *adunco ... cornu*), and *fraudes* (qualified by the adjective *magicae*). Then follows a consecutive *ut*-clause (set up by *tantum*). Its main verb is *vincant*; it takes four subjects: *voces* (qualified by the adjective *femineae*), *insania* (which comes with the participle phrase *mota ... vino*), *greges* (qualified by the adjective *obsceni*), and *tympana* (qualified by the adjective *inania*). The accusative object of *vincant* is an implied *vos*, which functions as the antecedent of the relative pronoun *quos*. The verb of the relative clause is *terruerit*; it takes three subjects: *ensis* (qualified by the adjective *bellicus*), *tuba*, and *agmina* (with the further specification *strictis ... telis*).

For Pentheus, the situation is tantamount to an invasion, and his language sets conventional terminology of warfare, in which he reckons his Thebans to excel, against the perverse and effeminate (from his point of view) Bacchic incursion:

	Regular warfare	Bacchants
Weaponry	*bellicus ensis, strictis ... telis*	*magicae fraudes, insania*
Musical instruments	*tuba*	*aera, tibia, tympana, femineae voces*
Military Formation	*agmina*	*obsceni greges*

Pentheus insists that the martial vigour of his compatriots (expressed with the resounding triple *anaphora of *non* in 534–35) ought to dispatch the effeminate and unwarlike Bacchic 'invaders'. By his obsessive military logic, *ensis* and *tela* ought easily to rout *magicae fraudes* and *insania*, the *tuba* should easily drown out the cacophonous racket produced by Bacchic instruments (on which more below) and female shrieking, and a properly drawn-up army (*agmina*) ought to make short shrift of a disorganized effeminate hord (*obsceni greges*).

532–34 aerane ... ut. The adverb *tantum* goes with *valent* and sets up the *ut*-clause: 'Are x, y, and z so powerful that …'

The formulation *aerane ... aere repulsa* is very similar to Lucr. 2.636 *pulsarent aeribus aera* ('they clashed bronze upon bronze'), which may have been Ovid's inspiration (if this isn't Ennius' epic resounding through both of them). Here, as often, *aes* ('copper or bronze') is used by metonymy for 'a musical instrument made of bronze' (cf. 586 *calamus*, 621 *pinus* with nn.). Since *aera* is nom. pl. and *aere* abl. sing., we have 'bronze (instruments) struck by bronze (instruments)'. The instruments in question (fig. 5) are cymbals, which were used in the worship of Bacchus, along with the Phrygian flute (*tibia*, also mentioned here) and kettledrum (*tympanum*, mentioned at 537). The participle *repulsa* ('beaten back') neatly captures the action of the cymbals clashing. The *polyptoton, the enjambment, and the 'echo' in *ae-re re-pulsa* help to join in the rhythmic beat of the percussion.

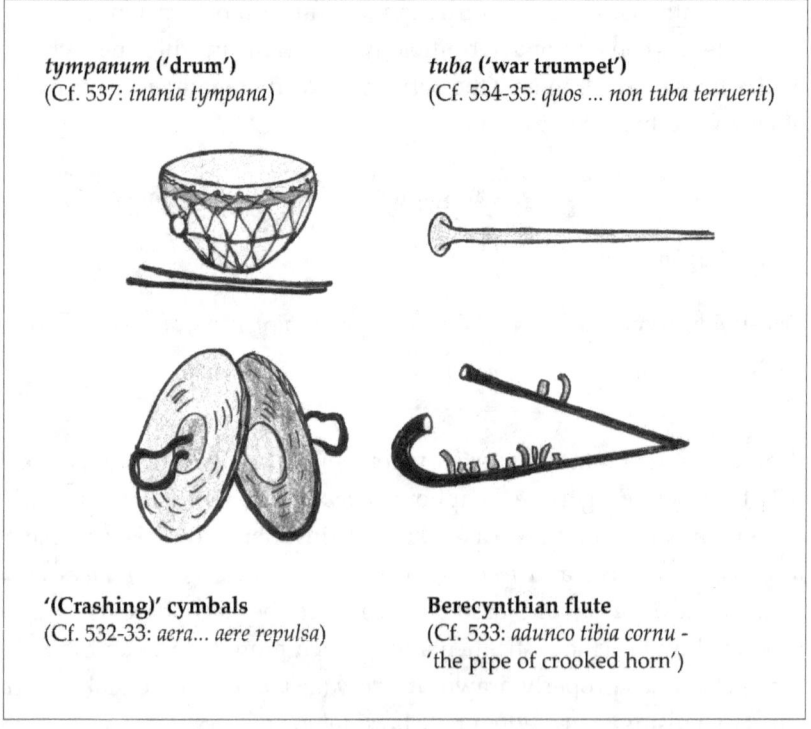

Fig. 5 Musical instruments.

The musical instrument indicated by **adunco tibia cornu** is the so-called Phrygian (or Berecynthian) flute, used in the cult of Bacchus/ Dionysus as well as that of the goddess Cybele. *adunco ... cornu* is ablative of description, a frequent construction in Ovid (we see it again at 607): the *tibia* was a straight wind instrument that ended in an upwards-bending horn (which magnified the sound produced).

Literally rendered, ***magicae fraudes*** would yield 'magical frauds', but since *fraudes* cancels out the claim to supernatural power implied by *magicae*, a better rendering might be 'charlatanry'. Pentheus regards any pretension to efficacious magic on the part of Bacchus as fraudulent — hardly surprising given his conviction that the latter is an impostor. The charge recalls a passage in Euripides' *Bacchae*, where Pentheus comments scornfully on reports that a 'wizard conjurer' (γόης ἐπῳδός, 234) has arrived from Lydia. The Greek formulation is slightly more ambiguous since it leaves open the possibility that the alleged wizardry is genuine — an ambiguity reinforced by the equivocal focalization (the people whose report Pentheus is reporting most likely believe in the supernatural powers of the stranger, whereas Pentheus clearly does not). Charlatanry was no doubt a common charge levelled against various mystery cults in historical times (as Livy's account of followers of Bacchus in early 2nd century BCE Italy illustrates: see Intro. §6). The sense of secrecy and, of course, mystery with which these cults shrouded their rites naturally suggested the idea of magic to outside observers.

534–35 quos ... telis. In the middle of the long rhetorical question we get, buried in a relative clause, an evocation of the martial spirit of the Thebans, the overpowering of which by Bacchus is the immediate cause of Pentheus' dismay. Ovid plays with the assonance of *t* (*tuba* — *terruerit* — *strictis* — *telis*), to recreate the sound of the *tuba*. This device is in the tradition of Ennius' *Annals*, where it was used to more extravagant effect: *at tuba terribili sonitu taratantara dixit* ('and the trumpet in terrible tones blared "taratantara"', *Ann.* 140 Sk); *Africa terribili tremit horrida terra tumultu* ('Africa, a rough land, trembled with a terrible tumult', *Ann.* 310 Sk).

Note the progression from equipment (***ensis***) to the signal to attack (***tuba***) to the actual onslaught of the enemy in rank and file (***agmina***) with weapons drawn (***strictis ... telis***). Pentheus here seems to refer to an occasion in which the Thebans faced an enemy army in regular battle without fear. It is difficult to match this occasion with any event in Thebes' very young history: ancient myth records no such encounter, and Cadmus' battle with the dragon or the civil war among the Spartoi (the military scenarios that defined the foundation of the city) do not fit the bill. ***terruerit*** is perfect subjunctive, an instance of 'subjunctive by attraction' arising from the fact that the relative clause containing *terruerit* is dependent on the subjunctive *vincant* in 537. Relative clauses that depend upon subjunctives and constitute an integral part of the thought will themselves take the subjunctive (AG §593).

536–37 femineae ... vincant? Despite the fact that Pentheus blames Bacchus for upsetting the strict separation of male and female, the dominant group participating in Bacchic rites are women. As he makes clear later in his speech (esp. 553–56), Pentheus regards Bacchus as deficient in masculinity: the emphatic use of *femineae* calls into question the virility of any man in his entourage.

We might translate ***mota insania vino*** as 'wine-induced madness'. The participle *mota* has the sense 'occasioned' or 'excited' (*OLD* s.v. *moveo*, 16). Bacchus, god of the vine, was of course well known for inducing states of inebriation and ecstasy in his worshippers; Pentheus acknowledges the phenomenon, but deprives it of any religious significance by characterizing it as what we might now term 'substance abuse'. In his view, Bacchus' followers are intoxicated miscreants who conceal their sozzled antics under a veneer of ritual piety.

Pentheus' contempt is clearly expressed in ***obsceni... greges***: the word *grex*, like English 'herd' is often disparaging when used of human beings. The original sense of *obscenus* seems to have been 'ill omened' (so Ovid has *obscena puppis* at *Her.* 5.119, of the ship that conveyed Helen to Troy), whence it came to mean 'detestable, repulsive', and eventually something like 'obscene' in the modern sense. Sexual license and like transgressions were widely attributed to Bacchic cult practice (see e.g. Eur. *Bacch.* 215–23; Liv. 39.8.7 *stupra promiscua*, 'widespread adultery' with Intro. §6).

The *tympanum* is a kettledrum (fig. 5), basically a hollow circular frame with parchment stretched over it, held in one hand and struck with the other. The mention of this instrument, for which *inanis* ('hollow') is clearly an appropriate epithet (but perhaps a double entendre), completes the list of musical instruments associated with the cult (532–33 n.). As McNamara (2010, 179) observes, Pentheus 'begins and ends his list with the actual musical paraphernalia of Bacchic worship (*aera ... tibia ... tympana*), while he places the more abstract Bacchic associations (*fraudes ... femineae voces ... insania ... obscenique greges*) between these. He thus "buries" his less tangible concerns within the brackets of these "real" items. For these concerns (magic, insanity, obscenity, femininity) are the standard accusations levelled at Dionysiac/ Bacchic rites by those who often represent more traditional authoritative religion'.

The force of **vincant** is — for the reader at any rate — metaphoric. The reference in context must be to religious conversion vel sim., but here and elsewhere the use of military language and martial imagery exemplifies Pentheus' martial obsession. Rather more subtly, it could also involve mythographic play with an older version of the tale, predating Euripides' *Bacchae*, in which Pentheus responds to the arrival of Dionysus by leading an army into the mountains, only to be defeated in battle by a troop of Maenads.

538–42 vosne ... decebat? The main verb is **mirer**, a deliberative subjunctive ('should I not wonder at ... ?') taking a matched pair of accusative objects in *anaphora: *vosne* (538) and *vosne* (540). The interrogative particles *-ne ... -ne* are attached to the words Pentheus wishes to emphasize: the two occurrences of *vos*. Taken literally, Pentheus is pondering which of the two age groups he should marvel at; but, as the alternatives are clearly not mutually exclusive, it is best to understand an implicit adverb such as *magis*: 'should I be [more] bewildered at *you* ... or at *you*?' Note that each *vos* is followed by a vocative (*senes; acrior aetas, o iuvenes, propriorque meae*) and a relative clause (*qui ... posuistis, sinitis ...; quos ... decebat*).

538–40 vosne ... capi? The first group Pentheus singles out from the citizen body is that of the older men who arrived with Cadmus from Tyre (Ovid may have had his eye on Pentheus' address to Cadmus and Tiresias at Eur. *Bacch.* 248–54: see 531–63 n.). This group cannot have been very large — in fact, it comes as something of a surprise that, excepting Cadmus, it exists at all. At the opening of Book 3, Ovid gave the impression that all of Cadmus' companions were killed (3.46–59), before he went on to found an entirely autochthonous community by means of the dragon's teeth. For the same reason, they are difficult to include among the *anguigenae* or a *proles Mavortia* that Pentheus addresses at the outset of his speech. These inconsistencies begin to make sense if we see them as a deliberate attempt on *Ovid's* part to align the founding of Thebes with the founding of Rome, which also has a discrepant 'double origin': arrivals from elsewhere (Aeneas and his fellow Trojan refugees) and a founding hero descending from Mars (Romulus). Reminiscences of the *Aeneid* reinforce the parallel: (i) *longa per aequora vecti*: thematically *Aen.* 1.3 *multum ille et terris iactatus et alto*; lexically 1.375–76 *diversa per aequora vectos*, 1.379 (cited below); (ii) *profugos ... penates*: *Aen.* 1.2 *fato profugus*; 1.68 (cited below); 1.378–79 *sum pius Aeneas, raptos qui ex hoste penates | classe veho mecum*; 3.86–88; *penatibus et magnis dis;* (iii) *Tyron ... posuistis*: the notion of *translatio imperii*.

The verses are rhetorically wrought: there is the emotional gemination *hac ... hac* (both modifying *sede*), further reinforced by *hyperbaton; the powerful *alliteration *profugos posuistis ... penates*; along with some subsidiary alliterative touches (*vosne ... vecti; sinitis sine*).

The participial phrase **longa per aequora vecti** is a variant on Cat. 101.1 *multa per aequora vectus*. The past participle *vecti* agrees with *qui*; Cadmus' original companions, initially forming a search party, had sailed with him from Phoenicia (513–14 n.); but as just noted, none of these should still be alive at this point.

With *hac Tyron, hac profugos posuistis sede penates*, Ovid evokes in particular Virgil's description of Aeneas at *Aen.* 1.68 *Ilium in Italiam portans victosque penates* ('bringing Ilium and his defeated household gods to Italy'), where *Ilium* is an alternate name for his native Troy. Tyre (Latin *Tyrus*; *Tyron* is the accusative form) was a city of Phoenicia, the original homeland of Cadmus and his followers. Pentheus' meaning is that they have in this location founded a 'new Tyre' (i.e. Thebes). The **penates** were, properly speaking, the guardian deities of a Roman household, closely associated with Vesta, goddess of the hearth, and worshipped in the home; there was a corresponding cult of public *penates* as well. Note that **profugos** (much like *victos* in *Aen.* 1.68) is a transferred epithet: it is not the *penates* who were exiled (or defeated)

Commentary 527–71: Pentheus' Rejection of Bacchus   147

but their human wards. All in all, Pentheus' statement is decidedly odd: not only are *penates* a Roman rather than Greek religious notion, but there would have been little reason for Cadmus and his followers to bring their *penates* (in the form of statues, which stood in the *penetralia*, or central point of a Roman home) with them because they originally left Phoenicia to search for Europa, not to found a new homeland (for the 'backstory' to this episode, see Intro. §5). Ovid has clearly worked against the grain, then, to have his mythical founding of Thebes evoke that of Rome. Speaking more broadly, it is worth noting that elements of Roman culture show up in the strangest places in the *Metamorphoses*: early in Book 1, for example, Ovid rather audaciously ascribes *penates* or household gods to the domiciles of the Olympian gods (1.173–74) — one of his strategies for insinuating the Roman telos of his poem in the early stages of his narrative (see Intro. §3d, and, for Ovid's 'triangulation' of Thebes-Troy-Rome, Intro. §5 n. 46).

The (accusative) subjects of **capi** are *Tyron* and *penates*. Pentheus laments not merely the fact of capitulation, but that it comes **sine Marte** — without a violent struggle. Here, as often, *Mars* stands by metonymy for 'war', 'battle'. This particular form of metonymy, in which a god stands for an activity or item with which he or she is associated (e.g. *Bacchus* = 'wine'; *Ceres* = 'bread') is also known as *denominatio*.

540–42 vosne ... decebat? The main verb continues to be *mirer* (538). Pentheus now turns to the younger generation of Theban men, and ratchets up the rhetorical effects. In poetry the interjection *o* (again in the set text at 579, 613, 641 and 713) inserted before a vocative — as here with *iuvenes* — creates a loftier form of address than the vocative by itself. The term *iuvenis* is a rather vague indicator of age, and one to which the English expression 'young man' does not exactly correspond. Roman thought generally divided a man's life into four stages (ranges are approximate): *infantia* (0–2 years), *pueritia* (3–16), *iuventus* (17–45), *senectus* (46 +). Hence **iuvenes** can be thought of as designating men of fighting age. Both *acrior* and *proprior* (which takes a dative) contrast the younger men with the elderly; the former term (here in the comparative form) means something akin to '(more) warlike'. As **acrior aetas** stands in apposition to *vos* and *o iuvenes*, it must be abstract-for-concrete, a figure whereby a quality is abstracted from the concrete form in which it exists (similarly 617 *tutela* with n.). In English this can be rendered with the genitive: 'young men *of* a more warlike age'. With **meae** supply *aetati* (a form of *ellipse common in Latin and English). With this fleeting personal aside, Pentheus bears out that he has come to the throne at a young age, but Ovid provides no further indications of his age (beyond what can be surmised from the mention that his grandfather Cadmus is still alive, and the fact that his mother and aunts are still sufficiently vigorous to tear him limb from limb with their bare hands). Euripides seems to make him a young man of about 20, or perhaps a bit less (see *Bacch.* 974, 1185–87, 1254).

The relative pronoun **quos** (whose antecedent is *iuvenes*) functions both as accusative object of **decebat** and subject accusative of the indirect statement introduced by it (with **tenere** and **tegi** as infinitives; they are linked by the *-que* after *galea* and by alliteration). This construction can be retained in English translation: 'whom it used to befit to …' (note the reproachful force of the imperfect tense: 'it *used to* befit …'). The indirect statement combines parallelism with variation: we get two antitheses along the pattern: alternative 1 (*arma* + *galea*) — verb (*tenere* + *tegi*) — negation (*non* + *non*) — alternative 2 (*thyrsos* + *fronde*). But the first is active (*tenere*) with accusative objects (*arma, thyrsos*), the second passive (*tegi*) with instrumental ablatives (*galea, fronde*).

A *thyrsus* (fig. 6) is a wand twined with ivy and/ or vine branches (both plants were sacred to Bacchus) carried by the god, as well as by his followers during the god's rites. It was one of the most recognizable accoutrements of Bacchus and his cult. Along with carrying the *thyrsus*, the god and his worshippers would crown their heads (whence **tegi**, a pres. pass. infinitive) with wreaths of ivy leaves, or a combination of vine and ivy leaves (whence **fronde**, a 'collective' singular) during the god's rites. Bacchus himself is later described as 'wreathed with clustering grapes' (666–67 with n.).

Fig. 6 A *thyrsus* ('A staff tipped by a pine cone').

543–48 este ... decus. Pentheus continues to address the younger generation(s) — those, who, like himself, are descendants of the dragon's teeth. He begins with an elaborate reminder of their serpentine ancestry (543–45); the overall design of the verses is chiastic: (a) imperative (*este ... memores*) + (b) relative clause (*qua ... creati*) ‹› (b) relative clause (*qui ... unus*) + (a) imperative (*sumite*). Then he draws two contrasts to underscore the triviality of dealing with Bacchus by comparison with the high stakes faced by the serpent and the heroic feats required of it:

	Serpent	Thebans
Contrast 1	*pro fontibus ille lacuque interiit*	*at vos pro fama vincite vestra*
Contrast 2	*ille dedit leto fortes*	*vos pellite molles et patrium retinete decus*

Again *alliteration (in particular of 's': *sitis, stirpe, sumite, serpentis* — reinforced by the endings in the same letter of *memores, illius, animos, multos, unus, serpentis*) generates formal coherence. McNamara (2010, 181) detects in the highly sibilant diction an evocation of the heroic serpent. Pentheus holds up the primordial monster as a civic role model for the Thebans to emulate. The appreciation of the monster that on its own (*unus*) slaughtered many (*multos*) companions of Cadmus illustrates Pentheus' mindset: he values martial prowess and merciless butchery wherever and however they manifest themselves. Why does he not praise Cadmus? The killer of the serpent is still alive — indeed, he is present (564–65 n.). See Hardie (1990, 225 and 229–30) discussing the comparison with Rome, James (1991, 87–89), Feldherr (1997, 50).

543. The plea ***precor*** is 'parenthetical' and so does not affect the syntax of the clause, which is a command (*este* is 2nd pers. pl. pres. imperative of *sum*): 'Be mindful!' Note the interlaced word order of the indirect question (more regular would be *qua stirpe creati sitis*). The compound verb form ***sitis ... creati*** is in the subjunctive (2nd pers. pl. perf. pass.) because of the indirect question, which is introduced by the interrogative adjective *qua*, modifying *stirpe*, an ablative of origin. Phaethon uses a like formulation at 1.760 *si modo sum caelesti stirpe creatus* ('if I am indeed born of heavenly stock ...').

544–45 illiusque ... serpentis! The *-que* after *illius* links the imperatives *este* and *sumite*. *illius* modifies *serpentis* in a striking instance of *hyperbaton: the 'framing' genitive encloses the noun on which it depends (i.e. *animos*, the object of the clause), the relative clause for which it is the antecedent, and the main verb (*sumite*).

Variations on the theme of one against many (*multos perdidit unus*) recur throughout the set text, starting with Pentheus opposing the Bacchus-worship of the citizens of Thebes (513 *ex omnibus unus* with n.). Here the contrast between *multos* and *unus* subtly prepares the isolated position Pentheus finds himself in at the end of his speech.

545–48 pro fontibus ... decus! After appealing to the Theban citizens' serpentine genealogy, Pentheus develops an elegant *antithesis, reinforced by *anaphora, contrasting the heroics of the dragon (*ille ... ille*, also picking up *illius ... serpentis*) with the lesser feats he asks of the Theban men (*at vos ... vos*). The *-que* after *lacu* links *fontibus* and *lacu*. For lower stakes (*pro fontibus ... lacuque* vs. *pro fama vestra*), the dragon undertook a more daunting task: he killed brave men (*ille dedit leto fortes*), whereas the Thebans merely have to drive away weaklings (*vos pellite molles*). Moreover, the dragon perished in defence of his realm (*interiit*), whereas the Thebans can expect to emerge victorious (*vincite*) and unscathed. Pentheus ends the sentence with an appeal to ancestral honour: *patrium retinete decus*. This is, as it were, Pentheus' variation on Horace's well-known line *dulce et decorum est pro patria mori* ('sweet and honourable it is to die for one's country', *Carm.* 3.2.13): the ancestral dragon died in defence of his realm, a point made emphatic by enjambment of the crucial verb *interiit* and the trithemimeral *caesura that follows it.

The declaration **ille dedit leto fortes** has an elevated, epic ring arising partly from the use of *letum*, an archaic and poetic synonym for *mors* ('death'), and partly from the periphrastic formulation itself ('gave over to death' rather than simply 'killed'). With *fortes* supply *viros* (referring to Cadmus' companions): this is the direct object of *dedit*; *leto* is the indirect object. The account of the serpent's slaughter of Cadmus' companions was narrated earlier at 3.46–49.

Like *fortes*, **molles** is used substantively: 'weaklings' or 'softies'; Pentheus will apply the adjective to the cult again at 555. Speaking more generally, *mollitia*, a hallmark of Bacchic revellers and associated with Eastern culture more broadly, was a quality that Greeks, and the Romans after them, regarded with suspicion: see further 555–56 n. Pentheus' language is, in effect, attempting to appeal to a kind of ethnic boundary. For *patrium ... decus*, see 591–92 n.

548–51 si fata ... sonarent. Pentheus here utters a somewhat unusual conditional statement, featuring an imperfect indicative in the protasis (*si fata vetabant stare diu Thebas*), followed by a counterfactual wish for the present (*utinam* + imperf. subjunct.: *diruerent, sonarent*) as the apodosis. The imperfect indicative *vetabant* almost seems to endow Pentheus with tragic foreknowledge of Thebes' fated destruction (cf. *Met.* 15.429 *Oedipodioniae quid sunt, nisi nomina, Thebae?* 'What is the Thebes of Oedipus now except a name?'), and, in entertaining the possibility that Thebes might be doomed, he momentarily adopts a more reflective stance. This is a striking moment in Ovid's text, but it must be remembered that Pentheus himself is merely engaging in an extravagant metaphor that equates the spread of Bacchic cult in Thebes with the city's physical eradication by warfare. The latter scenario is, in Pentheus' view, clearly more wholesome and honourable, and hence more desirable, than falling under the sway of Bacchus and his worshippers.

The acc. + infin. combination **stare diu Thebas** is governed by ***vetabant***. Note that, like 'Athens' (*Athenae*), 'Thebes' is a plural noun in Latin (*Thebae*) as in Greek (Θῆβαι), and so always has plural forms. The *-que* after *viri* connects the two subjects (*tormenta* and *viri*) of ***diruerent***, the *-que* after *ferrum* connects the two verbs of the *utinam*-clause, i.e. *diruerent* and *sonarent*, and the *-que* after *ignis* connects the two subjects (*ferrum* and *ignis*) of *sonarent*. Overall, the picture is one of martial activity and clamour. ***tormenta*** are siege-engines; the choice of ***viri*** (here in the sense of 'soldiers') is loaded: Pentheus implies a contrast with the effeminate followers of Bacchus, whom he considers *semiviri* ('half-men') at best; *ferrum* and *ignis* seem to form a *zeugma with ***sonarent*** — only the clash of iron on iron generates a martial soundtrack, unless *ignis* refers to the collapse of buildings set on fire.

551–52 essemus ... carerent. This is, in effect, the compound apodosis of a present contrary-to-fact condition, whose protasis is unstated but implied from what precedes: *si viri moenia diruerent* ('if *men* were tearing down our walls ...') etc. As noted above, Pentheus would be less perturbed if Thebes were being sacked and razed to the ground by an invading army. The sense of **sine crimine** is *sine culpa*, i.e. if the city were duly sacked by superior forces, the Thebans would be wretched, but free from the imputation of cowardice for shamefully submitting to an unworthy adversary (a *puer inermis*, 'an unarmed boy', as Pentheus goes on to say in 553).

Pentheus here evokes a thematic nexus typical of tragic discourse: 'modes of guilt/ transgression' + 'an emotional state of wretchedness'. Ovid explores variants thereof throughout his Theban history. Thus he introduces the tale of Actaeon (Pentheus' cousin), who accidentally stumbled upon the goddess Diana at her bath, only to be turned into a stag by the enraged divinity and torn apart by his own hounds, as follows: *at bene si quaeras, Fortunae crimen in illo, | non scelus invenies; quod enim scelus error habebat?* ('But if you seek the truth, you will find in this a fault of Fortune, not a crime; for what crime was there in a misstep?', 3.141–42).

The passive periphrastic **sorsque querenda, non celanda foret** elaborates on what preceded: a military defeat, since honourable, would not have to be hushed up in shame (a notion spelled out explicitly in the subsequent clause), it could be bewailed openly. *foret* is an alternate form of *esset*, so imperfect subjunctive (as befits a present contrary-to-fact condition). **lacrimae** are the tears to be shed over the downfall of the city: they could pour forth without any sense of shame. **pudore** is an ablative of separation with **carerent**.

553–58 at nunc ... fateri. The subject and verb of the main clause are *Thebae capientur*, with *a puero ... inermi* an ablative of agent. *puero* is the antecedent of the two relative clauses that follow: (i) *quem ... aurum*, with *iuvant* as verb and two antithetical sequences of nouns as subjects: first the things Bacchus does not like (*bella, tela, usus equorum*); then those he does (*madidus ... crinis, molles coronae, purpura, intextum ... aurum*). Pentheus dwells on the latter, devoting two lines to Bacchus' 'likes' (some of which he pads out with graphic attributes) and only one to his 'dislikes'; (ii) *quem ... fateri*, with *cogam* as verb, *quem* as accusative object, and *fateri* as complementary infinitive. It is probably best to understand *adsumptum* (with *patrem*) and *commenta* (with *sacra*) as predicative, with *esse* as the infinitive to be supplied. (Alternatively *fateri* could be seen as introducing an indirect statement, with *patrem* and *sacra* as subject accusatives and *adsumptum* (sc. *esse*) and *commenta* (sc. *esse*) as infinitives.)

553. After the contrary-to-fact flight of fancy, **at nunc** ('but as it is') marks Pentheus' return to present reality. For *Thebae* (nom. pl.), see 548–51 n. The verb **capientur** is 3rd pers. pl. *fut.* indic. pass. Note the iconic word order, with noun (*puero*) and attribute (*inermi*) 'enclosing' the city as if putting it under siege. The phrase conveys a twofold indignity: not only is Bacchus a mere boy (***puero***), he is also unarmed (***inermi***), a fact underscored by the hyperbaton, the double verbal paradoxes in the juxtaposed *puero* — *Thebae* and *capientur* — *inermi*, and the position of the attribute at the end of the line. For Bacchus' youthfulness and boyish appearance, see Intro. §5b-iii.

554 quem ... equorum. Bacchus' lack of bellicosity — which Pentheus here expresses with a scathing *tricolon — was a conventional attribute: cf. Eur. *Bacch.* 416 ὁ δαίμων ... φιλεῖ δ᾽ ὀλβοδότειραν Εἰρήναν, κουροτρόφον θεάν ('The god [sc. Dionysus/ Bacchus] ... loves Peace, giver of riches, goddess who nourishes youths').

555–56 sed madidus ... aurum. The combination *madidus murra crinis* is quasi-formulaic: Ovid has *madidos murra ... capillos* (of Athis) at 5.53. Here *crinis* is a so-called 'collective singular'. ***murra*** (myrrh) is a fragrant gum resin obtained from trees found predominantly in Arabia, used in unguents to produce a kind of scented hair oil (nicely conveyed here by the 'dripping' *m*-alliteration). Its use by men was unproblematic on festive occasions (see Gibson 2003, 280–81 on *Ars* 3.443–44); but habitual use was a sign of effeminacy, which the Romans associated with the Near East, in particular the regions of Phrygia (where Troy was situated) and Lydia. In the *Aeneid*, the titular hero is regarded as an effeminate dandy by both the African Iarbas and the Italian Turnus, with the latter speaking derisively of Aeneas' hair 'curled with heated iron and drenched in myrrh' (*crinis | vibratos calido ferro murraque madentis, Aen.* 12.99–100). In the Western cultural imaginary, 'effeminacy' and 'eastern' often go together in what Edward Said has labelled the discourse of 'Orientalism' (the nexus of preconceptions and prejudices that Western authors and thinkers have tended to project onto Eastern cultures).

mollesque coronae speaks to the crowns of ivy (or ivy and vine) leaves worn by Bacchus and his followers (for which see 540–42 n.). Pentheus scathingly attributes the same quality of *mollitia* ('softness') to the leafy crowns that he earlier attributed to those who wear them (547 with n.). For a Roman reader the epithet *molles* might have been particularly striking, as the Romans awarded a range of *coronae* for exceptional military service, including the *corona civica* (made of oak-leaves) awarded for saving the life of a fellow-citizen and killing an enemy in the process, and the *corona triumphalis* (a small golden crown in the shape of a laurel wreath with dangling ribbons) that emperors awarded in imperial times to victorious generals (in lieu of a full-blown triumph).

The ***purpura*** was a shellfish that yielded a purple dye, and the word came to be used both of the purple dye itself, and, as here, of purple-dyed cloth. The dye was expensive to make, and the colour purple therefore came to signify wealth and power, often in extravagant quantities. Kings and emperors used it; and, like myrrh, it carried connotations of Eastern decadence. The sense of ***pictis intextum vestibus aurum*** is 'gold (i.e golden thread) woven into embroidered/ painted garments'. Note that *pictis ... vestibus* is dat. pl. The assertion of Henderson (1979, 98) that *pictis* (perf. pass. part. of *pingo*, 'adorn with colours, paint, embroider') is 'proleptic' in sense is certainly correct if *pictis* is understood as speaking to embroidery (and so anticipating the result of *intextum ... aurum*), but less clearly so otherwise, since the gold thread could merely be adding further colour to already dyed garments.

An alert Roman reader might have caught in verse 556 a veiled reference to the so-called *toga picta*, a garment dyed entirely in purple and embroidered with gold, which was worn (so legend has it) by the original kings of Rome and also by triumphant generals and high magistrates on special occasions (including the emperor in imperial times). See Liv. 10.7.9 and 30.15.11–12 for generals wearing the *toga picta* during their triumph and Liv. 28.4.11, 30.15.11, and 31.11.12 for kings clad in purple. From the (anachronistic) perspective of Ovid's contemporary readers, then, allusion to such a garment would subtly — and ironically — reinforce Pentheus' framing of the advent of Bacchus in terms of military conquest and enhance the status of Thebes as a failed prefiguration of Rome.

557–58 quem ... fateri. The archaic adverb ***actutum*** ('forthwith, immediately, without delay') is frequently found in comedy and the fragments of Republican tragedy, but is very rare in epic, found only once in Virgil's *Aeneid* (9.255), and only here in the *Metamorphoses*. As Currie (1981, 2717) observes, 'Ovid's handling of the Pentheus story owes something to Pacuvius ... and the use of *actutum* ... in the context of Pentheus and his misfortunes is possibly meant as a hint of *color tragicus*, perhaps recalling for the alert and informed reader Pacuvius, and maybe even an actual line or phrase from the dramatist's treatment of this particular myth'. The alacrity Pentheus has in mind is neatly evoked by means of two elisions: *quid(em) eg(o) actutum*. This metrical peculiarity may also have specific generic evocations: as Henderson (1979, 98) points out, 'nowhere else does Ovid construct an initial dactyl of three words which before elision amount to five syllables. The scansion smacks not of epic, but of dramatic poetry'. In short, there is a reasonable chance that Ovid here echoes a now lost Roman drama, such as Pacuvius' *Pentheus*.

The relative pronoun ***quem*** again takes *puero ... inermi* (553), i.e. Bacchus, as its antecedent. The imperative clause ***modo vos absistite*** in parenthesis is more vivid than a subordinate conditional clause implied by *modo* (~ *dum modo absistatis*: 'only provided that/ so long as ...': see *OLD* s.v. *modo* 3c). It is probably best to take ***adsumptum*** (from *assumo*, 'lay false claim to') and ***commenta*** (from *comminiscor*, 'contrive, fabricate') as predicative (see 553–58 n.). Pentheus dismisses Bacchus' claim to Jovian paternity as false (as he does more expansively at Eur. *Bacch*. 242–45, identifying Semele, Bacchus' mother, as the source of the 'falsehood') and the rites devised for his followers a religious sham, and intends to use force to compel a confession (***cogam ... fateri***). Such ruinous scepticism regarding the authenticity of the new god recurs in the following book, where one of the daughters of Minyas makes the same charge in similar language: '*dum cessant aliae <u>commentaque sacra</u> <u>frequentant</u> ...*' ('While other women shun work and participate in the fraudulent rites ...', *Met*. 4.37).

559–61 an satis ... Thebis? Here *an* introduces a direct question and expresses indignation: 'Can it really be that ...?' The question falls into two adversative parts, which are (yet again) juxtaposed asyndetically:

satis ... portas (with *est* as verb and *contemnere* and *claudere* as epexegetic infinitives, as explained below), *Penthea ... Thebis* (with *advena* as subject and *terrebit* as verb).

Acrisius is a mythical king of Argos, father of Danaë and grandfather of Perseus (whose adventures are narrated in Book 4). According to legend he was initially, like Pentheus, resistant to Bacchus' advent, shutting his gates and refusing to admit the god or his worship. In the transition from the Theban narrative to the Perseus episode Ovid offers what amounts to a gloss on Pentheus' mention of Acrisius here, describing the latter as *qui moenibus arceat urbis | Argolicae contraque deum ferat arma genusque | non putet esse Iovis* ('who forbade the entrance of the god [sc. Bacchus] within the walls of his city, Argos, who violently opposed the god, and did not admit that he was born of Jupiter', 4.608–10). In having Pentheus adduce the case of Argos, Ovid unusually denies to Thebes the status of first Greek city visited on his return from Asia. This is in direct contradiction to the prologue of Euripides' *Bacchae*, spoken by Dionysus himself, where the god identifies his mother-city Thebes as his first port of call in Greece (ἐς τήνδε πρώτην ἦλθον Ἑλλήνων πόλιν, 'this is the first city of Greece I have come to', *Bacch.* 20). Another version, reported at Apollod. 3.5.2, has Acrisius' twin brother Proetus behind the Argive resistance to and sacrilegious exclusion of Bacchus — but again this happens right *after*, rather than (as here in Ovid) before, events in Thebes.

The subject of the first clause is **satis** (here used as a noun), with **animi** a partitive genitive dependent on it: one way to translate would be 'sufficient courage'; **Acrisio** is dative of possession. **contemnere** and **claudere** are so-called 'epexegetic' infinitives (i.e. infinitives that 'explain' what Acrisius' courage, according to Pentheus, consisted in), linked by alliteration and position in the verse. It should be noted that *contemnere* is the verb-equivalent to the noun *contemptor*, used earlier of Pentheus (514 with n.). For **vanum numen** we would say *'false* god' (*OLD* s.v. *vanus* 3, though our passage is listed s.v. 2, 'containing no real significance or force', 'empty', 'hollow', 'illusory'); for *numen* see 524 n. The participle **venienti** is dative (of disadvantage) with *claudere portas*; it refers to Bacchus and agrees with an implied *ei*.

Note that **Penthea** is acc. sing., the appropriate form for a *Greek* 3rd declension noun, as again at 706 and 712; like other Roman poets, Ovid regularly retains the Greek declension for Greek names and loanwords (again at 595 *Taygeten, Hyadas, Arcton*; 636 *Naxon*). Pentheus' scathing rhetorical question is made more forceful by reference to himself in the 3rd person, a device of emphasis: *Penthea* is more compelling here than *me*. The expression **cum totis ... Thebis** is an alternative, and more striking, way of saying *et [totas] Thebas*. If the overall expression fleetingly constellates a vision of unity — of the king and his city as one — the verb **terrebit** attributes this imagined unity to shared fear, which Pentheus dubiously imputes to his fellow Thebans, who have in fact been swept away by genuine religious enthusiasm (527-30). **advena** picks up etymologically (~ *ad-venio*) on *venienti* in the previous line. Pentheus' use of the term ('visitor from abroad', 'newcomer', 'stranger') may have been inspired by Euripides, where Pentheus refers to Dionysus/ Bacchus as ξένος (*Bacch*. 233 etc.), which has much the same sense. The scathing anonymity of *advena* stands in sharp contrast to the respectful cult name *Liber* used earlier by Tiresias and Ovid as narrator (519-20, 528).

562-63 ite ... vinctum. Pentheus orders his servants to put 'the leader' (*ducem*) of the commotion in chains (*vinctum* is perf. pass. part. of *vincio*, 'bind'). The same figure issues much the same command at Eur. *Bacch*. 352-55 οἳ δ᾽ ἀνὰ πόλιν στείχοντες ἐξιχνεύσατε τὸν θηλύμορφον | ξένον ... κἄνπερ λάβητε, δέσμιον πορεύσατε δεῦρ᾽ αὐτόν ('Go through the town and track down the woman-like stranger ... and once he is caught, bind him and bring him here ...'). As with *advena* in the previous sentence, *ducem* is used scathingly here, suggesting a mortal rabble-rouser rather than a divinity. By avoiding the god's names and cult titles, Pentheus implicitly rejects Bacchus' claim to divinity.

The parenthetical aside **famulis hoc imperat** ('he gives this order to his attendants') on the part of the poet reads almost like a stage direction (and perhaps enhances the dramatic-tragic qualities of the episode). The adjective *citi* (nom. m. pl. of *citus*, 'fast') is used here in lieu of an adverb (*cite, celeriter*). The **-que** after *ducem* connects the imperatives **ite** (second occurrence) and **attrahite**.

Wills (1996, 101), in a discussion of the iteration of *ite* in sacral contexts, points to a possible irony in Pentheus employing ritual language (if it be such) in ordering an assault on a divinity. He also points out that

Ovid has here reassigned to Pentheus words uttered by the Euripidean chorus at *Bacch.* 83–87 ἴτε βάκχαι, ἴτε βάκχαι, | Βρόμιον παῖδα θεὸν θεοῦ | Διόνυσον κατάγουσαι | Φρυγίων ἐξ ὀρέων Ἑλλάδος εἰς εὐ- | ρυχόρους ἀγυιάς, τὸν Βρόμιον ('Go, bacchants, go bacchants, bring the roaring son of a god, Dionysus, from the Phrygian mountains to the streets of Greece, broad for dancing! Bring Bromios!'). All told, then, Wills sees Pentheus inadvertently slipping into a religious register, while ventriloquizing the god's female worshippers (Euripides' chorus consisted of Asian bacchants). The boundary Pentheus erects between himself and the 'other' he seeks to annihilate seems already to be dissolving.

563 iussis ... abesto. In Latin the future imperative is normally used when there is a distinct reference to future time (AG §449); here, however, the future imperative *abesto* (of *absum*, 'be absent') merely imparts a heightened authoritative tone. This supplementary command brings out Pentheus' irritation and impatience, and perhaps hints at reluctance on the part of the *famuli*.

564–65. The two verses are elegantly constructed. In the first we have a *tricolon abundans of nominative subjects structured around the triple *anaphora of the pronoun *hunc* (= Pentheus) as recurring accusative object. This tricolon is arranged climactically in terms of length, but anti-climactically in terms of familial authority, as we move from grandfather (*avus* = Cadmus) to the maternal uncle (Athamas is the husband of Agave's sister Ino) to an unspecified assortment of relatives (*turba suorum*). Line 565 is dominated by the two finite verbs that enclose it, and which operate on the subjects and objects of the preceding verse. The use of the present tense adds vividness and imparts a sense of urgency.

The sense of *corripiunt* is 'rebuke' (*OLD* s.v. 6), a common poetic usage, also found in prose; the ablative *dictis* clarifies the discursive application of the verb (cf. Suet. *Aug.* 53 *correptus voce magistri*), but is not strictly necessary: Ovid has *Acmona corripimus* at *Met.* 14.497. The verb *laborant* is construed with the infinitive (*inhibere*).

In terms of familial attempts at dissuasion, Ovid has here 'upped the ante' vis-à-vis Euripides, who records only the efforts of Cadmus from among Pentheus' relatives to overcome the young king's opposition to

Dionysus/Bacchus (*Bacch.* 329–41). The elaboration of kinship terms and names in 564 calls to mind the genealogical structure of Ovid's Theban History (see Intro. §4): Cadmus stands at the beginning and the end; the destruction of Ino and Athamas concludes the series of fatalities that hit his daughters and grandchildren. Note, finally, the subtle proleptic force of *turba suorum*: it is precisely a crowd of (female) relatives turned maenads — a *turba furens* (716) — that will tear Pentheus apart at the conclusion of the episode.

566–67. A rather unusual sequence, in which three verbs in the present (*est, inritatur, crescit*) are followed by an imperfect (*nocebant*) that sums up the series. The subject of *est, inritatur,* and *crescit* is *rabies*, which is modified by the attribute *acrior* and the past participle *retenta*. The *-que* after *inritatur* links *est* and *inritatur*, the *-que* after *moderamina* links *crescit* and *nocebant* (which takes *moderamina ipsa* as subject).

admonitu is ablative of cause with **acrior est**: the very attempts to restrain Pentheus fuel his anger: as often, Ovid proves himself a keen student of human nature. The *alliteration *acrior admonitu* underscores the thematic nexus stylistically. **retenta** is perf. pass. part. of *retineo*, modifying *rabies*. Just like the ablative *admonitu*, the participle has causal force, operating on both **inritatur** and **crescit rabies**: the efforts to make Pentheus see reason only worsen his condition: 'his fury, *because it has been detained*, is roused and grows'. After *admonitu* and *retenta*, **moderaminaque ipsa nocebant** constitutes Ovid's third and culminating articulation of the consequences of trying to constrain Pentheus.

568–71 sic ego ... ibat. Ovid now proceeds to illustrate the psychological phenomenon by way of a simile drawn from the observation of nature. Comparing the irascible king to a river creates another subtle connection (526 n.) with the ancestral dragon, which was earlier likened to a river swollen with rain (3.79–80 *inpete nunc vasto ceu concitus imbribus amnis | fertur*: 'now he moves on with huge rush like a river in flood'). The present simile features two scenarios, introduced by, respectively, *qua* and *quacumque*: (i) the river is unobstructed and flows freely; (ii) the river is obstructed and becomes fiercer as a result. The second scenario corresponds to the case of Pentheus, with his relatives' attempt at dissuasion corresponding to the obstruction. The two halves of the simile are balanced across the adversative particle *at*, which functions as pivot. Each half reflects, with variation, the elements of its counterpart (*qua nil obstabat eunti ~ quacumque trabes obstructaque saxa tenebant; qua ~ quacumque; nil ~ trabes obstructaque saxa; obstabat ~ tenebant; eunti ~ [implied object of tenebant]; lenius et modico strepitu ~ spumeus et fervens et ab obice saevior; lenius ~ saevior; modico strepitu ~ spumeus et fervens; decurrere ~ ibat*). Note also that *obstabat* is also taken up by *ab obice*, and *ibat* harks back to *eunti*.

> Additional Information: Shakespeare evidently felt great admiration for Ovid's river simile, for he offers a beautiful, if less symmetrical, reworking of it in the *Two Gentlemen of Verona*, put in the mouth of Julia: 'The current that with gentle murmur glides, | Thou know'st being stopped impatiently doth rage; | But when his fair course is not hindered, | He makes sweet music with th' enamell'd stones, | Giving a gentle kiss to every sedge | He overtaketh in his pilgrimage | And so by many winding nooks he strays | With willing sport to the wild ocean' (*Two Gentlemen of Verona* ii. vii. 25–34).

568–69 sic … vidi. Here *ego* is, technically speaking, superfluous and so emphatic: Ovid injects the authorial 'personal voice' into his narrative at an unusual moment (on which more below). *vidi* (in final position) introduces an indirect statement, with **torrentem** as subject accusative and **decurrere** as infinitive. Note that *torrens*, which functions here as a substantive, can mean 'a rushing stream' or 'torrent' or, as here, 'the current (of a river)'; it is a graphic image that well captures Pentheus' youthful rashness and lack of emotional self-control, an effect reinforced by *strepitu*. **qua** here means 'where'; the subject of the relative clause is **nil**. With **eunti** (pres. act. dat. part. of *eo*, and indirect object of *obstabat*), supply *torrenti*.

The intrusion of the narrator in the first person (*ego … vidi*) is highly unusual for the epic genre, which tends to avoid the authorial 'personal voice', outside of invocations, or apostrophes. In the *Metamorphoses*, however, such authorial intrusions, which take various forms, are relatively frequent, and some critics have seen them as imparting a sense of unity to the disparate narrative content of the poem. For Solodow (1988, 37) it is Ovid's distinctive narrative voice that 'we learn to recognize as we read the poem; we feel him present everywhere mediating the transmission of the stories, we rely on him as a kind of guide through the vast confusion of the world' (see also Solodow 1988,

55 for discussion of the present passage). This approach yields valuable insights, but it is misguided to see these scattered authorial intrusions as the chief — or in Solodow's insistent formulation the *only* — unifying feature of the poem (see further Intro. §3d).

Looking beyond narrative epic, parallels for the present authorial intrusion can be found in Virgil's didactic poem, the *Georgics*, in the first book of which, for instance, the narrator remarks that he has often seen a clash of winds at harvest time (*saepe ego ... omnia ventorum concurrere proelia vidi*, G. 1.316–18).

570–71 at ... ibat. Ovid is describing a dam constructed from timber and stone: **obstructa** (perf. pass. part. of *obstruo*, 'build in the way of, obstruct') modifies **saxa**, but bears on **trabes** as well by implication (the *-que* attached to the participle connects the two nouns). Classical Latin poetry, and epic in particular, frequently employs simplex verb forms that had been replaced by compounds in general usage, as here with **tenebant** (we would expect *retinebant*); later in the set text we have *ducere* for *educere* (587), *mittere* for *omittere* (614), *ponere* for *deponere* (634). With *tenebant* supply an accusative object, such as *torrentem*. In the *tricolon **spumeus et fervens et ... saevior** all adjectives are used adverbially to qualify *ibat*, and all are deftly chosen to enhance the analogy between the natural and the psychological that underpins the simile. **ab obice** could be an ablative of cause (equivalent to *propter obicem*) or, perhaps less likely, an ablative of source (i.e. the preposition speaking to an origin or starting point).

572–691
The Captive Acoetes and his Tale

The *famuli* return, not with Bacchus, as Pentheus had ordered, but with a different prisoner — or so it would seem. This captive, who gives his name as Acoetes, proceeds to explain, in a lengthy inset narrative, how he became a follower of Bacchus.

Ovid has evidently borrowed the motif of a follower of Bacchus taken prisoner by Pentheus from Euripides' *Bacchae*, where the prisoner, who never gives his name, is the god himself in disguise. In Ovid, by contrast, the captive identifies himself as Acoetes (582), which name was evidently taken from Pacuvius' lost tragedy *Pentheus* (or *Bacchae*). Moreover, the metamorphic story that Ovid's Acoetes goes on to tell derives from the tradition represented by the long *Homeric Hymn to Dionysus*. For a full discussion of these intertextual complexities (and the full text of the *Hymn*), see Intro. §5a. Irrespective of the compound literary genealogy of the prisoner Acoetes, the fact that in Euripides the (unnamed) prisoner was the god in disguise suffices to raise the question: is the Ovidian Acoetes Bacchus in disguise? For a detailed discussion of this intriguing possibility, see Intro. §5b-iv. It is certainly true that various details (e.g. 582–83, 658–59, 699–700 with nn.) offer support for an affirmative answer, but the fact remains that Ovid never explicitly resolves the riddle of Acoetes' identity. At a minimum, though, it must be granted that the text gains in richness, irony, and complexity if we recognize the likelihood that Bacchus and Acoetes are one and the same. In this shifting and slippery narrative about Bacchus, the god never appears in his own guise, but his presence is felt throughout, and equating him with Acoetes yields the culminating stroke of his metamorphic ubiquity. No matter how one reads the captive's identity, Ovid follows Euripides in constructing a striking contrast between this cool, calm and collected figure and his enraged captor Pentheus, whose impatience and agitation mount as the interview unfolds (577–78, 692–93 with nn.). The resulting contrast in verbal style between the two antagonists could hardly be greater: whereas the restive, no-nonsense Pentheus manifests terseness and alacrity, Acoetes becomes ponderous and long-winded — irritatingly so, as a fuming Pentheus will later declare (692–93).

572–73. The interjection *ecce* marks a sudden and surprising development. Pertinent here is the observation of Austin (on Virg. *Aen.* 2.57) that this interjection often 'marks a sudden disruption, in a manner familiar from Comedy, when a character unexpectedly appears, or when there is some disconcerting development'. That the elided subject of **redeunt** is *famuli* ('servants') — i.e. those to whom Pentheus earlier issued the arrest order (cf. 562 *famulis hoc imperat*) — is made clear by **domino**.

The overall syntax is a little convoluted: **quaerenti** modifies *domino* and governs the indirect question (hence the subjunctive) **Bacchus ubi esset**; at the same time, (*quaerenti*) *domino* serves as the indirect object of **negarunt**, which introduces an indirect statement, with subject accusative (*se*) elided and **vidisse** as infinitive, with **Bacchum** the internal accusative object of *vidisse*.

Note the unusual switch in tense from present *redeunt* to perfect *negarunt* (a syncopated 3rd pers. pl. perf. form = *nega-ve-runt*). With regard to the latter, a present participle (here *quaerenti*) would normally denote incomplete action contemporaneous with that of the verb, which does not match the normal progression of question-and-answer. This could imply that the servants interrupt Pentheus or that he keeps pressing them while they try to answer. But it might have no such implication: the stress on contemporaneity in the use of the present participle is not as pronounced for the oblique cases (as here with dative *quaerenti*).

If the indirect report represents Pentheus' actual query, this would be the first time that he mentions the god by name. That name, in any event, registers emphatically here thanks to the *hyperbaton that places *Bacchus* in front of the *ubi*-clause to which it belongs, and the reiteration with *polyptoton (*Bacchus* ... *Bacchum*). The text registers the god's presence even as Pentheus' henchmen report his absence.

That the servants return 'blood-stained' (***cruentati*** is the perf. pass. part. of *cruento*, 'stain with blood'), would seem to imply some manner of struggle with Bacchus' worshippers. Ovid does not elaborate on this encounter, but may have been thinking of Eur. *Bacch.* 760–63, where a messenger reports on a skirmish between armed (male) villagers and (female) Bacchants, in which the latter rout the former, inflicting serious wounds while themselves remaining unscathed. In any event, the graphic detail is an ominous sign that contributes to the 'gore-nographic' build-up of the set text (521–23 n.).

574–76 hunc ... secutum. Ovid here switches from indirect to direct speech. In an inversion of the sequence at 572–73, the verbs now progress from perfect (*dixere* is an alternate 3rd pers. pl. perf. form) to present (*tradunt*). The concessive particle ***tamen*** is an apologetic touch on the part of the servants: although they did not see, let alone capture Bacchus, they nevertheless do not come back empty-handed. ***hunc ... comitem famulumque sacrorum*** designates the same individual, their captive, in a mildly pleonastic fashion (Ovid will promptly ratchet up the *pleonasm with *sacra dei quendam ...secutum* — note the *polyptoton of *sacra* — which supplies no new information). The term *comes* here designates a follower in Bacchus' retinue, whereas *famulus* is used in the religious sphere of functionaries charged with carrying out parts of the sacred rites. Presumably all *famuli* are *comites*, but not every *comes* is a *famulus*. It is difficult to judge where to situate *famuli* within the hierarchy of Bacchus' entourage: are they subservient factota or privileged religious ministrants? It is at any rate suggestive that Ovid uses the same term of both the henchmen that Pentheus sent out to capture Bacchus (562 *famulis* *hoc imperat*) and the religious functionary of Bacchus whom they bring back. The ablative absolute ***manibus post terga ligatis*** indicates attendant circumstances; *terga* ('back') is a 'poetic' plural. To place a follower of Bacchus/ Liber ('the Freer') in chains is not without a measure of irony — all the more so if we understand the captive to be the god himself in disguise (see Intro. §5b-iv).

quendam is the accusative object of ***tradunt***; it is modified by ***secutum*** (perf. pass. part. of the deponent *sequor*, 'follow'), which takes *sacra dei* as internal accusative object: 'someone who followed the rites of the god'. This tells us nothing that we didn't already know, but the throwaway designation *quendam* ('someone or other') is a wonderfully arch metaliterary touch given Ovid's elusive play on the identity of this figure (see Intro. §5b-iv). ***Tyrrhena gente*** is ablative of origin, qualifying *quendam*. The adjective *Tyrrhenus*, used of Acoetes again at 696, means 'Etruscan' or 'Lydian'. Why? According to Hdt. 1.94, the Tyrrhenians were a 'Pelasgic' race, one of the pre-historic people inhabiting the Aegean, which originally settled on the coast of Lydia but later migrated to Italy to become the ancestors of the Etruscans. The Greeks continued to designate them 'Tyrrhenian', and Roman authors frequently followed suit, as here. Other terms for 'Etruscan' include *Etruscus* (*Met.* 15.557), *Tuscus* (found later in the set text at 624) and the poeticism *Maeonius* (cf. 583 *Maeonia* with n.). The double Lydian/Etruscan geographical identity of Acoetes enables Ovid subtly to link Euripides' *Bacchae* (in which Dionysus twice declares his Lydian origins: see 582–83 n.), Pacuvius' *Pentheus* (with the character Acoetes), and the second *Homeric Hymn to Dionysus*, where the helmsman remains anonymous, but the crew is collectively designated 'Tyrrhenian' (Τυρσηνοί, *Hymn. Hom.* 7.8).

577–78 adspicit … differt. The placement of the verb (*adspicit*) in initial position, both within its verse and its sentence, neatly marks the incipit of Pentheus' interview with the captive, which occupies lines 577–700 (including the long inset narrative). The *et* after *fecerat* links *adspicit* (577) and *ait* (580), the two main verbs of the sentence.

hunc, repeated from 574, designates the captive, who will identify himself as Acoetes in 582, but, as already observed, may well be Bacchus in disguise (see Intro. §5b-iv). Pentheus' meteoric anger already features in Euripides (e.g. *Bacch.* 670); Ovid here imagines its manifestation in his gaze: his eyes are, literally, 'to be feared' (***tremendos***, gerundive of *tremo*). Epic heroes are sometimes described as having blazing or shining eyes, particularly in the heat of battle, where they are prone to manifest what Lovatt (2013, 311) terms an 'assaultive gaze', the essence of which is 'looking at someone with the intention of committing violence against them'. The belligerent Theban king seems to be following the generic paradigm here. But it should not be forgotten that this is also a *genetic* paradigm: cf. the description of his serpentine ancestor at 3.33 *igne micant oculi*: '[the dragon's] eyes flashed with fire' (on Pentheus' 'genetic' connection to the dragon, see 526 n.). As Hardie (1990, 225) observes, 'Pentheus' rage is as elemental in its fury as the violence of the serpent'. The implication of *poenae vix tempora differt* is that Pentheus is torn between the desire immediately to execute the prisoner and the more rational course of acquiring some intelligence about the cult of Bacchus and its followers first; *vix* indicates that he just barely musters the necessary self-control to follow the latter course.

579–80 o periture ... morte. Pentheus begins with a characteristically nasty vocative address: the lofty tone of the opening interjection *o* (on which see 540–42 n.) is promptly dispelled by a redoubled 'promise' of execution, which he expects to set an example for other perceived miscreants. *periture* and *dature* are future active participles in the vocative. They are linked by *-que* (which has migrated to *tua*). *documenta*, the accusative object of *dature*, has the sense 'example, warning', with *tua... morte* an ablative of means ('by your death'; note that the verse position of *tua* requires that it scan as an iamb [∪ —], so it must be abl. sing., agreeing with *morte*, rather than acc. pl., agreeing with *documenta*).

580–81 ede ... frequentes. The imperative *ede* ('declare') governs three accusative objects (*nomen, nomen parentum, patriam*), as well as the indirect question (whence the pres. subjunct. *frequentes*) introduced by *cur*, which is appended to the list by the *-que* after *moris*. In the corresponding scene, Euripides' Pentheus starts the interrogation with a rather less elaborate question (πρῶτον μὲν οὖν μοι λέξον ὅστις εἶ γένος, 'But first tell me of your origins', *Bacch.* 460). The sense of *morisque novi sacra* is 'new fashioned rites': *moris... novi* is genitive of quality qualifying *sacra*.

582–83 ille ... parentes. The unruffled prisoner — *metu* is an ablative of separation dependent on *vacuus* ('free from') — begins his lengthy narrative, which occupies more than one hundred verses, by obliging Pentheus with a response to his multi-faceted query. He is asyndetically brief and to the point, with both the pronoun (*mihi*, dative of possession) and the verb (*est*) operating **apo koinou* over the three clauses (notwithstanding the plural subject of the final clause: *sunt* is strictly needed, but the license is a common one).

The name 'Acoetes' is Greek in form (Ἀκοίτης), but occurs nowhere in extant Greek literature. Etymologically, it might suggest 'husband', 'bedfellow' (ἀκοίτης) or 'unresting' (ἄκοιτος), neither of which shed much light on Ovid's figure; if it is a 'speaking name', its significance may have been clarified in Pacuvius' lost *Pentheus* (on which see Intro. §5b-iv). **Maeonia** is properly a district of Lydia, in the neighbourhood of Mount Tmolus, where, according to some mythic accounts, Bacchus/ Dionysus spent his childhood; the term was also used by poets as a synecdoche for Lydia, and here it almost certainly means, by a further poetic extension, 'Tyrrhenian' or 'Etruscan': cf. Virgil's reference to the Etruscan Mezentius' troops as *Maeoniae delecta iuventus* (*Aen.* 8.499). For the array of terms for 'Etruscan' used by Ovid, see 574–76 n. By the choice of this term Acoetes emphasizes 'historical' Lydian origins as against Etrurian habitation, a suggestive self-characterization in the intertextual context. Euripides' Dionysus twice states that he hails from Lydia: in the prologue (*Bacch.* 13), and in the scene to which the present passage corresponds when, disguised, he declares to Pentheus Λυδία δέ μοι πατρίς ('Lydia is my fatherland', *Bacch.* 464); Acoetes here offers a close Latin equivalent to the second statement — and one that might even be deemed more 'Dionysian'. His declaration of Lydian origins would thus seem to connect him to both Euripidean instantiations of the god, thereby fuelling the suspicion that he is indeed Bacchus in disguise (see Intro. §5b-iv).

humili ... plebe amounts to a mild *tautology in the context. Acoetes' emphasis on his humble origins is somewhat unusual for ancient epic; of course if this self-characterization is a 'front', then the archetype would be Odysseus assuming the guise of a beggar upon his return to Ithaca. In a Bacchic context, moreover, the low social rank of the internal narrator is appropriate, recalling the mixing of 'commoners' and princes in the religious festivities (*vulgusque proceresque ignota ad sacra feruntur*, 530); there is also perhaps a moral dimension to a plebeian figure speaking enigmatic truth to tyrannical power. Note that *plebs* is a technical term of Rome's political culture, referring to the body of Roman citizens who were not patricians. Ovid uses such Roman idiom throughout the *Metamorphoses* in both the human and divine realms (so Jupiter in his attempted seduction of Callisto promises her safety *praeside ... deo, ... nec de plebe deo* ('under a god's protection — and no plebeian god at that', *Met.* 1.594–95). Such terrestrial and cosmic analogies subtly prepare Ovid's narrative culmination, in which the city of Rome has subsumed and become coextensive with the world (see Intro. §3c).

584-87 non ... pisces. Acoetes specifies the profession he 'inherited' from his father in a roundabout fashion, first mentioning two livelihoods — farming and pasturing — that were *not* his father's and then identifying fishing as the case at hand. These were, in fact, the three principal ways by which a rural inhabitant of ancient Italy might earn a living. Once again, the point is to underscore Acoetes' humble station: land and cattle were the essential constituents of rural wealth; the fisherman's condition was regarded as one of pauperdom.

584-85 non mihi ... reliquit. The pronounced *hyperbaton presents something of a challenge; a more natural word order for the essential sequence would be *non mihi arva, quae duri iuvenci colerent, ... pater reliquit*. In other words, *pater* is the subject of the main clause; the principal verb *reliquit* takes three accusative objects: *arva* (the antecedent of *quae*, though coming after it), *lanigeros... greges*, and *ulla armenta*. Note also that **quae duri colerent ... iuvenci** is a relative clause of purpose (AG §530.2), whence the subjunctive verb. The sense of jerkiness and imbalance is further increased by the double (rather than triple) *anaphora of *non*, and the fact that the first and the second accusative objects (*arva* and *lanigeros greges*) are linked by *-ve*, whereas the second and third (*lanigeros greges* and *ulla armenta*) follow each other *asyndetically.

lanigeros... greges, literally 'wool-bearing flocks', speaks to sheep. *laniger* is a compound epithet (from *lana* + *ger*) of a type quite frequent in epic, which likes constructing adjectives by adding either *-fer* or *-ger* (both contributing the sense 'bearing') to a noun; later in the set text Ovid has *racemifer* ('cluster-bearing', 666).

586-87 pauper ... pisces. The key to sorting out this sentence is untangling the connectives. The *-que* after *lino* links the two main verbs *fuit* and *solebat*. Then we have two complementary infinitive phrases dependent on *solebat*, both taking *salientis pisces* as accusative object (an *apo koinou construction): *lino et hamis decipere* and *calamo ducere*. The *et* between *solebat* and *hamis* thus links *lino* and *hamis*, the *et* between *decipere* and *calamo* links *decipere* and *ducere*.

Henderson (1979, 102) understands *et ipse* in the conventional manner as setting up a comparison: 'he too', i.e. 'like me'. But this seems pointless, even inept on Ovid's part, in the wake of the previous three lines. Bömer's solution seems preferable: he assumes that we are dealing with yet another transposition and should understand *et pauper ipse fuit et solebat* etc. ('he himself was poor and was accustomed to ...'). Rather than using a verb for 'fishing' (*piscari* vel sim.), Acoetes provides a circumlocution elaborating the two stages of that activity: catching the fish with a hook on a line (**lino ... et hamis decipere**), and then drawing the struggling creatures out of the water with the fishing rod (**calamo ... ducere**). *calamus* (= κάλαμος) is a reed, but can stand by metonymy for an object made thereof (cf. 532 *aera*, 621 *pinus* with nn.). The sense 'fishing rod' is common in both Greek (e.g. Theoc. *Id.* 21.43) and Latin. *ducere* is a simplex form (570–71 n.), standing for *educere* ('to draw out'). Note that **salientis** is acc. pl. of the pres. act. part. (AG §118; most modern readers would expect *salientes*, because the *-es* termination had largely supplanted the original *-is* by the Augustan Age); it modifies *pisces*: the image is that of fish on the hook struggling to free themselves. The mini-vignette of a fisherman in his moment of triumph could reflect authorial zeal: there is extant a fragment of some 130 lines of a *Halieutica* (a handbook on the art of fishing) ascribed to Ovid (on which see Richmond 1962). At the same time, the reader might catch a whiff of allegory here: anglers practise their proverbial craft of baiting hooks then tricking and landing prey by paying out plenty of line. If we sense something fishy about Acoetes' autobiography, Pentheus seems to fall for it — hook, line, and sinker.

588 ars ... erat. Strictly speaking, the **census** was a registration of the property of every Roman citizen, performed every five years by the censors, in order to classify citizens according to wealth. From this technical sense, the term came to be used in a broader metonymic sense for 'property in general, wealth, substance' (*OLD* s.v. 3), as here. Since his father has no material property — if he were actually assessed in a Roman census he would be placed in the lowest category, the *capite censi*, those 'registered by their head' because they owned nothing — Acoetes applies the term to his technical skill as a fisherman as part of an elaborate metaphor that is further developed by the terms *traderet*, *successor*, *heres*, *reliquit* and *paternum*. Use of the term *census* at this point in Ovid's cosmic history is of course anachronistic, but such anachronisms are part of Ovid's broader strategy of anticipating Rome's eventual global dominance (see Intro. §3c). ***illi*** is dative of possession. ***sua*** is, as Bömer (1969, 591) puts it, 'indirectly reflexive' (i.e. referring to *illi*, rather than the subject of the sentence); or as Henderson (1979, 103) puts it, '*sua* refers to the "logical", not the grammatical, subject of the sentence, as often'.

588–90 cum ... opes. We have a quotation (***dixit***, with which supply *pater* as subject from 584) within Acoetes' direct speech. The quotation is anchored chronologically by **cum traderet artem** (with which understand *mihi*), but the verb *traderet* is playfully inept. Acoetes refers to his father *teaching* him how to fish, but this could not occur as a single process as the coordination of the *cum*-clause with *dixit* requires (*traderet* is imperfect subjunctive with circumstantial *cum*, so expressing contemporaneous action). Thus we are caught between *trado* in the sense 'teach' and its more common meaning 'hand over, bequeath'. Ovid may be having a bit of fun with the traditions of didactic poetry in the spirit of his own *Ars Amatoria* (*ars* meaning a codified body of teachable knowledge), as well, perhaps, as the *Halieutica* ascribed to him (on which see 586–87 n.). The (postponed) antecedent of the relative pronoun ***quas*** is ***opes***, which is also accusative object of ***accipe***. The grand, pretentious-sounding vocative ***studii successor et heres*** ironically evokes notions of intellectual accomplishment, social rank, material wealth, or political power being handed down from one generation to the next; but the *studium* bequeathed in this case is the lowly art of fishing.

591–92 moriensque ... paternum. This restatement of Acoetes' 'inheritance' maintains the ironic pose: where others inherit land, his father left him nothing but the waters he fished in (which were of course available to all). The non-specificity of ***aquas*** subtly prepares for Acoetes career change from fisherman to navigator. Notice that the adjective ***paternum*** is in predicative position, correlated with ***unum hoc*** by ***appellare***: it can be translated substantively as 'inheritance'. L-S s.v. *paternus* notes that it is used 'of the property, possessions, external relations, etc. of a father', whereas its near synonym *patrius* 'is used of that which belongs to his nature, dignity, or duty' — much as we saw earlier with *patrium ... decus* (548).

592–96 mox ... aptos. There are two main verbs in this sentence, linked by the *et* between *flectere* and *Oleniae*: *addidici* (593) and *notavi* (595). The latter governs the following accusative objects, all linked by *-que* save the last, for which Ovid uses *et*: (i) *sidus pluviale*, (ii) *Taygeten*; (iii) *Hyadas*; (iv) *Arcton*; (v) *domos*; (vi) *portus*. If Acoetes has to this point used banalities to raise Pentheus' blood pressure, he now switches modes and taxes the king's patience with recherché learning, set out in excruciating detail.

592–94 ne scopulis ... flectere. The negative purpose clause marks Acoetes' decision not to follow in his father's footsteps. With *scopulis ... isdem* understand *where my father had fished before me* (vel sim.). The prefix of **addidici** (from *addisco = ad + disco*, 'learn besides') indicates skills *in addition to fishing*, which he had learned from his father. The skills in question belong to the *métier* of helmsman or navigator. **regimen** ('guiding, steering') is used concretely by Ovid here (and again at *Met.* 11.552), by an unusual poetic metonymy, to designate the component by which one does the steering, i.e. the rudder (or, more precisely 'steering-oar'; *moderamen* will have the same sense at 644); it is the accusative object of *flectere*. **dextra moderante** is an ablative absolute, here taking the place of a clause of accompanying circumstance (AG §420.5), but in truth adding nothing of significance: Acoetes is becoming annoyingly (or amusingly) prolix. The termination of the present participle in *-e* (rather than *-i*) indicates verbal (rather than adjectival) force, and so is the usual form in an ablative absolute construction.

Latin epicists tend to avoid the 'obvious' prosaic word *navis* for 'ship', using instead a wide range of more elevated terms, as here with the synecdoche *carina* (literally 'keel'; again at 604 and 639), which is widespread in poetry from Enn. *Ann.* 376 Sk onwards. Other poetic synonyms for 'ship' found in the set text are *pinus* (621 with n.), *puppis* (596 with n.) and *ratis* (687 with n.).

594–96 et Oleniae ... aptos. Here Acoetes enumerates in indirect and learned fashion the various cognitive skills, all essential for navigation in the ancient world, that he acquired: (i) observation of stars or constellations (Capella, the Pleiades, the Hyades) whose rising or setting marked the beginning of the rainy season when sailing was dangerous and so should be avoided; (ii) use of the Great Bear constellation to chart one's course; (iii) anticipation of wind patterns and other meteorological activity; (iv) recognition and/ or knowledge of good harbours. The importance of these particular stars and constellation to sailing is evident from Virgil's statement that it was sailors who gave them their names: *navita tum stellis numeros et nomina fecit,* | *Pleiades, Hyadas, claramque Lycaonis Arcton* ('the sailor then counted the stars and gave them names, the Pleiades, the Hyades and Lycaon's Arctos', G. 1.137–38).

594–95 Oleniae ... notavi. Henderson (1979, 103) draws attention to *Oleniae sidus pluviale Capellae*, calling it 'an enclosing appositional structure', the genitive *Oleniae ... capellae* being in apposition to (or defining) *sidus pluviale*. Ovid employs a very similar expression with the same structure at *Fast.* 5.113 *Oleniae signum pluviale Capellae*.

Oleniae ... Capellae designates the goat star, so named from the creature, usually called Amalthea, that, according to legend, suckled the infant Jupiter. The goat was afterwards rewarded by being changed into a star called Capella (sometimes Capra) in the constellation Auriga. The epithet *Olenius* is variously explained as arising (i) from the fact that Amalthea was born near the town of Olenos (Ὤλενος), or (ii) from the fact that the owner of the goat, a nymph sometimes herself identified as Amalthea, was the daughter of Olenos, or (iii) from the fact that the goat, when translated to heaven, was placed in the elbow (ὠλένη) of the constellation Auriga. The star rises at the beginning of the rainy season (October), whence the label ***sidus pluviale***. From the point of view of sea navigation, the rising of this constellation signalled dangerous sailing conditions. Virgil mentions the importance of the observation of this sign by mariners at G. 1.204–07.

Taygeten designates one of the Pleiads, a cluster of seven stars located in the sign Taurus. Ovid here uses a single star synecdochically of the whole constellation, the setting of which (around the beginning of November) caused it to be associated with autumn storms (e.g. Arat. *Phaen.* 1064–66; Luc. 8. 852; Stat. *Theb.* 4.120, 9.460–61; *Silv.* 1.6.22). Already Hesiod uses the morning setting of this constellation to mark the end of the (safe) sailing season (*Op.* 618–23), and this remained the rule in the Roman period. *Taygete* is a Greek loanword (Τηϋγέτη) which scans as quadrisyllabic ($- \smile \smile -$), with both the initial *a* and the final *e* standing in for the long Greek vowel 'êta' (η). Notice that *Taygeten* is a Greek accusative form (559–61 n.), the first of three in the verse.

The *Hyades* (f. pl.; gen. *Hyadum*; the acc. pl. **Hyadas** follows the Greek declension, as with *Taygeten*) were a group of seven stars in the head of the constellation Taurus, whose morning rising and setting were associated with rainy weather (hence their name: *huein* is Greek for 'to rain'). Like the Peliades, the Hyades were thought to be daughters of Atlas.

Arctos is Greek for 'bear' (**Arcton** is yet another Greek accusative form), and is the name of the two northern constellations, the Great and Little Bear (Ursa Maior and Ursa Minor). These constellations were crucial for seafaring, as ancient navigators steered by them, using either one or the other to determine orientation, as well as approximate geographic position (Luc. 8. 174–81 elaborates on the technique). Ursa Maior is mentioned in the context of navigation as early as Hom. *Od.* 5. 270–73.

596. The verb continues to be *(oculis) notavi*, though it may suit its penultimate object, **ventorum... domos**, less well than the preceding celestial bodies (which would be a mild case of *zeugma). This expression does not refer to the mythological conception of the wind gods as incarcerated in a mountain cave under the supervision of Aeolus, king of the winds (as we find, e.g., in Homer's *Odyssey* and Virgil's *Aeneid*). Ovid seems rather to be thinking of the geographical or celestial region from which each wind blows as its individual 'abode' (the plural *domos* indicates separate 'houses'); in the cosmogony at the start of the epic, the domains of the individual winds were treated in such a geographical manner (*Met.* 1.61–66). An important precedent for the present expression is Virgil's *Eurique Zephyrique ... domus* (G. 1.371), with use of the verb *tonat* ('thunders') indicating that each wind's 'abode' is the part of the heavens from which it blows.

puppibus is dative with **aptos**, a predicative adjective modifying **portus**. The term *puppis* (literally 'stern' or 'poop') is a frequent poetic synecdoche *(pars pro toto)* for 'ship', found again in the set passage at 651 and 660. For other poetic terms used to avoid the 'obvious' prosaic word *navis* for 'ship', see 592–94 n. The alliteration and assonance of *p* and *t* in *portus puppibus aptos* provide a resonant flourish to bring this segment of Acoetes' speech to a close.

Commentary 572–691: The Captive Acoetes and his Tale   175

597–99 forte ... harenae. With a striking ellipse, Acoetes' autobiography abruptly transitions from his acquisition of navigational skills and knowledge to their concrete application. What is missing is his securing gainful employment as a helmsman: perhaps the marine transportation sector was awash with job opportunities; then again, as we'll see, Acoetes wasn't especially fussy about the kind of outfit he signed on with. In any event, he now proceeds to tell of a particular voyage — the one, indeed, that brought his seafaring career to an end and made him a devotee of Bacchus. Though this sentence exhibits Acoetes' stylized prolixity — he takes three full verses to say 'on the way to Delos, I made landfall at Chios' — it maintains the momentary impulse towards narrative compression by omitting both the point of departure and the reason for the journey, evidently details of no consequence for his tale.

The adverb *forte* is often used in narrative to introduce a chance event or circumstance: 'as it happened' or 'as luck would have it' (see *OLD* s.v. 2). Notice that the participle *petens* is used here to indicate *final* destination ('on my way to ...', 'as I was heading towards ...'), while the finite verbs indicate an event *en route* (in this case a stopover); for this convenient syntactical structure cf. Val. Max. 2.6.8 <u>Asiam petens</u> Iulidem oppidum intravi ('on the way to Asia I stopped in at the town of Iulis'). *Delos* is a Greek noun of the 2nd declension (Δῆλος; see AG §52), which admits two accusative forms in Latin: **Delon**, (as here), and the Latinized *Delum* (as at, e.g., Virg. *Aen.* 4.144). Delos is an important Aegean island, nearly in the centre of the Cyclades, celebrated as the birthplace of the gods Apollo and Diana. Its significance here, if any, is unclear; in the long *Homeric Hymn to Dionysus* (see Intro. §5a), the island where the pirates make landfall and come upon the god is not identified. In the *Aeneid*, the Trojans sail to Delos and obtain a riddling oracle that sends them circling around the Aegean ... Ever been had?

Henderson (1979, 104) rightly calls **Chiae telluris ad oras** a 'grandiose circumlocution': Acoetes does not simply say 'Chios', but 'the *coast* of the *land* of Chios'. The verb *applico* is a nautical technical term ('direct, steer, or bring to land') which takes an accusative object (*navem* vel sim.) in the active voice, but is used absolutely in the passive voice (as here with *applicor*) when it is 'middle' in sense (see further L-S s.v. *applico*). *adducor* is likewise middle in force: 'I sail (my ship) to' (*OLD* s.v. *adduco*, 1c). The use of *litora* as a simple accusative of the end of motion (i.e.

without a preposition) is an unusual license (L-S s.v. *adduco*, 2; *TLL* 1.596.71). **dextris ... remis** probably means 'with the right hand oars', i.e. those on the starboard side of the ship, and speaks to manoeuvring to make landfall on Chios. Henderson (1979, 104) voices suspicion over the 'technical and precise' nature of this specification, but Roman epic is strongly inclined to technical terminology and precise detail in its treatment of seafaring — and the internal narrator Acoetes has already demonstrated the same propensity. Con artists work with the 'reality effect' guaranteed to accrue from circumstantiality. But let's just notice that the *wine* of Chios was the best Greece had to offer ...

The *-que* after *do* links it with *adducor*. The combination *do* + noun (in place of a verb) is a mild periphrasis of a familiar poetic kind, though **do ... saltus**, equivalent to *salio*, which occurs again in the set text at 683, is not common before Ovid: Virgil has it only once (*Aen.* 12.681 *saltum dedit*). **levis** is best rendered 'nimble' (*OLD* s.v. 2). Note that *levis saltus* is acc. pl. (*levis* = *leves*); since one leap would presumably suffice, we should understand a 'poetic' plural. This nautical leap might strike some readers as a bit fishy: fish 'leap' (cf. 587 *salientis ... pisces*) and so, especially, do acrobatic dolphins (as we shall soon see, 683). The *-que* attached to *udae* links *do* and *inmittor*. After *applicor* and *adducor*, **inmittor** is yet another passive form used in a reflexive or middle sense ('I jump onto'), here taking the dative (***udae ... harenae***).

600–04. After an indication of a night's rest and a new day dawning, Acoetes describes preparations for resuming the voyage: he orders his companions to fetch water and then climbs a hill to get a sense of which way the wind is likely to blow. The reference to crewmen — first implied by the verbs *admoneo* and *monstro* and then explicitly mentioned with *comitesque voco* — brings these individuals into the narrative picture at precisely the moment when their conduct will bear on the course of events. Not until verse 687 are we told their number: *viginti* (20).

The syntax is arranged *chiastically: we get three main verbs in paratactic sequence linked by *-que* (*exsurgo, admoneo, monstro*), followed by a subordinate clause (*quae ducat ad undas*); then we get a subordinate clause (*quid aura mihi tumulo promittat ab alto*), followed by three main verbs in paratactic sequence linked by *-que* (*prospicio, voco, repeto*).

600–01 nox ... coeperat. Acoetes emerges as something of an 'Odyssean' internal narrator here, telling the tale of his sea voyage in a manner reminiscent of Homer's very own 'sole survivor' yarn-spinning seafarer Odysseus. His account of the events of the fateful day begins with the breaking of dawn, *aurora rubescere primo | coeperat*, which is reminiscent of the standard Odyssean incipit ἦμος δ' ἠριγένεια φάνη ῥοδοδάκτυλος Ἠώς ('when rosy-fingered dawn appeared ...'). The adverb *primo* usually indicates the first stage in a sequence (and is often followed by *deinde* vel sim.), i.e. 'at first', 'firstly', which is clearly not the case here: it is perhaps best translated 'as soon as'.

601–02 laticesque ... undas. The *-que* after *latices* links *exsurgo* and *admoneo*, here with the sense 'exhort', governing the infinitive *inferre*. This infinitive construction is a license largely confined to poetry through the Augustan period: like *hortor* and its compounds, *moneo* and *admoneo* are normally followed by an *ut/ ne* clause. *latices ... recentis* (= *recentes*) is the accusative object of *inferre*. The word *latex* (pl. *latices*), which can be used of any liquid, is almost exclusively poetic, often occurring in contexts of drinking and libations. Here it serves as an elevated synonym for 'water'; the adjective *recentis* indicates that 'fresh' or 'drinking' water is meant, for use on the voyage. *undas* is probably best translated 'spring' (*OLD* s.v. 2), which would be a preferred source of drinking water. From *monstro... viam* etc. it is clear that Acoetes knows his way around the island.

603–04. The pronoun *ipse* underscores the distinction between Acoetes, who concerns himself with the 'technical' task of reading the weather conditions, and the rest of the crew, to whom he assigns more mundane tasks. The main verb *prospicio* introduces the indirect question *quid aura mihi ... promittat* ('what the breeze promises to me', i.e. what sort of weather I might anticipate). Virgil describes Aeneas' helmsman Palinurus assessing sailing conditions in much the same fashion: *surgit Palinurus et omnes | explorat ventos et auribus aera captat* ('Palinurus arose to test the winds, his ears taking in their first stirrings', *Aen.* 3.513). Such forecasting, which was an important part of the navigator's repertoire (594–96 n.), was best undertaken at or before dawn, ideally from an elevated position, whence *tumulo ... ab alto*. The straightforwardly paratactic follow-up *comitesque voco repetoque carinam* again imparts a sense of Acoetes' authority over the crew and his firm control of events — a perfect set-up for the anarchic disruptions that follow as Acoetes' crewmembers decide to take matters into their own hands — a recipe for disaster, as readers familiar with the *Odyssey* will recognize. For the poetic synecdoche *carina*, see 592–94 n.

605–07. Ovid, with what appears to be mock scrupulousness, will end up naming about a dozen of the 20-man crew. In strict narrative terms there is no need for the nomenclatural profusion — no crewmembers are named in the *Homeric Hymn* — but epic likes catalogues and similar effects, and Ovid evidently could not resist the temptation here (see esp. 617–20 and n.). There seems to be no rhyme or reason to the drawn-out enumeration, and John Henderson is surely right to see it as 'typical Ovidian bait for academics with the *Oxford Classical Dictionary* to hand, and the rest of us can enjoy imagining the quest to "authenticate" this profusion of smallest fry. Here is an epic trait that *this* epic means to send up. Obsessively'.

In these lines we are introduced to Opheltes, who is represented as the ringleader throughout — whence **_primus sociorum_**. The designation *socii* ('companions') for these characters creates a suggestive parallel with Odysseus and *his* companions (ἑταῖροι) — not least since Homer instantly qualifies Odysseus' companions as fools (νήπιοι) who lost their lives because of their foolish conduct vis-à-vis the gods (*Od.* 1.6–9 'Yet even so Odysseus could not save his companions, even though he greatly desired to, for through their own blind folly they perished — fools, who consumed the cattle of Helios'). At the end of his tale, Acoetes, like Odysseus, will be the last man standing. Only more so: Acoetes will be the *last man* (the only crewmember not transformed into a dolphin) *standing* (the only crewmember still possessing legs).

The word order is somewhat jumbled, starting with Opheltes' pronouncement **adsumus en**: the interjection would normally precede the verb (as famously with the declaration of the goddess Isis at Apul. *Met.* 11.4 _en adsum_ *tuis commota, Luci, precibus*); the inversion here is *metri gratia*. The *-que* after *ut* links the two main verbs of the sentence, i.e. *inquit* and *ducit*. Note that **ut putat** ('as he believes') glosses **praedam**: Acoetes signals at once that his comrades have badly misjudged the situation. To modern sensibilities, the conduct of the crew in abducting a seemingly defenceless youth and regarding him as 'booty' seems loathsome; in antiquity, such activity was quite widespread (as the opening pages of Herodotus' *Histories* attest; cf. also Hom. *Od.* 14.297, 15.427 and, for a Roman example, Plut. *Caes.* 2), as well as extremely lucrative: the kidnapping victim could be sold on the slave-market or (if from a wealthy family) ransomed. Notice that Acoetes does not criticize the abduction as such; it is rather the choice of victim that he finds fault with. In a poetic universe in which the gods (still) mingle with humans, if it looks too easy ... well, suffice it to say that right now, Acoetes has his very own 'prize beauty' well and truly *hooked*.

The circumstances of Bacchus' capture are surprising: he was wandering about in a deserted field (***deserto ... in agro***) when the sailors abducted him; in the *Homeric Hymn to Dionysus* he is said to be wandering on the shore (*Hymn. Hom.* 7.2). ***virginea ... forma*** is an ablative of description, qualifying ***puerum***. Barchiesi (2007, 227) points out that the attribute *virginea* ('referring to a girl of marriageable age') introduces an element of gender-ambiguity into the portrayal that is absent from the *Hymn*, where the god appears 'in the likeness of a youth in first manhood' (νεηνίῃ ἀνδρὶ ἐοικώς | πρωθήβῃ, *Hymn. Hom.* 7.3–4), but chimes well with the decidedly androgynous Dionysus of Euripides' *Bacchae*. Indeed, one might add that *virginea ... forma* looks very much like a Latin gloss on θηλύμορφος ('woman shaped'), used of Dionysus/ Bacchus at Eur. *Bacch.* 353. 'Acoetes' thus casts Bacchus in Euripidean terms that resonate powerfully with the frame-narrative in the *Metamorphoses*, while feeding Pentheus' prejudices — almost a *captatio benevolentiae*.

In terms of versification, notice that an adjective and its corresponding noun (*virginea ... forma*) 'frame' verse 607, which is designed symmetrically around a central verb in a quasi-'golden' arrangement. The attractive *forma* of the verse reflects that of the boy it describes.

608–09 ille ... sequi. The pronoun ***ille*** designates the as yet unidentified Bacchus, with ***mero somnoque gravis*** standing in apposition. The weight metaphors with wine and sleep(iness) are longstanding, in Greek (e.g. Hom. *Od.* 3.139 οἴνῳ βεβαρηότες) as well as Latin. Elsewhere in the poem Ovid has *somno gravis* (1.224) and *vino gravis* (10.438); the combination of the two here (*mero* being equivalent to *vino*) suggests (the appearance of) an advanced state of inebriation. The *-que* after *vix* links *titubare* and *sequi*; both infinitives depend on ***videtur***. The first infinitive, implying a loss of motor control, prepares the second (***vixque sequi***: he seems 'to follow with difficulty'). In the *Homeric Hymn* account, the sailors attempt to put the god in chains (*Hymn. Hom.* 7.13–15); in Acoetes' account, by contrast, Bacchus is evidently too drunk for the sailors to bother with physical restraints. But of course *videtur* here and *veluti* at 630 imply that the god is merely feigning a state of inebriation, making this a case of divine testing of mortal goodness, whereby wicked behaviour is induced in order to be punished promptly thereafter. We call that entrapment, but it's hard to mount an affirmative defence when you've been transformed into a dolphin.

609–10 specto ... videbam. Once again (cf. 572–73 n.) we have a change of tense in mid-sentence, this time from vivid present (*videtur, specto*) to the more reflective imperfect (*videbam*). Acoetes discerns three aspects of the stranger that manifest a more than human nature: the elegance or refinement of his overall physical appearance (***cultum*** is perhaps best taken as a reference to the stranger's body, i.e. *cultus corporis*, rather than the adornment of his attire), his countenance (***faciem***), and his gait (***gradum***). The individual elements of the *tricolon add up to an impressive whole, which is further enhanced by the absence of attributes: it is left to the audience to visualize the appearance of, say, a (perfectly elegant and beautiful) body, a (translucent) face, and a (divine) gait — even though the last attribute sits oddly with the earlier description of the youth staggering along (*titubare*) in a drunken stupor.

Verse 610 constitutes a relative clause of characteristic (AG §535), with ***nil*** the antecedent of ***quod***; the overall statement is similar in form to Cic. *Fam.* 9.16.3 *nihil video quod timeam* ('I see nothing to fear'). ***ibi***, an adverb of place ('there') refers to the stranger, or more specifically his *cultus, facies*, and *gradus*. These, along with the voice, are 'standard' epic ways of spotting a deity in disguise: cf. Virg. *Aen.* 5.647–49, identifying <u>vultus</u> *vocisque sonus vel* <u>gressus</u> *eunti* as *divini signa decoris*. The use of a passive form of *credo* (here ***credi***, pres. pass. infinitive) suggests the common-sense validity of Acoetes' observations, thereby underscoring the obtuseness of Opheltes and the rest of the crew, evidently blinded by greed — as blind as Pentheus, at this moment, who can't see that he is right in this story, facing a sight that *shouldn't* look like 'anything mortal' (610).

611–12. The simple paratactic statement *et sensi et dixi* conveys the rapidity of Acoetes' reaction: 'I no sooner felt than said …' The interrogative adjective *quod* (modifying *numen*) begins an indirect question (hence the subjunctive *sit*) dependent on *dubito* (here: 'I am uncertain'). Acoetes drives his point home with a *chiasmus (*numen* … *corpore* … *corpore* … *numen*). The anastrophe *corpore … in isto* in the second half ensures that *numen* resides within 'that body' also on the formal level. Acoetes does not know *which* divine power dwells in the youth, but, unlike his comrades, he is dead sure that one does. The anonymous protagonist of the *Homeric Hymn to Dionysus* is similarly sure of the stranger's divine nature, but uncertain of the precise identity of the god before him, speculating that he might be Zeus, Apollo, or Poseidon (*Hymn. Hom.* 7.19–20).

613–14 quisquis … veniam. Acoetes now addresses the stranger, whose divinity he has recognized, in prayer. As Bömer (1969, 598) points out, the all-encompassing *quisquis es* ('whoever you are') both accords with Roman practice — such precautionary language avoids a misrecognition that might offend the deity in question (cf. e.g. Virg. *Aen.* 4.576–77 *sequimur te, sancte deorum,* | *quisquis es*) — and suits the narrative situation. The interjection *o* (for which see 540–42 n.) creates an elevated tone, appropriate for an address to a god. The *-que* after *nostris* links *faveas* and *adsis*, which are instances of the 'polite' 2nd pers. sing. subjunctive, sometimes referred to as the 'precative' subjunctive because typical of prayer-language (cf. e.g. Virg. *Aen.* 4.578 *adsis o placidusque iuves*): Acoetes prays for the divinity's benevolent disposition and help. **nostris… laboribus**, which has an epic ring — *labores* are what heroes such as Hercules undertake — should probably be understood in reference to Acoetes alone, since the immediately following **his quoque** refers to the case of his crew as a separate matter, with **veniam** acknowledging a transgression on their part. Come on Pentheus, take the hint.

614–16 pro nobis … relabi. Ovid now introduces a second member of the crew, Dictys. The name is Greek (Δίκτυς), and found of various figures in myth, including a centaur appearing much later in the *Metamorphoses* (12.327), and a fisherman who caught in his nets the babe set adrift in the box, i.e. Perseus. Ovid is surely indulging in (false) etymological play with δίκτυον/ *diktyon* 'fishing net'. ***mitte precari*** is a poetic form of prohibition, much like *parce* + infinitive (the prose equivalent would be *noli* + infinitive). Here simplex *mittere* stands for *omittere* (cf. Hor. *Epod.* 13.7 *cetera mitte loqui*); on the use of simplex for compound verb forms, see 570–71 n.

For good measure, if somewhat inconsequentially, Acoetes specifies the skill at which the blasphemous Dictys excelled, thereby individuating his role on the vessel. Put simply, Dictys' allotted task while at sea is taking care of the rigging of the sail yard, for which he would need to be agile at scampering up the mast, making the required adjustment, and then sliding back down again. The ship will prove to be the 'net' that catches the crew, including this expert 'Netski' who knows all the ropes. *Then*, there'll be no more of *these* acrobatics … (664).

The combination ***quo non alius*** + comparative adjective is a convenient hexametric formula found earlier in Virgil (*G.* 4.372–73 *Eridanus, quo non alius … violentior amnis*) that continues to find favour with post-classical writers (including the Renaissance humanist Desiderius Erasmus). In this formula, the antecedent of the relative pronoun *quo* (ablative of comparison with the comparative adjective) is the immediately preceding name (here *Dictys*). Note that ***conscendere*** and ***relabi*** are epexegetical (explanatory) infinitives dependent upon *ocior*. Such dependence of infinitives upon adjectives is largely confined to poetry in Ovid's day, a syntactic form found in early Latin that was displaced in prose by gerundive constructions. It is widespread in Augustan poetry, and its preservation is at least partly attributable to Greek influence. ***antemnas*** refers to the 'yard', or long crossbeam at the top of the mast from which the sail was hung. It usually consisted of two spars lashed together, whence the interchangeability of singular and plural forms (the sense here is singular). *rudens* can designate a rope of any kind; in a nautical context, it could refer to any of the ship's tackle, including ropes attached to the yard. The sense of ***prenso rudente relabi*** is 'in sliding down again (while) grasping a rope'; *prenso rudente* is an ablative absolute, here merely instrumental in force.

617–20. Acoetes now devotes four verses to listing, in a kind of mini-catalogue, four members of the crew who voice approval of Dictys' scornful riposte — before wrapping up with the catch-all *omnes alii*. The main verb throughout is *probat* (though with the concluding subject *omnes alii* we need mentally to switch to plural *probant*). There is an interlacing pattern for the named sailors: for the first (Libys) and the third (Alcimedon) we get the name only; for the second (Melanthus) and the fourth (Epopeus), we also get physical characteristics and their sphere of nautical competence. Those whose role is not mentioned will be rowers (both the most common and the humblest occupation on an ancient ship). The fourfold *anaphora of *hoc* (throughout the accusative object of *probat*) works slightly differently: the third *hoc* goes with two of the named sailors (Alcimedon and Epopeus), the fourth with *omnes alii*. The catalogue effect, the intricate word order, the insistent anaphora, the concluding generalizing *sententia* — all contribute to the creation of a compelling picture of the many, spurred on by vocal ring-leaders, turning into a mob and overpowering a lone voice of reason (for the leitmotif one-versus-many in the set text, see 513–14 n.).

617–18 hoc Libys ... Alcimedon. The pronoun *hoc* refers to Dictys' brief utterance at 614. The name **Libys** (Λίβυς) means 'Libyan', which ought to raise an eyebrow or two. The *Homeric Hymn to Dionysus*, to which Acoetes' inset narrative broadly conforms (see Intro. §5a), bluntly declares the company to be 'Tyrrhenian [i.e. Etruscan] pirates' (ληισταὶ ... Τυρσηνοί, *Hymn. Hom.* 7.7–8), thereby conforming to an ancient ethnographic stereotype that associated the Etruscans in particular with piracy (not that any one nationality held a monopoly on such activity!). Other than himself (583 with n.), Acoetes explicitly identifies Lycabas as Etruscan (624 with n.), so that the name *Libys* raises a scruple as to how far we should pursue the analogy of the *Homeric Hymn to Dionysus*. But we have already noted a penchant for geographical mystification in this episode (582–83 n.), and will soon see that speaking names have a tendency to misspeak.

flavus ... Melanthus appears to entail a bilingual witticism: the Latin epithet (equivalent to Greek ξανθός), here speaking to blond hair, ill-suits the Greek name Melanthus (Μέλανθος, 'the Black one'). The poet may also have had in mind a nominal/zoological connection to Melantho, daughter of Deucalion, who is mentioned later by Ovid as seduced by Neptune in the form of a dolphin (the very species into which Melanthus will soon be transformed): *sensit delphina Melantho* (*Met.* 6.120). In any event **prorae tutela** stands in apposition to *Melanthus*, designating him as the 'lookout' or bow officer (*proreta*, Greek πρῳράτης), stationed on the small foredeck of the ship, whose job was to be on the lookout for hazards and sound the depths — both crucial for a vessel sailing among the islands and reefs of the Aegean — as well as to report changes in wind direction. Notice that *tutela* is an instance of abstract for concrete (540–42 n.), with the abstracted quality ('guardianship') standing for the concrete form — in this case *tutor* ('guardian') vel sim.

618–19 hoc probat ... Epopeus. The Greek name *Alcimedon* is compounded from ἀλκή (*alkê*), meaning 'strength, might, power' and μέδων (*medôn*) meaning 'lord, ruler'. It is the name of several characters in Greek mythology, and affords an ironic epic ring to this inconsequential figure, probably a lowly rower on Acoetes' nondescript vessel.

In contrast to Alcimedon, about whom we are given no explicit information, Epopeus' role on the vessel is fleshed out via the relative clause *qui requiemque modumque | voce dabat remis*, which precedes its antecedent *Epopeus*. The clause identifies him as the boatswain, that is, the officer who gives time to the rowers, to ensure synchronized rowing strokes. This could be done by a musical instrument or a small hammer called a *portisiculus*, or simply by the sound of the boatswain's voice — as the ablative *voce* indicates here. *requiemque modumque* ('rest and rhythm'; for the correlating *-que ... -que*, see 521–23 n.) neatly expresses the cadence Epopeus' voice imparts: *requies* corresponding to the retraction of the oar above the water, and *modus* to the 'measured stroke' of the submerged oar-blade that propels the vessel. Note that Epopeus is said to give (*dabat*) time to the oars (*remis*) rather than the rowers, but the former stand for the latter by an easy metonymy. After the descriptive relative clause, **animorum hortator**, which stands in apposition to *Epopeus*, provides a technical specification: the boatswain was called κελευστής (*keleustês*) by the Greeks and *pausarius* or *hortator* by the Romans. Note that the objective genitive *animorum* activates the verbal root of the technical term — cf. Plaut. *Merc.* 4.2.5 *solet hortator remiges hortarier* ('the boatswain is accustomed to urge on the rowers') — as well as creating a more lofty epic expression.

The name *Epopeus* is again Greek (ἐπωπεύς — note that the *o*, corresponding to ω, is long), meaning something like 'watcher'. It is somewhat incongruous for a boatswain — one would expect a figure so named to be the lookout (cognate ἐπωπή actually means 'look-out place, observation post') rather than Melanthus, whereas the name Alcimedon seems more suited to a *hortator animorum*. Ovid seems playfully to be developing verbal incongruities — speaking names that misspeak, as it were — as he enumerates members of the crew. All is not as it *sounds*; *im*proper names abound: 'Pentheus' works (see Intro. §5b-ii) in the frame narrative, but does anything in Acoetes' inset tale — 'Acoetes' included?

620 praedae ... est. The objective genitive *praedae* depends on *cupido*, with *tam caeca* a predicative complement. Blindness, both literal and metaphorical, is a prominent theme of the Pentheus-episode from the outset (515–16, 516–18, 525 with nn.) and, more generally, of Ovid's Theban narrative, complementing the focus on sight, vision, and the gaze. The phrasing here harks back to an earlier Theban episode: at 3.225, right after listing many of the names of the hounds of Actaeon (who had just been transformed into a stag), Ovid says that *ea turba* ('this pack') pursues its metamorphosed master *cupidine praedae* ('in lust for prey'): they desire to tear him to pieces. A frenzied crowd eager to commit outrage is a recurring motif of Ovid's Theban History; in Acoetes' tale, though, the apparent victim(s) will ultimately emerge unscathed.

621–22. The adversative particle *tamen* and the prepositionally 'strengthened' main verb (*perpetior* = *per* + *patior*), here rendered even more forceful by enjambment and scansion (a choriamb followed by a strong trithemimeral *caesura), underscore Acoetes' determined opposition to the crew's scheme. A prohibitive tone is also imparted by the staccato effect of the rapid-fire alliteration on *p* (*pondere pinum perpetiar ... pars*).

non ... perpetiar ('I will not suffer', i.e. 'I will not permit') introduces an indirect statement with *pinum* as subject accusative and *violari* as infinitive (the regular construction: *OLD* s.v. 2; cf. AG §563c). The implication of *violari* is that the (coerced) presence of the god would render the ship religiously impure — and Acoetes will have none of it. Note that *hanc* agrees with *pinum* (trees are almost invariably feminine nouns in Latin, just as rivers are almost exclusively masculine). *pinus*, the pine-tree, can stand metonymically for objects made out of pine-wood (cf. 532 *aera*, 586 *calamo* with nn.); since that material was much used in shipbuilding, *pinus* is a common poetic term for 'ship' (cf. 592–94 n.). ***sacro ... pondere*** refers to the captured youth, whom Acoetes has correctly identified as a god. Note the use of an adjective (here a transferred epithet: it is not the weight that is 'holy', but the deity) instead of an attributive genitive (e.g. *pondere dei*). Great weight was a traditional attribute of gods that frequently features in epic; so, for instance, when Juno visits the underworld in Book 4 the threshold groans under her weight (4.449–50 *sacro... a corpore pressum | ingemuit limen*, 'the threshold groaned beneath [the weight of] her sacred body').

pars ... maxima takes the partitive genitive ***iuris***; supply the verb *est* with ***mihi*** (dative of possession). Note that ***hic*** is not the pronoun, but the adverb (with long vowel) meaning 'here' — i.e. on the ship. Hence: 'the greatest part of authority here belongs to me'. Acoetes invokes his superior rank as helmsman or captain of the ship — an office that afforded him broad authority for averting dangers to the vessel and its crew.

623–28. The situation escalates to physical confrontation, when, with the crew evidently about to bring Bacchus on board, Acoetes follows up his verbal rebuke by attempting to block access to the ship — in this context ***aditu*** ('entrance') would be the 'gangplank'. Acoetes is promptly and violently cast aside by Lycabas, a particularly felonious member of the crew. The juxtaposition in 623 of the verbs ***obsisto*** and ***furit***, representing the two antagonists, separated by a strong penthemimeral caesura neatly enacts on the level of verse the initial confrontation. In addition, the consecutive elisions in *inque aditu obsisto* may be meant to evoke Acoetes' unsuccessful attempt to block access to the vessel. After a two-verse elaboration on Lycabas' murderous past, Acoetes proceeds to recount the physical assault he suffered at his hands. The language and verse design are highly dramatic: we get the brutal verb *rupit* in enjambment (627); and in the conditional sequence, the apodosis (*excussum misisset in aequora*) comes first, summoning up the shocking picture of the helmsman hurled overboard, before the negated protasis (*si non = nisi*; the two monosyllables at the end of the verse are a sign of unsettled discourse and set up the enjambment of *haesissem*).

John Henderson observes that the attempt of Acoetes, champion of righteousness, to quell mob violence 'must insinuate a bogus parallel with Pentheus' attempted stand to stop the stampede into perceived fanaticism. Throughout, the stock metaphor analogizing ship to state underpins the story's function as parable, captain to king. Just like the *Odyssey*, like the "Odyssean *Aeneid*"'. What we get in Ovid's '*Thebaid*', in other words, is the shipwreck of state.

623–25 furit … luebat. Acoetes ominously supplements the main clause (*furit … Lycabas*) in two ways. First, the appositional phrase *audacissimus omni* | *de numero* foregrounds Lycabas' particular notoriety within Acoetes' miscreant crew (the partitive use of the preposition *de* after the superlative is an unusual construction, highlighted by enjambment, which puts the emphasis on *omni*). More sinister still is the relative clause documenting Lycabas' homicidal past: the initial **Tusca pulsus ab urbe** speaks to Lycabas' banishment (*OLD* s.v. *pello* 4) while affirming his Etruscan origins (a nod to the *Homeric Hymn*: cf. 617–18 n.); this is fleshed out by **exilium … poenam … luebat**, which amounts to 'was suffering exile as punishment' (*exilium* is best taken in apposition to *poenam*); finally, **dira … pro caede** explains what prompted the banishment: Lycabas committed some manner of homicide. All this, as Anderson (1997, 400) points out, is reminiscent of Virgil's villain Mezentius, a vicious Etruscan exile and murderer.

Exile is a recurring theme and motif in the *Metamorphoses*: from Io in the first book to Pythagoras in the last, the epic repeatedly features the travails of protagonists banished from their homeland (in the context of Ovid's Theban narrative, of course, it should be recalled that Cadmus founded Thebes as a Phoenician exile). In most cases the exiles are innocent victims suffering unjustly; Lycabas is a rare instance in which the banishment was merited. Exile was a common punishment in the ancient world for various forms of homicide, though premeditated murder was not usually included among them, so we should perhaps imagine Lycabas 'flying off the handle' in the earlier offence, just as he does here — and with nearly the same result.

626–27 is … rupit. The high-stakes showdown between the two adversaries is nicely developed by the initial juxtaposition of pronouns and the verb *resto* ('hold one's ground', *OLD* s.v. 2; for the combination with *dum*, cf. Prop. 3.8.31 *dum restat barbarus Hector*). But the thuggish Lycabas dispatches Acoetes without breaking a sweat. The precise sense of **guttura … rupit** is difficult to pin down. Ovid has the expression again at *Met.* 15.464, where it means 'throttle to death', a sense clearly inadmissible here. Bömer (1969, 601–02) suggests taking *rupit* as counterfactual, with indicative used in lieu of subjunctive (*rupit ~ rupisset*); but *excussum* and *amens* would stand awkwardly without a preceding factual (i.e. indicative) report of a forceful blow sustained by Acoetes, e.g., 'dealt (me) a crushing blow to the throat' (Henderson 1979, 107) or, more colloquially, 'smashed (me) in the throat' (Anderson 1997, 401). Note that *guttura* is poetic plural, which, like *pectora* in 631, provides a convenient dactyl in the fifth foot. ***iuvenali pugno*** is ablative of instrument; *iuvenalis* is best understood in a derived sense as speaking to physical power; cf. *Met.* 10.674 (of Hippomenes) *iecit ... nitidum iuvenaliter aurum.*

627–28 et excussum ... retentus. A past contrary-to-fact condition (whence the pluperfect subjunctives) with the apodosis (*misisset*) coming before the negated protasis (*si non* = *nisi*). Lycabas would have sent Acoetes tumbling into the water, had the latter not managed to cling to the ropes (sc. of the ship's tackle). The mildly tautological participle ***excussum*** (from *excutio*) modifies an implied *me*, the object of ***misisset***: 'he would have sent me, having been knocked off (sc. the gangplank), into the sea ...' The sense of ***quamvis amens*** is probably 'though stunned *by the blow*'. The implication of ***in fune retentus*** is that Acoetes, after being sent flying by his adversary, manages to grab hold of a rope or more likely he gets 'caught in the ropes'.

629 inpia ... factum. Earlier the crowd expressed its approval (*probat,* 618) at the blasphemous words of Dictys, here they approve the phyal outrage committed by Lycabas: we move from *dicta* to *facta,* from words to deeds.

629–31 tum denique ... sensus. The sprawling main clause *tum denique Bacchus ... ait* (extending through 632) sets up the direct speech at 632–33. *Bacchus enim fuerat* is a parenthetical gloss on the part of the internal narrator Acoetes. Bömer suggests that pluperfect *fuerat* is here used in lieu of the imperfect *erat,* but Henderson (1979, 107) rightly insists on the point of the pluperfect here: 'for it had been Bacchus *all along*' (our italics). The stranger, now positively identified as Bacchus, acts as if the noise of the brawl is returning him to his senses. ***veluti*** (= *velut + si,* 'as if') introduces a so-called 'clause of comparison' (AG §524), which normally takes present and/ or perfect subjunctive verbs — as here with ***solutus sit*** and ***redeant*** (linked by the *-que* attached to the preposition *a/ ab*). Notice that the clause of comparison expresses an *interpretation* of Bacchus' behaviour: Acoetes, maintaining his guise of pious devotee, modestly refrains from claiming to know for a fact what the god was up to, but, as earlier with *videtur* (608 with n.), his language implies the suspicion that Bacchus' inebriation is feigned (see also OLD s.v. *veluti* 5, for use in the context of pretence). The subject of *redeant* is the long-delayed **sensus** (nom. pl.): Bacchus' senses seem to return *a mero* ('from drunkenness', by metonymy) *in pectora* (translate 'to him': in ancient thought the breast was regarded as the seat of reason and of the feelings). As with *guttura* in 626, *pectora* is a stock 'poetic' plural that conveniently supplies the requisite dactyl in the fifth foot of the verse.

So 'it had been Bacchus all along' ... *and probably is right now, talking!* It's *déjà bu* all over again: Bacchus is the wine (*mero*), he is frenzied yelling (*clamore*), he is release (*solutus*). Time to come to our senses.

632–33 quid ... paratis? Bacchus stays 'in character', playing to perfection the part of a bewildered youth awakening from a drunken stupor to find himself in unfamiliar surroundings. Befuddlement is conveyed through four rapid-fire questions, each introduced by a different interrogative pronoun, adjective, or adverb: *quid* ...? *quis* ...? *qua* ... *ope*? *quo* ...? In the midst of this sequence of queries the parenthetical command **dicite, nautae** (in which the vocative reinforces the imperative) heightens the sense of urgency, as deeds and noise (*factum* ... *facitis*; *clamore* ... *clamor*) prompt their correlative, words (*dictis*). The question **quis clamor?** is equivalent to *qui clamor est?*; for the interrogative *quis*, see 531–32 n. The noise in question is the crews' shouts of approval for the violence visited on Acoetes by Lycabas (629). **qua ... ope** amounts to 'by what means' — a common sense.

634–35 pone ... petita. There is some uncertainty here about the individual speaking: most modern editions capitalize **Proreus**, taking it as a proper name. The alternative would be to understand *proreus* as an occupational designation, rendering the Greek technical term πρῳρεύς, used of a ship's 'lookout' or bow officer (i.e. synonymous with πρῳράτης, discussed at 617–18 n.; this is the view of OLD s.v. *proreus*). Understood this way, *proreus* would amount to a second mention of Melanthus, who featured earlier at 617 (see 617–18 n.). But it seems more in keeping with what proceeds to take *Proreus* as a proper name individuating a new member of the crew via a 'speaking name' that misspeaks, by referring to a different figure's nautical role (cf. 618–19 n.). At any rate, this figure endeavours to conceal the crew's malicious intentions from Bacchus, assuring him that he will be dropped off wherever he wishes. In this tricksy story, the dunces think to trick the master who holds all the tricks.

et links the two imperatives *pone* and *ede*. The former is a simplex poetic form for *depone* (570–71 n.): *pone metum/ metus* is a frequent command in epic (elsewhere in *Met.* at 1.735, 5.256, 15.658). The latter ('tell us') governs the indirect question *quos contingere portus velis* (cf. 580–81 n.). In the closing reassurance *sistêre* is an alternative form of *sistêris*, i.e. 2nd pers. sing. fut. indic. pass. of *sisto* (this form occurred earlier at 522 *spargêre*) in the sense 'put ashore'. *terra ... petita* is ablative of place.

636–37 Naxon ... tellus. For *Liber* as a designation of Bacchus, see 520 n. The god continues to play along, instructing the crew to direct its course to Naxos (*cursus ... vestros* is 'poetic' plural). Note the Greek accusative form *Naxon* (559–61 n.), here an accusative of direction without a preposition (as we are dealing with a relatively small island: AG §427). Naxos is one of the Cycladic islands, celebrated in antiquity for its vineyards; it was as such sacred to Bacchus (cf. Stat. *Ach.* 1.678 *Bacchica Naxos*), and a key centre of his cult. In terms of mythology, it was the island where he rescued Ariadne after her abandonment by Theseus, and, according to some sources, it was Bacchus' birthplace (*Hymn. Hom.* 1.2). The strong associations of the god with the island afford his statement *illa mihi domus* an underlying appropriateness.

638–39 per mare ... carinae. The *-que* attached to *me* links *iurant* and *iubent*. It is probably best to construe the adjective *fallaces*, referring to Acoetes' crew members, substantivally here ('the liars') rather than predicatively ('they swear, *lying*'). The miscreants swear *per mare* and, with dramatic irony, *per omnia numina*, unwittingly invoking their addressee, that they will do his bidding. *iurant* introduces the indirect statement *sic fore* (= *sic futurum esse*), which is missing a subject accusative (supply *id*). *iubent* governs an accusative (*me*) + infinitive (*dare*), as often. With *vela dare* supply *ventis* as indirect object (Ovid has the full expression at *Met.* 1.132 *vela dabant ventis*), with *pictae ... carinae* a genitive of possession: i.e. 'give the sails of the painted ship to the winds'. For the poetic synecdoche *carina*, see 592–94 n. *pictus* is a stock epithet for ships (Ovid has it again at *Met*. 6.511), usually referring to the encaustic paint that was applied during the waterproofing stage of a vessel's construction (for details see Zissos 2008. 152). Notice the power inversion achieved through the mutiny: the crew is now issuing orders to the helmsman. Just like Thebes? Not in Pentheus' Thebes — *if* he had anything to do with it.

640–43 dextera Naxos ... susurro. An amusing mime is acted out on board, as the crew endeavours to indicate to Acoetes that he is to steer the opposite course from that just promised to Bacchus, without tipping off the latter. Acoetes, meanwhile, seeks to fulfil Bacchus' wish and ignore the wicked plot hatched by his crew. The use of the present tense throughout these verses adds to the 'dramatic' effect.

> Additional Information: In Tarrant's Oxford Classical Text of the *Metamorphoses*, these lines look very different: 'Dextera Naxos erat; dextra mihi lintea danti | 'quid facis, o demens? quis te furor' inquit Opheltes | 'persequitur?' retinens 'laevam pete!' maxima nutu | pars mihi significat, pars quid uelit aure susurrat. (Naxos was on the right; as I was trying to give sail to the right, Opheltes held me back and said: 'what are you doing, madman? What frenzy addles your brain? Go to the left!' The greater part signals with nods, the rest whisper into my ear what they want.).

640–42 dextera Naxos ... pete. Notice that ***dextera*** is an adjective (nom. f. sing.), the predicative complement of ***Naxos***, whereas the syncopated form ***dextra*** in the following sentence is a noun ('the right hand side'). The unsettled word order of the second sentence reflects the agitation of the crewmembers, who evidently assume that Acoetes is slow on the uptake rather than still daring to resist their plan. To construe the Latin, it might be helpful mentally to reorder as follows: *dextra mihi lintea danti pro se quisque dixit: 'quid facis, o demens? quis te furor, Acoete, tenet? laevam pete!* The pronoun ***mihi*** serves as the indirect object of *inquit* in the following verse; agreeing with it is the participle ***danti***, which takes ***lintea*** (a stock metonymy for *vela*) as its object; ***dextra*** is ablative of place (a regular usage without a preposition), here qualifying the participial phrase. An English rendering might be something like: 'As I was setting sail to the right ...' Acoetes explicates his action in rational terms: Naxos was on the right: *ergo* he tried to sail to starboard. The formula

pro se quisque (literally 'each for himself') often has the weakened sense 'everyone', as here. The verb of speaking, ***inquit***, introduces the pair of rhetorical questions and the abrupt command with which the crew members assail Acoetes. For the interjection *o* before a vocative address, see 540–42 n. Their imputations of insanity (***demens, furor***) are of course, freighted with irony; *quis ... furor* recalls Pentheus' query to his fellow-citizens at 531, thereby reinforcing the analogy between his imperception and that of Acoetes' crew. The command ***laevam pete***, literally 'seek the left', means of course 'steer to the left' (cf. 597–99 n.).

642–43 maxima nutu ... susurro. Like *pars ... alii*, the combination *pars ... pars* is a standard formula of distribution, meaning 'some ... others'. Here the distribution is made asymmetrical by the adjective ***maxima*** modifying the first *pars*: in effect, we have a *pars maior* and a *pars minor*. Each group is assigned its own verb and ablative of means, while ***quid velit***, an indirect question (AG §573–75; hence the subjunctive *velit*) is the shared (*apo koinou) object of both verbs.

> Additional Information: Although the manuscript reading *ore* creates a neat balance of ablative complements (*nutu ... ore*), it is otherwise somewhat lacking in point, and many editors prefer the variant *aure* (a poetic shortening of *in aure*; in prose we would expect *in aurem*).

644–45 obstipui ... removi. The *-que* after *capiat* (in the original Latin, the quotation marks would of course have been absent) connects *obstipui* and *dixi*. The *-que* after *me* connects *dixi* and *removi*. To construe the initial sentence, reorder as follows: *obstipui et dixi: 'aliquis moderamina capiat'*. The indefinite pronoun ***aliquis*** ('someone') here has the emphatic implication 'someone *else*' — i.e. 'someone other than me'. Having already suffered physical assault, Acoetes now opts for passive resistance. ***capiat*** is a hortatory subjunctive (AG §439); its object ***moderamina*** ('poetic' plural) is probably used concretely here of the rudder (as again at 15.756), much as *regimen* was earlier (593 with n.). In English we would say 'take the helm'.

me is the accusative object of ***removi***, with ***ministerio*** an ablative of separation (AG §401). For the correlating *-que ... -que*, coordinating the two genitive attributes of *ministerio*, see 521–23 n.; this pair of genitives produces a mildly zeugmatic and hendiadic effect: '(I removed myself) from *service* of their crime and the *exercise* of my skill (sc. as helmsman)' — that is, *from helping them in their crime with my skill*. The versification reflects Acoetes' brisk, punctilious response: lines 644 and 645 are almost entirely dactylic, with just a single spondee in the fourth foot of the second verse.

646 increpor ... agmen. The *-que* after *totum* links *increpor* and *inmurmurat*. Notice that this verse constitutes a so-called 'theme-and-variation', with the second clause essentially reformulating the first (cf. 515 with n.): *increpor* is synonymous with *inmurmurat*, *a cunctis* with *totum ... agmen*. This is a device of emphasis; in addition, the switch from Acoetes as passive subject to the crew as active subject subtly prepares for the emergence of a ringleader from the group, who takes charge of matters with Caesarean vigour and decisiveness.

647–48 e quibus ... ait. The relative pronoun is 'connecting': *e quibus* is equivalent to *ex iis*, and depends on *unus* understood. As with the previous instances, the name **Aethalion** is Greek; αἰθαλίων (*aithaliôn*) means 'burning, blazing'. His utterance is dripping with sarcasm, rendered explicit by the particle **scilicet** and underscored by the hyperbaton of *te ... in uno* (giving mocking prominence to the 2nd person pronoun) and of *omnis ... nostra salus* (giving mocking prominence to the hyperbolic *omnis*).

648–49 et subit ... relicta. The *-que* after *meum* links *subit* and *explet*; the *-que* after *Naxo* links *explet* and *petit*. The sense of **subit** is 'succeeds me, takes my place' (cf. *Met*. 1.114 *subiit argentea proles*, of the silver race succeeding the gold); *explet* can be rendered 'performs'. **Naxo... relicta** is an ablative absolute (the Greek proper noun *Naxos* is f., as is the rule for islands). As earlier at 642, **petit** has the sense 'direct one's course'; *diversa*, its object, can be understood as modifying an implied *loca*, or as neuter adjective used as a noun, in which case it could be rendered in English with an adverbial clause: 'in the opposite direction'.

650–52 tum deus ... similis. The primary verb for this sequence is *ait* in 653. In the elaborate build-up, the circumstantial participle *inludens* governs a clause of comparison (AG §524) introduced by the comparative particle **tamquam** ('as if'), which takes a subjunctive verb (*senserit*); the sense of **modo denique** is 'only then' (i.e. 'then for the first time'). Here *puppe* is meant literally rather than synecdochically:

Bacchus is standing at the stern. The epithet *adunca* arises from the fact that on the ancient ship the keel was raised up at the stern (just as it was at the front; cf. *Met.* 1.298 <u>curvae</u> *carinae*).

The dative participle *flenti* (from *fleo*) is dependent on *similis*: as he proceeds to address the crew, Bacchus is 'akin to someone crying'. It was generally held by the ancients that the gods were incapable of crying; but of course Bacchus is acting here. Indeed, the god, who was the divine patron of the theatre, does that patronage proud by continuing persuasively to play the part of the defenceless youth, on whom the criminal intent of the crew is only now beginning to dawn. Notice the pronounced alliteration on *p* in 651.

653–55 tum ... unum. Bacchus' brief speech is direct, with repetition and 'doubling' used to powerful rhetorical effect (1a: <u>non haec mihi</u> <u>litora</u> ... *promisistis* — 1b: <u>non haec mihi</u> *terra rogata est*; 2a: *quo merui poenam facto?* — 2b: *quae gloria vestra est ...?*; 3a: *si puerum iuvenes* [sc. *fallitis*] — 3b: *si multi fallitis unum*).

The first *mihi* (652) is the indirect object of *promisistis*; the second *mihi* is dative of agent ('by me') with perfect passive *rogata est* (AG §375). In Bacchus' first query, *quo* is an interrogative adjective modifying *facto*, forming a causal ablative ('on account of what deed ...?'). In the second, *quae* is an interrogative adjective, modifying *gloria*, with *vestra* in predicative position ('what glory is yours if ...?'). Bacchus emphasizes the shamefulness of the crew members' exploit by means of subject-object pairs, arranged *chiastically, that underscore their superiority in age (*iuvenes ... puerum*) and number (*multi ... unum*).

> Additional Information: The differentiation between the Latin terms *puer* and *iuvenis* is starker than it might appear to modern readers (thanks in no small part to modern cognates like 'juvenile'). Roman thought generally divided a man's life into four stages (ranges are approximate): *infantia* (0–2 years), *pueritia* (3–16), *iuventus* (17–45), *senectus* (46 +). Hence the age range of the *iuvenis* (someone in the stage of *iuventus*) extends into what we would classify as 'middle-age', and we should imagine Acoetes' crewmembers surpassing the apparent age of their captive by a considerable margin.

656–57 iamdudum ... remis. Whereas Bacchus only simulates weeping (*flenti similis*), the pious Acoetes has long since dissolved into genuine tears of despair (for the tense of *flebam*, see AG §277b); notice the appropriate metrical articulation of Acoetes' sobbing: all of the syllables in *iamdudum flebam* scan long. True to type, the crew, ominously characterized as a ***manus inpia*** ('blasphemous band'), makes fun of his tears (***nostras*** is 'poetic' plural, hence: 'my'). The sense of ***impellit*** is 'strikes' or perhaps 'sets in motion', speaking to the 'shovelling' of the sea by the oars (***properantibus ... remis***).

658–60 per ... fide. The inset tale has reached its pivotal moment, with Bacchus about to cast off the victim's role to exact miraculous metamorphic punishment on the crew (for the formal requirement that every episode of the poem include a metamorphosis, see Intro. §3b). Acoetes portentously introduces this new narrative phase with an affirmation of veracity in the form of an oath sworn by the avenging god himself, delivered to his internal audience (***tibi*** is addressed to Pentheus), but naturally aimed at the reader as well. Challenges to the reader to overcome (steep) thresholds of disbelief in the face of the marvellous are a key feature of the *Metamorphoses*, an epic poem that insists on making prima facie incredible forms of (divinely induced) transformative change part of the record of universal history. Anticipation of incredulity on the part of the audience is one of the strategies by which Ovid tries, tongue-in-cheek, to endow his narrative with credibility.

The separation of the preposition from the noun it governs is a peculiarity of Latin poetry. Within this broad phenomenon, the separation of ***per*** from its case (here ***ipsum***, with which understand *deum*) is particularly frequent in adjurations: Bömer (1969, 608) provides a list of parallels. In the parenthetical aside, ***illo***, referring to Bacchus, is ablative of comparison after ***praesentior***. In supernatural contexts, *praesens* has a quasi-technical sense, speaking to a deity making its power manifest (cf. *OLD* s.v. 3); hence the implication would be 'no god is more powerful than he'. But for those recognizing Bacchus in Acoetes, this declaration can be taken literally: 'no god is more present than he', an arch double-entendre that clearly — and fatally — sails over Pentheus' head.

Acoetes insists on the truth of the marvel he is about to recount in a decidedly counterintuitive fashion. The indirect statement *tam me tibi vera referre | quam veri maiora fide* is dependent on ***adiuro***; the subject accusative is ***me***, the infinitive ***referre***. The latter takes two accusative objects, ***vera*** and ***maiora*** (both are n. pl. adjectives used substantivally), which are coordinated by ***tam... quam***. Finally, ***fide*** is ablative of comparison after *maiora*, and *veri* an objective genitive dependent on *fide*. Taken altogether, we have 'I swear that the things I tell you are just as (*tam*) true as (*quam*) they are greater than belief in the truth', i.e. beyond belief.

660–61 stetit … teneret. The miraculous developments begin with the ship (for the synecdoche *puppis*, see 596 n.) suddenly standing still (*stetit*) on the open sea as if it were resting in dry dock (*siccum navale*). This eerie prelude appears to be Ovid's invention (cf. *Hymn. Hom.* 7.32–34). The imperfect subjunctive *teneret* is the usual form for this kind of conditional (or 'hypothetical') comparison; the general rule is that *quasi* and *tamquam* are followed by the present and perfect subjunctive, while *quam si* (as well as *ut si*, etc.) is followed by the imperfect and pluperfect subjunctive, as here (cf. *Met.* 15.331 *haud aliter titubat quam si mera vina bibisset*, 'he staggered as if he had drunk unmixed wine'). Since Latin idiom has the vessel 'holding' dry dock rather than the reverse, the subject of the clause remains *puppis*, with *siccum navale* the accusative object.

662–63 illi admirantes … temptant. Acoetes now describes the unavailing efforts of the astonished crew (*admirantes* is a circumstantial participle) to restore the ship's motion. This report takes the form of a *tricolon, structured around the verbs *perstant* — *deducunt* — *temptant*. The *-que* after *vela* links *perstant* and *deducunt*, the *-que* after *gemina* links *deducunt* and *temptant*. The first colon captures the attempt at rowing; the second the unfurling of the sails; the third sums up the first two: they try to overcome the eerie standstill through this twofold effort (*gemina ope*).

Persisting in a given activity is regularly expressed by *perstare in* + abl. (*OLD* s.v. 3), as here with **remorum in verbere perstant**. Here, though, the sense is 'persist *in the attempt* at rowing', since Acoetes promptly reveals that the oars are held fast by ivy (664). The metaphoric use of *verber*, *verberare* etc. in reference to rowing strokes, figured as a kind of 'lashing' of the sea, is quite common in Latin poetry (Görler 1999, 273); Ovid uses the same conceit of swimming strokes at *Her.* 18 *dare verbera ponto*. In addition to rowing, the crew makes an equally futile attempt to harness the winds: **vela deducunt** speaks to the unfurling (or letting down) of the main sail, which was tied to the yard (the horizontal beam attached to the top of the mast). That this measure is supplementary to the rowing is underscored by **gemina ope** ('with double aid', i.e. with the aid of both oars and sail). Acoetes sets the crew's double effort in relief because it was not normal ancient seafaring practice simultaneously to resort to both means of propulsion. The application of ***currere*** to the progress of a ship through water is a standard poeticism (*OLD* s.v. 3a), attested as early as Naevius but enjoying particular currency in the Augustan and later periods. It belongs to a set of nautical metaphors systematized by Virgil, including 'flying', used of rapid sailing (on which see further Zissos 2008, 226–27).

664–65 inpediunt ... corymbis. Bacchus' power is now made manifest through a miraculous botanical metamorphosis, the onset of fast-spreading ivy (a plant associated with the god: see 540–42, 555–56 nn.). Here Ovid has simplified the account of the *Homeric Hymn to Dionysus*, which begins with a miraculous geyser of wine (*Hymn. Hom.* 7.35–37), and then features a combined incursion of ivy and vines: 'All at once a vine spread out in both directions along the top of the sail, with many clusters hanging down from it, and a dark ivy-plant twined about the mast, blossoming with flowers, and with rich berries growing on it' (αὐτίκα δ᾽ ἀκρότατον παρὰ ἱστίον ἐξετανύσθη | ἄμπελος ἔνθα καὶ ἔνθα, κατεκρημνῶντο δὲ πολλοὶ | βότρυες: ἀμφ᾽ ἱστὸν δὲ μέλας εἱλίσσετο κισσός, | ἄνθεσι τηλεθάων, χαρίεις δ᾽ ἐπὶ καρπὸς ὀρώρει, *Hymn. Hom.* 7.39–42).

Notice that *hederae* is the subject of all three verbs, whose sequence produces a *tricolon structure (the *-que* after *nexu* linking *inpediunt* and *serpunt*). The rapidly spreading ivy 'obstructs' (***impediunt***) the oars — without, it would seem, growing out of them, as we find in other accounts (e.g. Sen. *Oed.* 452–56, quoted below). In the second colon, the enjambment of ***serpunt*** neatly reflects what is being described: the ivy is crawling all over the place; the instrumental ablative ***nexu recurvo*** speaks to the 'intertwined formation' of the ivy. In the final colon, the sense of ***distinguunt vela corymbis*** is 'deck the sails with clusters of ivy berries' (for *distinguo* in this sense, cf. Hor. *Carm.* 2.5.11 *distinguet Autumnus racemos purpureo varius colore*). The Greek loanword *corymbus* (κόρυμβος) designates a cluster of ivy-berries. The basic meaning of *gravidus* is 'pregnant' and then, metaphorically, 'laden, swollen, teeming with', 'rich, abundant'.

Additional Information: Writing in the later Neronian Age, Seneca offers a ramped-up version of this scene: *hinc verno platanus folio viret | et Phoebo laurus carum nemus; | garrula per ramos avis obstrepit. | vivaces hederas ramus tenet, | summa ligat vitis carchesia* ('so there were plane trees green with spring foliage, and laurels whose groves are dear to Phoebus; birds chattered among the branches, the oars were covered with vigorous ivy, grapevines twined at the mastheads', *Oed.* 452–56). His twofold elaboration of the initial miracles — ivy on the oars and a vine at the top of the mast — makes for an attractive botanical 'division of labour'. Notice that *vivaces hederas remus tenet* is a neat variation on Ovid's *inpediunt hederae remos*, which emphasizes the metamorphic without insisting on the sudden immobility of the vessel (a detail also absent from the *Homeric Hymn*).

666–67 ipse racemiferis ... hastam. As the epiphany continues, the god himself — *ipse* refers to Bacchus — acquires a couple of his familiar accessories: a garland and the thyrsus. The elaborate formulation can be stripped down to a simple core: *ipse* (subject) *agitat* (verb) *hastam* (object). The participle *circumdatus* agrees with *ipse* and governs *frontem*, which is a synecdochical or 'Greek' accusative used to denote the part affected (AG §397b, so named as a construction thought to have entered Latin in imitation of Greek practice), and the instrumental ablative *racemiferis ... uvis*. The latter defies literal translation: a *racemus* is a cluster of grapes (or other fruits); the compound adjective *racemifer* (from *racemus* + *fer*; for such epithets in *-fer* and *-ger*, see 584–85 n.) means 'bearing clusters (of grapes)'. Its application to the noun *uva* is decidedly odd; perhaps translate '(with) clustering grapes'.

As already indicated, *hastam* does not designate a real spear but rather the thyrsus (on which see 540–42 n.), a metaphoric usage found earlier in Virgil (*Ecl.* 5.31; *Aen.* 7.396) and later in Statius (*Theb.* 9.796; *Ach.* 1.261). The participle *velatam*, agreeing with *hastam*, governs *pampineis ... frondibus*, another instrumental ablative: '... a spear veiled in vine-leaves' is an attractive indirect formulation for the thyrsus. The trope is freighted with foreboding for Pentheus, as his mother Agave will begin the murderous onslaught on her son by hurling her thyrsus at him as if it were a spear (712 with n.). But here as elsewhere, Acoetes' imperious interlocutor *misses the point*.

668–69 quem circa ... pantherarum. The god's bestial entourage is now added to the epiphany; Ovid opts for more theologically 'appropriate' — if less concrete — species than the *Homeric Hymn to Dionysus*, which states that the god metamorphosed into a lion and a bear materialized at his side (*Hymn. Hom.* 7.45–46). The creatures in question here — tigers, lynxes, panthers — became associated with Bacchus (and were added to his train) as a result of a body of legends attributing the conquest of India to the god (on which see Intro. §5b-iii n. 76; although Ovid does not develop this alternate, 'martial' version of the god, these oblique allusions could be yet another hint that Bacchus isn't the pushover Pentheus has assumed: cf. 553–58 with nn.). The lynx in particular came to be seen as the Bacchic animal *par excellence*. In a retrospective section of the 'Hymn to Bacchus' with which he opens Book 4, Ovid mentions a chariot drawn by lynxes as one of the divinity's preferred means of transportation, right after his punishment of the Etruscan sailors: *Tyrrhenaque mittis in aequor | corpora, tu biiugum pictis insignia frenis | colla premis lyncum* ('you send the Tyrrhenian bodies into the sea, you press the necks of lynxes yoked in pairs with multi-coloured reins', *Met.* 4.23–25).

The verb *iacent* has three subjects — *tigres, simulacra, corpora* — linked, respectively, by the *-que* after *simulacra* and *pictarum*. The pronoun **quem** is a so-called connecting relative, equivalent to *et eum*. It occupies emphatic initial position (of both verse and clause) by virtue of the *anastrophe of its preposition **circa**.

Whereas **tigres** are mentioned without qualification, the expression **simulacra... inania lyncum** raises the possibility that all these creatures are apparitions — which would not be inappropriate to Bacchus, as a god of illusion. A *simulacrum* is an image formed in the likeness of something else. Depending on the context this could be a work of art (such as a portrait or statue), a mirror-image, something seen in a dream (shade, phantom) or in one's imagination, or, when the emphasis is the opposition to what is real or substantial, something flimsy or insubstantial (shadow, semblance, appearance). The attribute **inania** ('empty') reinforces the sense that the *lynxes* in question are mere apparitions. But one might justly wonder about focalisation: did the lynxes appear as *simulacra inania* to Acoetes at the time? Or is it Acoetes the narrator who retrospectively clarifies that what at the time seemed to him (as surely to the sailors) to be real lynxes were in fact phantom beasts. The sense of **pictarum** is 'spotted'.

Verse 669 exhibits some noteworthy stylistic features, starting with the attractive 'enclosing' arrangement of the alliterative epithet-noun pair *pictarum... pantherarum*. In addition, the four long syllables of *pantherarum* occupying the last two feet of the hexameter, produce something of a metrical monstrosity, turning verse 669 into a so-called spondaic verse (i.e. one in which the 5th foot consists of a spondee rather than the expected dactyl).

670–72 exsiluere ... flecti. In construing *exsiluere* (an alternate 3rd pers. pl. perf. form) the prefix should be afforded its full force: the men jump *out* of the vessel, i.e. *overboard*. After this dramatic declaration, Acoetes momentarily suspends the action to speculate on its motivation, entertaining two possibilities (*sive ... sive*): a fit of insanity or fear. This of course reminds us that Acoetes is (posing as) a non-omniscient narrator. On the metaliterary level, this equivocation could also be marking Ovid's departure from the tradition of the Homeric Hymn, in which the creatures that appear are only too real, and it is the lion's apparent assault on the helmsman — Acoetes' counterpart! — that prompts the fearful crew to jump overboard (*Hymn. Hom.* 7.51–52).

The *-que* after *primus* links *exsiluere* and *coepit*, which governs the two infinitives *nigrescere* and *flecti* (linked by *et*). **primus** is an adjective, agreeing with **Medon** (a Greek nominative form), used in lieu of an adverb: he is the first to exhibit symptoms of the metamorphosis subjected upon the entire crew; **corpore** is a somewhat otiose ablative of respect with **nigrescere**. The sense of **expresso spinae curvamine** (ablative absolute) is 'with the curve of his spine arching outwards' — an initial manifestation of his metamorphosis into a dolphin. Strictly speaking, this curve is not an anatomical feature of the species, but is dramatically in evidence when dolphins leap out of the water, and this captivating sight prompted many ancient artists and poets to conceive of — or at least represent — the dolphin as hog-backed: cf. Ovid's earlier reference to *curvi delphines* (*Met.* 2.265, which appears to be the inspiration for Christopher Marlowe's 'crooked dolphin' at *Hero and Leander* 2.234).

673–75 incipit ... trahebat. The text may well be corrupt here: see Additional Information below. If retained as transmitted, it will be necessary to supply *dicere* with **incipit**: 'he begins *to speak*'. This is an easy *ellipse in English as well as Latin, but here it sits very oddly with *dixit* at the end of the verse. *huic* refers to Medon, Lycabas' addressee. The sense of *in quae miracula* is 'into what strange shape ...?' *rictus* (nom. m. pl.) and *naris* (nom. f. sing.) are both subjects of *erat* (which is singular in correspondence with the nearer of the pair); they take *lati* and *panda* respectively as predicative complements. *loquenti* is a circumstantial present participle, agreeing with an implied demonstrative pronoun in the dative of possession. Taken together, we have 'as he was speaking his mouth became broad and his nose curved'. The sense of *squamam... trahebat* is 'took on scales, became scaly' (*squamam* is a collective singular). Here again — cf. 670–72 n. — we reach the limits of the poet's zoological competence: dolphins are mammals and, unlike fish, do not have scales. Ovid is evidently not speaking from personal observation. The compact combination of perfect participle (*durata*) + 'ingressive' imperfect (*trahebat*) neatly expresses a two-fold process: the skin hardens and then takes on scales. In describing metamorphoses Ovid regularly uses the verbs *traho* (*OLD* s.v. 13, 'take on, acquire (properties, attributes, etc.)'), as here: cf. *Met.* 1.412 *saxa ... faciem traxere virorum* ('the stones took on the form of men'). Another stock verb of transformation is *duco*, which is used in much the same way (cf. *Met.* 1.163 *ducere formam*, 'take shape').

> Additional Information: The juxtaposition of two main verbs in different tenses without any connectives in 673 (*incipit* — *dixit*) is difficult to parallel and make sense of. It may well be that the transmitted text is corrupt and some editors have put forward conjectures (as well as proposing alternative punctuation). Here is the text as printed by Tarrant in his Oxford Classical Texts edition: *exsiluere viri, sive hoc insania fecit | sive timor, primusque Medon nigrescere toto | corpore et expresso spinae curvamine flecti | incipit; huic Lycabas 'in quae miracula' dixit | 'verteris?' et lati rictus et panda loquenti | naris erat, squamamque cutis durata trahebat* (670–75). The differences are underlined: (i) *toto*, in lieu of the manuscript reading *coepit*, at the end of line 671 is a conjecture of Shackleton Bailey adopted by Tarrant; (ii) this conjecture entails changes in punctuation: Tarrant has no full stop after *flecti*, but puts a colon after *incipit*, with no punctuation after *Lycabas*. The conjecture and re-punctuation results in syntactical differences: (i) the *-que* after *primus* links *exsiluere* (670) and *incipit* (673), rather than *exsiluere* (670) and *coepit* (671); (ii) *incipit* governs the preceding infinitives *nigrescere* and *flecti* rather than being used in an absolute, elliptical sense ('he begins to speak').

676–78 at Libys ... vocari. The conjunction *at* does not have its usual adversative force here, merely signalling a transition to the next victim of transformation, Libys, who featured earlier at 617. The main verb *vidit* governs an indirect statement that falls into two parts, linked by *et* and arranged chiastically: *resilire* (verb) — *manus* (subject accusative) and *illas* (subject accusative) — *posse ... posse* (verb), with *vocari* a supplementary infinitive dependent on (both instances of) *posse*. This sequence is focalized through the metamorphic victim: Libys witnesses as he experiences the transformation of his own hands into fins. As Henderson (1979, 111) observes, 'Ovid gets inside the mind of Libys, whose rapidly changing definition of his own extremities is subtly brought out by the asyndetic *anaphora *iam* (*non*) ... *iam* ...' Notice how the line break helps to capture the eerie moment in which Libys' extremities have ceased to be recognizable as hands and have become recognizable as fins.

The verb of the *dum*-clause is **vult**, which takes *obvertere* as supplementary infinitive. Libys wishes to ply (**obvertere**) the oars (i.e. turn them against the water), but they are resisting the attempt (**obstantes**), i.e. they are immovable. The sense of **in spatium resilire ... breve** (literally 'to jump back into a small space') is 'to contract' or 'to shrink'. The use of *pinna* in the sense 'fin' (*OLD* s.v. 3) though not attested before Ovid in extant Latin literature, would appear to have been the regular term in both poetry and prose; cf. Plin. *NH* 9.7 *pinnarum ... quae pedum vice sunt datae piscibus* ('fins ... which are given to fish in place of feet').

679–82 alter ... lunae. Acoetes subtly generalizes the metamorphic phenomenon by describing the experience of an unnamed victim (*alter*). The first main clause is *alter ... bracchia non habuit*, with the present participle *cupiens* (which agrees with the subject *alter*) governing an infinitive construction that specifies what this individual wished to do with the arms he no longer has. The verb of the second main clause is *desiluit*, which is linked to *non habuit* by the *-que* after *trunco*. Ovid here underscores the quick sequence of events by interweaving description of the transformation (*trunco repandus ... corpore*) with portrayal of the behaviour it entails: *in undas ... desiluit*, across a line break, which enacts his jumping down from the ship into the waters.

intortos ('twisted') is a conventional attribute of ropes and cables, speaking to the braiding of individual strands during the manufacturing process (cf. Cat. 64.235 *intorti ... rudentes;* Virg. *Aen.* 4.575 *tortos... funis).* The sense of **dare bracchia** is *tendere bracchia*: this fellow wishes to reach out towards the braided ropes (*ad intortos ... funes*) — to what end is not altogether clear; perhaps to trim the sail or to perform some other nautical task. **trunco ... corpore** (speaking to the metamorphic loss of limbs) is ablative of respect with **repandus** ('curved backward'). **novissima cauda** denotes the extremity (or tip) of the tail; *novus* can bear a spatial as well as a temporal implication. **qualia** introduces a comparison; it agrees with **cornua**, the subject of the sentence, on which the genitive **dimiduae ... lunae** ('half-moon') depends: 'just as the horns of the crescent moon are bent'.

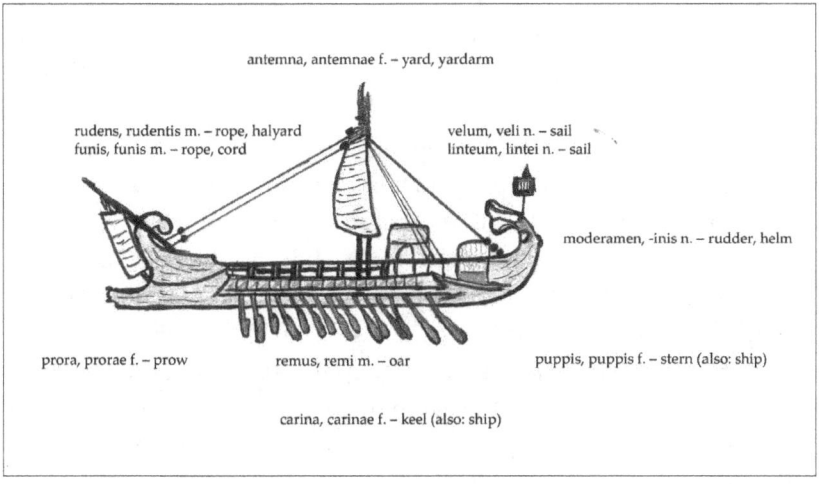

Fig. 7 Nautical terms.

683–86 undique ... efflant. These four verses constitute an extended paratactic sequence describing the newly formed dolphins — the subject is implied by the plural verb forms — frolicking in the sea. There are fully seven verbs, all in the vivid present: *dant, rorant, emergunt, redeunt, ludunt, iactant, efflant.* The initial five are linked by *-que* (after *multa, emergunt, redeunt, in,* and *lasciva*), the last two by *et* (this switch nicely 'closes out' the sequence). The sportive dolphins are in many ways the polar opposite of the vicious and depraved humans from whom they have been transformed. Ovid provides no indication that they have retained any vestige of their former human consciousness (as is explicitly affirmed in many of the transformations recounted in the *Metamorphoses*).

For the expression **dant saltus** (note that *saltus* is acc. pl.), see 597–99 n. The sense of **multa... aspergine rorant** is 'they shed moisture in a great spray'. The phrase captures the initial moment when a dolphin emerges above the surface of the sea in order to breathe, as a preliminary to which it vigorously 'chuffs' or exhales in order to clear its blowhole and the area around it of water. Acoetes well captures the repetitive character of the dolphins' disappearance beneath the water (**redeuntque**) and reappearance above it (**emerguntque**) through the adverbs *iterum* and *rursus* (the latter technically redundant after <u>red</u>*eunt*) — a dynamic in fact dictated by the need to breathe. Here **aequora** retains its primary connotation of *the surface* of the sea (L-S s.v.): Acoetes observes (and reports) from a vantage point above sea level. The expression **in chori ... speciem** constitutes a very brief comparison: the dolphins' activity resembles that of a band of dancers. The Greek loanword *chorus* (χορός) refers to the performance of group dancing (usually with musical accompaniment). The use of *in speciem* + genitive with the sense 'in the guise of/ giving the impression of' is widespread in Classical Latin (*OLD* s.v. *species*, 6b). A certain intricacy of expression is achieved by the separation of the preposition from its case (on which see 658–60 n.). The sense of **iactant corpora** is that the dolphins 'throw *their own* bodies about' in a playful manner (speaking to their leaping above the water); Ovid here uses an adjective (**lasciva**) in lieu of an adverb (**lasciviter**). Though a frisky and highly intelligent species, the dolphin's apparently playful activity is in this instance dictated by its need to breathe, as mentioned above. The statement *acceptum patulis mare naribus efflant* returns to the action of 'chuffing' briefly treated in 683 (as discussed above). **mare** is an instance of whole for part (a less common form of synecdoche), designating the seawater taken in (**acceptum**) while the dolphins are submerged; it is the accusative object of **efflant**: they blow it out again through a gaping nose (**patulis ... naribus**). The 'gaping nose' is an anatomically imprecise reference to the dolphin's blowhole (which, as a result of evolution, has migrated from its snout to the top of its head, facilitating breathing when partly submerged).

687–91. In the closing section of his account, Acoetes returns to his own situation: as the sole survivor, he is in a state of holy horror, almost beside himself — but is promptly reassured by the now benevolent divinity, whose follower he thereupon becomes.

687–88 de modo ... solus. The preposition *de* governs the indeclinable numeral *viginti* and has partitive force; *modo* is a temporal adverb here meaning 'just a moment ago': taken together we have 'out of twenty *who were there* just a moment ago ...'. Of the various poetic synonyms for 'ship' (592–94 n.), *ratis* is perhaps the least grandiose: it originally designated a raft (cf. Varr. *Ling.* 7.23), but from Enn. *Ann.* 515 Sk onwards serves as a poetic term for a sea-going ship (*OLD* s.v. 2), as here. Overall, the parenthesis glosses *viginti*: with **tot** supply *viros* as the accusative object of *ferebat*. Acoetes is once again being a stickler for precision. Twenty might be on the high side for such a vessel; Hyg. *Fab.* 134 reports a total crew of twelve. In any event, the contrasting numerical specifications *(de) viginti ... solus* neatly frame the sentence. The import of **restabam solus** is 'I alone remained *in unaltered form*' and/or 'I alone remained *onboard*' — an effective encapsulation of Bacchus' transformative intervention.

688–90 pavidum ... Dianque tene. The subject of the sentence is the long-delayed and climactic *deus*; the verb is *firmat*. What precedes is a long and complex accusative object: the adjective **pavidum** and present participle **trementem** (linked by the *-que* after *gelido*) agree with an implied *me*: 'the god reassures me, fearful and trembling as I am ...'. **gelido ... corpore vixque meo** is an ablative of description, with the noun *corpore* modified by two attributes (*gelido* and *vix meo*) linked by the *-que* after *vix*: 'with my body chilled and hardly my own'. Acoetes is obviously scared out of his wits — and almost out of his body as well: the phrasing here is poignant given what has just happened to the sailors and *their* bodies.

Bacchus proceeds to give two orders (linked by *-que* after *Dian*), in chiastic sequence: imperative (*excute*) — accusative object (*metum*) ‹› accusative object (*Dian*) — imperative (*tene*). *corde* is ablative of separation. **Dian tene** is short for *cursum tene ad Dian*, i.e. make for the island of Naxos (of which *Dia* is an old designation). Sol uses this abbreviated imperative in advising his son Phaethon at 2.140 *inter utrumque tene* ('steer a course between the two [sc. constellations]'). Notice that *Dian* is a Greek accusative form (the Latin equivalent, found in some manuscripts and retained in some modern editions, is *Diam*).

Additional Information: In his Oxford Classical Text, Tarrant prints *pavidum gelidumque trementem | corpore vixque meum*. On this reading, *pavidum, gelidum,* and *(vix) meum* (linked by the two *-que* after *gelidum* and *vix*) are the complements to the implied *me*. They are further qualified by the ablative of description *trementi corpore*, which stands **apo koinou* with all three: 'The god reassures me, fearful, chilled, and hardly myself as I was, with my body trembling all over'. (We added 'all over' to bring out the extra formal stress on this phrase achieved by the enjambment.)

690–91 delatus ... frequento. A curious feature of the closing statement of the inset narrative is the abrupt switch in subject (from Bacchus to Acoetes) and in voice (from active to passive). Indeed, in the wake of Bacchus' command to Acoetes to head for Naxos, it is natural to assume that the god continues to be the subject and it is only after ***accessi*** (1st pers. sing. perf. act.) that one grasps that ***delatus in illam*** ('having been brought to Naxos'; *illam* refers back to *Dian*) is in reference to Acoetes and involves an abrogation of agency. It is tempting to see this odd effect as a further conflation of Bacchus and Acoetes, and a final clue to Acoetes' true identity (see Intro. §5b-iv).

The *-que* after *Bacchea* links *accessi* and *frequento*. The switch from perfect (*accessi*) to present (*frequento*) distinguishes between a singular moment in the past when Acoetes first joined in the rites and his continuing participation, i.e. ***accessi sacris***: 'I joined the rites'; ***frequento***: 'I (still) attend'. The repetition of *sacra frequentare* indicates that Acoetes has at last managed to answer the question Pentheus posed at the end of *his* speech at 581 *morisque novi cur sacra frequentes*?

Additional Information. Some editors have suspected a corruption in the transmitted text on the grounds that *accedere sacris* is an unusual idiom and the repetition *sacris ... sacra* has struck some readers as a trifle clumsy. Hence some editions have substituted the conjecture *accensis aris* for *accedere sacris*. Alternatively, one could interpret the *polyptoton as indicative of Acoetes' devotion to the cult as well as a subtle pun on *frequento*, which implies repetition, thus rendering the reiteration of *sacra* thematically appropriate.

692–733
Pentheus' Gruesome Demise

With the completion of Acoetes' lengthy embedded tale, the narrative reverts to the 'frame' level, and proceeds at a quicker pace and in a terse — almost fragmentary — manner to its conclusion. Pentheus orders the captive to be taken away for torture and execution; but despite being chained and incarcerated, the stranger — so rumour has it — miraculously and effortlessly extricates himself. Pentheus then hastens to Mount Cithaeron, where he is assailed by a troupe of Bacchants led by his mother and aunts, and literally torn limb from limb. In Euripides' more detailed version, the build-up to the *sparagmos* is treated with ingenious psychological twists that Ovid has not explicitly included: Pentheus is persuaded by Dionysus/ Bacchus to dress up as a Bacchant before proceeding to Mount Cithaeron, and experiences hallucinations induced by the god (so that he famously sees two suns and two Thebes). After setting Pentheus in a tree on Cithaeron, ostensibly to afford him a better view of the rites, the god abruptly disappears, after signalling to the Bacchants that their prey is at hand. (For detailed comparison of the Euripidean and Ovidian versions, see Intro. §5a).

692–93 praebuimus ... posset. Ovid's separate embedding of subject (*Pentheus*) and verb (*inquit*) of the main clause within the direct speech they introduce is an intricate effect that visually encircles and ensnares the Theban king in *longis ... ambagibus* (explained below).

The mild circumlocution *praebuimus ... aures* is rather like the English idiom 'lend an ear'; the lofty tone is enhanced by the 'poetic' plural of the verb. The indirect object (that to which Pentheus lent his ears) is *longis ... ambagibus* ('*your* long winding account'). The figurative use of *ambages* (literally 'a circuitous path') extends to all forms of discourse (*OLD* s.v. 2): in the following book the Fury Tisiphone cuts off Juno when she needlessly adds justifications to her commands: *non longis opus est ambagibus; ... facta puta quaecumque iubes* ('No need for long explanations; consider done whatever you command', *Met.* 4.476–77). *ut* introduces a purpose clause whereby Pentheus explains why he sat through Acoetes' longwinded account: in case his wrath might have lessened through the delay (*mora* is ablative of means) — i.e. if Acoetes' (perceived) guilt had not been so great as to make that impossible. Ovid is clearly attempting to account for — or, perhaps better, archly to signal — the implausibility of Pentheus' impetuous anger allowing him patiently to sit through Acoetes' lengthy account.

694–95 praecipitem ... nocti. The *-que* after *cruciata* links the two imperatives *rapite* and *demittite*. **praecipitem** (modifying *hunc*) is used in lieu of an adverb, which would go with *rapite*. The insistent and unsettled syntax and the dactylic rhythm (verse 694 is metrically '*praeceps*') reflect Pentheus' agitated frame of mind. The *famuli* addressed here are no doubt the same attendants who were earlier ordered to arrest Bacchus (562–63, 572–73 nn.). In the second main clause we have interlaced word order reinforced by enjambment: attribute $_1$ (*cruciata*) — attribute $_2$ (*diris*) — noun $_1$ (*corpora*) — noun $_2$ (*tormentis*). **diris ... tormentis** is instrumental ablative dependent on the participle **cruciata**, which modifies the 'poetic' plural **corpora**. Much like *dare leto* (545–48 n.), ***Stygiae demittite nocti*** constitutes an elevated periphrasis for 'kill' (the prosaic term would be *interficere*). The adjective *Stygius* is formed from *Styx*, the Greek name — 'loathsome', from στυγέω — for one of the main rivers of the Underworld, the realm inhabited by the dead (or more precisely, by their 'shades' or ghosts); and *nox* is in itself a conventional metaphor for death in Latin poetry (e.g. Cat. 5.6; Hor. *Carm.* 1.28.15; Virg. *Aen.* 6.390). Pentheus' murderous commands are freighted with tragic irony, inasmuch as *he* is the one who will presently undergo bodily mutilation and death.

696–700 protinus ... catenas. Ovid creates an intriguing rift in his account of what happens next. Acoetes' initial experience, which is in conformity with Pentheus' orders, is reported in the vivid present (*clauditur, parantur*). But in proceeding to the miraculous liberation that follows, the poet seems to distance himself from the factuality of his account with *fama est* ('there is a story'). In fact, Ovid may be 'quoting' earlier literary versions here (on the probable literary implications of *fama est*, see Additional Information below). The statement introduced by *fama est* (i.e. 699–700) is strikingly similar to Euripides' account at *Bacch.* 447–48 'Of their own accord, the chains were loosed from their feet and keys opened the doors without human hand' (αὐτόματα δ᾽ αὐταῖς δεσμὰ διελύθη ποδῶν | κλῇδές τ᾽ ἀνῆκαν θύρετρ᾽ ἄνευ θνητῆς χερός), even if the situation is slightly different: see Additional Information below.

Notice the 'iconic' word order in 696–97, with *solidis ... in tectis* 'enclosing' the prisoner *Tyrrhenus Acoetes* and thereby illustrating the verb *clauditur*. For the epithet **Tyrrhenus**, see 574–76 n. The conjunction *et* (after *tectis*) is adversative in force. Although **crudelia instrumenta**, **ferrum**, and **ignes** are all subjects of **parantur** (all linked by *-que*), the last two explicate the first: the instruments of torture are iron and fire. **iussae ... necis** depends on *instrumenta*: 'of the death that had been ordered' (referring to Pentheus' command *Stygiae demittite nocti* at 695). **fama est** introduces an indirect statement that falls into two parts, linked by the *-que* after *lapsas*: infinitive (*patuisse*) + subject accusative (*fores*); infinitive (*lapsas*, sc. *esse*) + subjective accusative (*catenas*). **lacertis** is ablative of separation (the simple ablative without a preposition is a feature of poetic language: in prose *de* or *ex* would be used). The ablative absolute **nullo solvente** is concessive in force ('even though no one, i.e. no human, freed him'); it is semantically redundant after the emphatic *anaphora of **sponte sua** (equivalent to Euripides' αὐτόματα) at the beginning of verses 699 and 700, but contributes to the sense of wonder (or disbelief).

> Additional Information. *fama est* is a stock phrase, often used by Roman authors to signal awareness of earlier literary treatments: it functions as the poetic equivalent of a footnote. In a sense, then, Ovid is here outsourcing responsibility for the truth-value of his account, saying that he is covering material he has found elsewhere, without necessarily vouching for its veracity. Unfortunately, we cannot be sure which text (or texts) he is referencing here, not least since we do not have Pacuvius' play from which he took the name Acoetes (see Intro. §§5b-iv). There

is a similar scene of liberation in Euripides' *Bacchae*, though it features captured and imprisoned bacchants who are set free the moment that Pentheus' servants bring the bound Dionysus onto the stage: 'the Bacchae whom you shut up, whom you carried off and bound in the chains of the public prison, are set loose and gone, and are gambolling in the meadows, invoking Bromius as their god. Of their own accord, the chains were loosed from their feet and keys opened the doors without human hand' (Eur. *Bacch.* 443–48). At which point, Pentheus himself orders Dionysus' bonds to be loosened, reckoning him to have no means of escape, and in what follows he is *fooled* into thinking that he has the stranger imprisoned.

701–03 perstat … sonabat. The sense of ***perstat*** is that, Acoetes' cautionary tale and his miraculous release from bondage notwithstanding, Pentheus *persists* in his obtuse and impious rejection of Bacchus. The powerful simplicity of the verb is enhanced by its emphatic initial position in both verse and clause. For the patronymic ***Echionides***, identifying Pentheus, see 513–14 n. ***nec iam*** in combination with ***sed ipse*** signals the fateful transition: Pentheus no longer orders his attendants about, but opts rather to venture out in person and look into matters himself. ***iubet*** introduces an indirect statement with infinitive ***ire*** and a subject accusative (*famulos* vel sim.) implied from what precedes; cf. Pentheus' earlier command to his attendants at 562 'ite citi' (*famulis hoc imperat*), 'ite …'

Cithaeron, the subject of the *ubi*-clause, is a mountain range in the vicinity of Thebes associated with the worship of Bacchus, for which its wild character was well suited. The construction ***electus*** with ***ad*** + gerundive expressing purpose is prosaic: Bömer (1969, 619) detects hints of religious language here, which would be appropriate for what amounts to an oblique religious aetiology. ***bacchantum*** = *bacchantium* (from *bacchantes*, a substantive derived from the present participle of *bacchor*): the gen. pl. in *-um* is a common poetic licence for participles (AG §121b.2). Here the genitive stands **apo koinou* with both *cantibus* and *clara … voce*, which are causal ablatives with ***sonabat***. Notice how the repetition of the letter *c* in the *ubi*-clause (*ele<u>c</u>tus, fa<u>c</u>ienda, sa<u>c</u>ra, ba<u>cc</u>hantum, vo<u>c</u>e*) serves to enhances the already striking alliteration <u>C</u>ithaeron <u>c</u>antibus et <u>c</u>lara.

704–07 ut fremit … ira. Ovid now rolls out a simile, likening the impact of the ritual Bacchic shrieking on Pentheus to that of a military trumpet on a spirited war horse: in both cases, sound quickens the emotions, inducing an (automatic, unthinking) eagerness for hostilities. This reprises, on an abstract and figurative level, Pentheus' misconception of Bacchus' advent as a military incursion (531–63 *passim*), a culminating assertion of the mentality that proves to be the king's undoing. Ovid's protagonist is in this respect starkly different from his Euripidean counterpart, who goes up the mountain as a cross-dressing voyeur (see Intro. §5b-ii).

The formulation of the simile is conventional, with *ut* introducing the 'vehicle' (the war horse responding to the battle trumpet), and *sic* the 'tenor' (Pentheus reacting to Bacchic howling). In the first part, the *-que* after *pugnae* links *fremit* and *adsumit*; *acer equus* is the subject of both. The conjunction *cum* meaning 'when' takes an indicative verb to indicate a general case rather than a specific occurrence; the verb is frequently, but not always, in the present tense (AG §547). *fremo* is used of various animal noises occasioned by excitement or anger (*OLD* s.v. 1b), most often growling; in the case of horses, of course, it speaks to neighing. The sense of *acer* is 'spirited'; the application of this adjective to horses is found earlier at Lucr. 4.420. The military scenario, which the epithet **bellicus** promptly announces, is fleshed out in Roman terms (for such 'Romanizing' tendencies, see 538–40 n.). A **tubicen** is a trumpeter, i.e. one who sounds the *tuba*, a straight trumpet, which was one of the principal signalling instruments used in the Roman army (others include the *cornu* and the *bucina*, sounded respectively by the *cornicen* and *bucinator*). By additionally deploying the metonymic expression *aere canoro* ('tuneful/ melodious bronze') for the trumpet (quite literally an ablative of instrument!), Ovid etymologically connects the musician — *tubicen* is a compound derivative from *tuba* + *cano* — and his instrument. The signal (***signa*** is 'poetic' plural) in question here is of course the *battle* signal. ***pugnae*** is an objective genitive dependent on ***amorem***.

The 'tenor' of the simile is formulated with hyperbolic poetic indirection. Instead of saying that the Bacchic cries incite Pentheus (for the accusative form **Penthea**, see 559–61 n.), Ovid says that it is the sky, reverberating with the cries, that moves him (*audito clamore* in the following clause expresses the notion more mundanely). **aether** is a stock poeticism for 'the heavens' or 'the sky'; the idea of its reverberation is conveyed by the metaphor of it being 'struck' (***ictus*** is the perf. pass. part. of *icio*), by the long-continued howls of the Bacchants. For ***ululatibus*** applied to the ritual howling, see 528 n.; notice that ***longis*** is temporal in force. The prolonged sound-track moved Pentheus into action and his wrath flared up again. The simile concludes with an apt metaphor: ***recanduit*** ('grew white with heat again, rekindled') equates Pentheus' anger with fire. *Ira* ('wrath') is of course a quintessentially epic emotion — it provides the keynote to the *Iliad*.

> Additional Information. The epic simile is a conservative literary element that exhibits a high degree of continuity over time. The present example is a case in point, for the comparison of a hero to a horse is widespread in Greek and Latin poetry. Important precedents include Hom. *Il.* 6.506–11 (Paris) = 15.263–68 (Hector), Ap. Rhod. 3.1259–62 (Jason), Enn. *Ann.* 535–39 Sk (of an unidentifiable hero), Virg. *Aen.* 11.491–97 (Turnus). Ennius clearly follows Homer and Virgil both Homer and Ennius. All compare the war-like spirit of their heroes to a horse that has broken its tether and runs exultantly across the plain. Notice how Ovid has reversed the terms of the comparison vis-à-vis these predecessors: his hero is *not* going to war, whereas his horse is. Ovid refuses to engage in the explicit rewriting process that so conspicuously links Homer, Ennius, and Virgil; and in so doing he also refuses to insert Pentheus into a line of epic heroes that includes Paris, Hector, and Turnus.

With the respect to the 'vehicle' of the simile, Ovid's conception of the spirited war horse has suggestive parallels elsewhere in ancient literature, including a passage in the *Georgics* discussing various breeds in which Virgil suggests that the superior horse will rise to the sound of arms: *tum, si qua sonum procul arma dedere, | stare loco nescit, micat auribus et tremit artus, | collectumque premens volvit sub naribus ignem* ('Again, should he but hear afar the clash of arms, he cannot keep his place; he pricks up his ears, quivers in his limbs, and snorting rolls beneath his nostrils the gathered fire', Virg. *G.* 3.83–85). Another noteworthy treatment is found in the Bible at *Job* 39.20–25 '[the horse] paws in the valley and rejoices in his strength — he goes forth to meet armed men. He mocks at fear and is not affrighted. The quiver rattles against him, as do the glittering shield and the spear. He swallows up the ground with fierceness and rage; nor does he believe that it is the sound of the trumpet. He says "ha!" among the trumpets and he smells the battle far off, the thunder of the captains and the shouting'.

708–09 monte ... campus. Ovid prepares the grim denouement with a description of the setting in which Pentheus' dismemberment will occur. Such 'topographical introductions' (a type of ekphrasis), are stock elements of epic narrative, which serve, inter alia, to focus attention on what follows. They almost invariably open with *est*, which critics have dubbed the 'timeless' present, followed by either *locus* (the 'generic' formula, already attested at Enn. *Ann.* 20 Sk, reprised by Virgil at *Aen.* 1.530) or a particular landscape element, such as *nemus*, *specus*, etc. — as here with the long-delayed *campus*. Ovid brings the setting of the final showdown gradually into focus. ***monte fere medio*** (ablative of place) situates it about half-way up the mountain. ***cingentibus ultima silvis***, an ablative absolute, indicates that it is fringed with trees: *ultima* is n. acc. pl. with the sense 'edges', serving as object of *cingentibus*. Finally, the slightly odd-looking ***purus ab arboribus*** (the preposition is redundant) informs us that the field is itself free from trees. These characteristics turn the clearing into a natural theatre, perfectly suited for the performance of religious rites — or the denouement of a tragedy.

710–13 hic oculis ... sorores. The breathless, asyndetic sequence *videt*, *est ... concita, violavit*, punctuated by the powerful triple *anaphora of *prima*, reaches its climax with the postponed subject *mater*, surely one of the most devastating enjambments in Latin epic (for Pentheus' mother Agave, see 513–14 n.). Ovid seems here to have had his eyes on Eur. *Bacch.* 1114–15 πρώτη δὲ μήτηρ ἦρξεν ἱερέα φόνου | καὶ προσπίτνει νιν ('his mother was the first, as priestess of the rites, to begin the slaughter, and fell upon him ...'), the basic elements of which he has subjected to rhetorical intensification. Not to be overlooked here is the broader pattern of repetition initiated in these lines whereby successive verses open with the same word: just as verses 711 and 712 begin with *prima*, so 714 and 715 begin with *ille*, and 718 and 719 begin with *iam*. This is a very striking, and clearly deliberate, *anaphoric sequence, reminiscent of hymnic language.

hic is the adverb ('here'), rather than the demonstrative pronoun, connecting the narrative to the just completed description of the setting. Notice that the participle ***cernentem***, itself the accusative object of *videt*, has its own internal object ***sacra*** (n. acc. pl.): 'she sees (Pentheus) observing the rites'. ***oculis ... profanis***, an instrumental ablative, refers to the eyes (*pars pro toto*) of Pentheus, who is *uninitiated* in the

Bacchic rites, and therefore not permitted to be present (*pro* = 'before/ outside'; *fanum* = 'holy space'; cf. the Sibyl's ritual warning at Virg. *Aen.* 6.258 *procul, o procul este, profani!*). Euripides uses the more precise ἀβακχεύτοισιν ('uninitiated in the Bacchic rites', *Bacch.* 472) in a scene of enticement motivating Pentheus' spying that Ovid has excluded from his account (see Intro. §5b-ii). This compressed sequence nonetheless constitutes the realization of Tiresias' ominous prognostication at 517–18. The use of the reflexive adjective *suum* ('her own'), which modifies **Penthea** (for the 'Greek' accusative form, see 559–61 n.), sets up the aforementioned enjambed shocker *mater*, and is fraught with pathos. The import of *misso ... thyrso*, which functions instrumentally with *violavit*, is that Agave hurled her thyrsus as if a javelin — a (mis)application of the cult object prefigured at 666–67; at 542 Pentheus himself dismissed the *thyrsus* as a weapon: his contempt is now coming back to haunt him. For the interjection *o*, see 540–42 n. Agave calls upon her two sisters Autonoe and Ino (named at 720 and 722 respectively) to join in the attack: **geminae** here simply means 'twofold' (*OLD* s.v. 5; cf. 662 *gemina... ope* with n.), without implying a shared birth; none of Cadmus' daughters were twins. Notice that the kinship terms *mater* and *sorores* 'frame' verse 713.

In line with his cursory treatment of the denouement (692–733 n.), Ovid does not elaborate on why Bacchus selects Pentheus' mother and aunts (i.e. Agave, Ino, Autonoe) as executioners. Euripides motivates this detail by making Semele's sisters (i.e. the same trio) responsible for the calumny that Zeus/ Jupiter was not her lover, for which Dionysus/ Bacchus exacts revenge via the unwitting kin murder (*Bacch.* 26–31). Ovid's redeployment of the calumny as a 'suspicion' voiced by Juno (in disguise) to lure Semele to her doom (3.279–86) and his attribution to Ino of a secret role in the upbringing of the infant god (3.313–14) would seem to weigh against assuming that he is implicitly following the Euripidean version on this matter.

714–15 ille aper ... aper. Agave in her delusional condition misrecognizes her son, in effect 'transforming' him into a boar, and thereby making him a legitimate target for violence. It was entirely appropriate — indeed, it was regarded as a manifestation of divine inspiration — for Maenads to tear to pieces any wild animals they came across during ritual bouts of Bacchic frenzy. This becomes a popular theme in art: perhaps most famously, the Derveni Krater (4th century BCE) includes an image of Maenads tearing apart a deer. In Euripides *Bacchae*, Agave likens the maenads to hunting dogs and hunters (*Bacch.* 1189–90, 1202–04).

Although not an 'actual' metamorphosis in the fictional universe of Ovid's epic, Agave's 'delusional transformation' of Pentheus into a boar is only too 'real' in its consequences. Indeed, a few verses down Pentheus will respond to this perceptual metamorphosis by invoking the case of Actaeon, thereby comparing the Bacchants (turning them into) the hounds that tore apart their master. The Pentheus frame narrative thus crosses ontological lines via delusion and hallucination: both perpetrators and victim reduce each other to a sub-human level in their discourse and imagination.

The connections to the Actaeon episode are subtly reinforced by Agave's use of *errat* of the boar/ Pentheus: the creature has unwittingly wandered into the ritual space (*nostris ... agris*). Very much like Actaeon, who stumbled across Diana and her nymphs in the nude and paid for it with a canine *sparagmos*, the 'boar' is in the wrong place at the wrong time. As we already had occasion to note, Ovid insists at the outset of the tale that Actaeon did not mean to commit a crime: *quod enim scelus error habebat?* ('what crime was there in a mistake?', 3.142) And he reinforces the point later on in the narrative: *ecce nepos Cadmi dilata parte laborum | per nemus ignotum non certis passibus errans | pervenit in lucum: sic illum fata ferebant* ('lo! Cadmus' grandson, his day's toil deferred, comes wandering through the unfamiliar woods with unsure footsteps, and enters Diana's grove; for so fate guided him ...', 3.174–76).

From the point of view of word order, these one-and-a-half verses ingeniously convey the deranged condition of Agave's mind. Note (i) the migration of the attribute *maximus* into the relative clause; (ii) the repetition of *ille aper* and shift in stress from *áper* (714) to *apér* (715); (iii) the postpositive location of the relative pronoun *qui*; (iv) the hyperbaton *in nostris ... agris*; (v) the *ellipse of *est*. Rejigged in standard prose, the sentence would read: *ille maximus aper, qui in agris nostris errat, mihi feriendus est*. The effective use of *anaphora in the initial position of successive verses (see 710–13 n.) continues here with *ille*. The repetition of *aper* also helps to underscore the deviation from Euripides' account, in which Agave and her companions mistake Pentheus for a lion (additional variations are found in later Roman poets, with Valerius Flaccus opting for a bull at *Arg.* 3.264–66, and Martial a calf at *Ep.* 11.84.11).

maximus is a so-called superlative 'of eminence' (AG §291b), with no implication of a distinct comparison: 'this *very great* boar'. The gerundive *feriendus* is part of a passive periphrastic structure with *est* suppressed (as noted earlier), and *mihi* a dative of agent.

715–18 ruit ... fatentem. On the motif of many versus one, see 513–14 n. Deranged, murderous crowds are standard fare in mythic Thebes — indeed they are part and parcel of the city's very foundation, in the form of the mutual slaughter of the Spartoi (described earlier at 3.122–23 *exemploque pari furit omnis turba, suoque | Marte cadunt subiti per mutua vulnera fratres*, 'The same dire madness raged in them all, and in mutual strife by mutual wounds these brothers of an hour perished').

Notice how the word order mirrors the action in 715–16: *omnis ... turba furens* encircles *in unum*, an effect reinforced by the two attributes of *turba* (*omnis, furens*). The pattern of *anaphora at the beginning of successive verses (710–13 n.) continues with *iam* in 717 and 718, reinforced by a pair of additional mid-verse repetitions. The relentless, 'hammering' effect of the sequence *iam trepidum, ... iam ... loquentem | iam ... damnantem, ... iam fatentem* generates a sense of panic as it builds to a *climax. Adding to the effect is the repetition of *trepidum*, which contrasts pointedly with Pentheus' earlier scorn.

The *-que* after *trepidum* links *coeunt* and *sequuntur*; the accusative object of the second verb is an implied *eum* or *Penthea* with which **trepidum** agrees in predicative position: 'they follow him alarmed as he is now'. The implication of **sequuntur** is, of course, that the panicked Pentheus has taken to flight. The accusatives *trepidum, loquentem, damnantem*, and *fatentem* all stand in apposition to the implied *eum* just mentioned. All are linked by the *anaphora of *iam*, but Ovid varies the construction: first the lone adjective **trepidum** (picking up on the *trepidum* of the previous line if the text is sound), then two participles (**loquentem, damnantem**) with accusative objects (***verba minus violenta, se***), and finally a participle (***fatentem***) that governs an indirect statement (*se peccasse*) — all in another breathless asyndetic sequence. The three participial phrases brilliantly capture the progression in Pentheus' change of sentiment, culminating in a moment of 'recognition' (or to use Aristotle's term: *anagnorisis*). After his belligerent rejection of the new god and his rites, Pentheus at the moment of his demise acquires (and articulates) insight into his fatal blindness: *cognita res* (511)... Too late!

719-20 saucius ... umbrae. Whereas the first explicit plea of Euripides' Pentheus is addressed to his mother (*Bacch.* 1120-21, quoted below), here he demonstrates superior 'mythographic competence' by making his initial appeal to his aunt Autonoe, mother of Actaeon. This *prima facie* counterintuitive shift from his mother, who is leading the attack, enables Ovid to link the fate Pentheus is about to experience (gruesome dismemberment) to the fate of his cousin Actaeon, recounted earlier in Book 3: he was torn limb from limb by his own hounds after his transformation into a stag. The invocation emphasizes repetition: in Thebes, such horrific events not only occur, they re-cur. Only, *this time*, out in the wilds beyond the city, it's the big one, the king's turn, ultimately one more mother's son out of his league.

tamen should be understood with what precedes: although acknowledging his guilt, Pentheus nonetheless cries out for mercy. The vocatives *matertera* and *Autonoe* go together: Pentheus first specifies the kinship-relation, then adds the personal name of his addressee. *moveant* is a jussive subjunctive, taking *umbrae* (a 'poetic' plural), on which the genitive *Actaeonis* depends, as its subject and *animos* (supply *tuos*) as accusative object.

721-22 illa quis ... raptu. The *-que* after *dextram* links *nescit* and *abstulit*. *illa* refers back to Autonoe; *nescit* introduces the indirect question *quis Actaeon* (with *sit* omitted): she is so crazed that she does not recognize the name of her own son. *precantis* (a present participle) is dependent on *dextram* and indicates that Pentheus is holding out his right hand in entreaty, a pathetic gesture that compounds the horror. The shocking verb *abstulit*, the effect of which is (again) enhanced by enjambment, implies an immediately prior act of dismemberment; after ripping it out of its socket, Autonoe carries off the imploring limb. The subject of *lacerata est* is *altera* (sc. *manus*), i.e. the left arm. The adjective *Inoo* (from the name-based adjective *Inous, -a, -um*) modifies *raptu*, an instrumental ablative: translate 'by a wrenching heave from Ino'. The assonance *la̱cerata alte̱ra* evokes the mangling of Pentheus as his arm is torn from its socket.

723–25 non habet ... ait. The climactic encounter with his mother unfolds over six gut-wrenching verses, beginning here with Pentheus, now armless, making a final, futile appeal to his mother. Actaeon likewise found his gesture of supplication thwarted by a want of limbs (3.241), as did Io (1.635–36). Notice also the similarity to the metamorphic experience of the Tyrrhenian sailor described earlier at 3.679–81 *alter ad intortos cupiens dare bracchia funes | bracchia non habuit truncoque repandus in undas | corpore desiluit*. He, too, lost his arms (and experienced the wish of using these appendages no longer there) and was reduced to a 'trunk' — though of course retaining his life.

The two main verbs are *(non) habet* and *ait*, linked by **sed** (724). **bracchia** is the accusative object of **habet**, as well as the antecedent of the relative pronoun **quae**, which, together with the subjunctive **tendat**, forms a relative clause of purpose (AG §531.2). Since no later than Virgil's Dido episode, **infelix** is the stock epithet of a tragic protagonist turned victim.

The ablative absolute **dereptis ... membris** refers back to the sundered arms, informing the somewhat odd **trunca ... vulnera** ('mutilated wounds'), a bold instance of transferred epithet involving an elided noun (*trunca* properly applies to *corpora* vel sim.), which serves as accusative object of *ostendens*. The participle presents its own conceptual difficulties: how exactly does the armless Pentheus gesticulate? His speech is, at any rate, short and to the point: 'Look, mother!' Euripides' Pentheus makes a more fulsome plea to Agave: οἴκτιρε δ' ὦ μῆτέρ με μηδὲ ταῖς ἐμαῖς | ἁμαρτίαισι παῖδα σὸν κατακτάνῃς ('Have mercy, mother, and do not slay your son on account of his faults', *Bacch.* 1120–21).

725–28 visis ... nostra est. Following Pentheus' very brief appeal, the focus switches to Agave, with a sequence of four paratactic clauses linked by *-que* after *colla*, *movit*, and *avulsum*: *ululavit* (725) — *iactavit* (726) — *movit* (726) — *clamat* (728). The verbs focus very much on her — and none concerns her beheading of her son. Indeed, this act is elided: it has already happened when the reader gets to 727, where Agave is holding (*conplexa*) the torn-off head (*avulsum caput*) in her bloody fingers. This curious omission is certainly *not* due to squeamishness on Ovid's part — see above 521–23 n. — and could be meant as an ingenious metageneric nod to tragic performance, in which the decapitation would occur off-stage, so that the audience would be witness only to the aftermath. Notice the shift from perfect (*ululavit, iactavit, movit*) to present (*clamat*) just as the narrative skips over the moment when Pentheus loses his head.

With ***visis*** supply *vulneribus* from what precedes, and construe as an ablative absolute. ***colla... iactavit*** is unsettlingly ambiguous: whose neck is in agitated movement here? It could be Agave's neck as a manifestation of Bacchic frenzy (*collum iactare* = 'toss one's head about in ecstasy'); or the reference might be to her brandishing of Pentheus' head (though *colla* as a synecdoche or metonymy would be a bit unusual). If the plural *colla* is not 'poetic', then both necks could be understood. The next phrase is similarly equivocal: *movitque per aera crinem* indicates that Agave makes hair stream or flutter (in the air). The 'natural' reading (but what is natural here?) is that Agave does this to her own hair — and Bacchants did go about with hair unbound, as we are informed just a few lines later in the next episode (*crinales solvere vittas*, 4.6). But we are also free to imagine that, in brandishing her son's head, she makes *his* hair flutter in the air. The punchline that reinforces the ambiguity as an anticipation of the climax comes in the following verse: Pentheus' head is off (*avulsum caput*).

The exclamation ***io*** (Greek ἰώ) is used in various contexts in Latin. Fundamentally, it is a call to attract attention (so used earlier by Narcissus at 3.442 *io silvae!*, and later by Athamas at 4.513 *io, comites, his retia tendite silvis!*). Its specific use to express jubilation, as here, is seen in the quintessential Roman cry *io triumphe* (Hor. *Carm.* 4.2.49). ***victoria nostra*** is predicative complement to ***opus hoc***: 'this deed is our victory'. Agave's exultant declaration is an aggravation, very much in the Euripidean manner, of the catastrophe.

729–31 non citius ... nefandis. Ovid sums up the *sparagmos* of Pentheus with a simile likening the dispersal of leaves from a wind-blown tree in autumn to the disintegration of his body. The simile harks back to Tiresias' prophecy at the beginning of the set text that Pentheus would be scattered into a thousand pieces (521–23 and n.). Regarding the startling ease with which the women achieve the dismemberment, it is worth noting that Euripides describes a more strenuous act (*Bacch.* 1125–27) and offers an explanation absent from Ovid's account: Agave rips off one of her sons limbs 'not by her own strength, but the god gave facility to her hands' (οὐχ ὑπὸ σθένους | ἀλλ' ὁ θεὸς εὐμάρειαν ἐπεδίδου χεροῖν, *Bacch.* 1127–28).

The simile is structured around (*non*) *citius* and *quam*, introducing, respectively, its 'vehicle' and 'tenor'. The subject of the initial clause is the long-delayed *ventus*; the verb is *rapit*. It takes as accusative object *frondes*, which is modified by two participles (linked by the *-que* after *iam*): *tactas* (with *autumni frigore* an ablative of agency without *a/ ab*) and (*male*) *haerentes*, with the latter expressing the consequences of the former (the sense of *male* is 'barely'). *alta ... arbore* is ablative of separation — prose usage would require *ab* or *ex*. The topsy-turvy word order of the second clause evokes the disorderly multitude of hands grabbing and ripping off Pentheus' body parts. The clause is formulated in the passive voice, with *membra* the subject, *viri* (referring to Pentheus) genitive of possession, and *manibus nefandis* ablative of agent. Notice that the attribute *nefandus* (literally 'unspeakable', hence 'blasphemous') signals a switch from Pentheus committing a religious outrage to the unwitting women doing so. In tragic Thebes, everyone gets stained, the audience/reader, too.

> Additional Information: Many readers and critics have found fault with this simile, and in particular the stark disjunction, both in terms of ease and number, arising from the equation of the scattering of autumn leaves and the dismembering and dispersal of the parts of a single human body. Whatever its merits, the peculiarity of the simile is enhanced by the fact that Ovid has deployed a 'vehicle' belonging to an established tradition of anthropological reflection via similes that reaches back to Homeric epic (*Il.* 6.144–49, generations of men likened to leaves) and includes lyric poetry (Mimnermus fragment 2 West). (If 'Autumn Leaves' makes you think of the unforgettable song of romantic regret, take note that its original, the Jacques Prévert poem 'Les Feuilles Mortes', was written *in 1945*, when fighting to forget could only bring back a worldscape of tragic carnage.) Ovid's most immediate model is Virg. *Aen.* 6.305–14 *huc [ad cumbam]* <u>omnis turba</u> *ad ripas effusa* <u>ruebat</u> | <u>matres atque viri</u>, *defunctaque corpora vita* | *maganimum heroum, pueri innuptaeque puellae,* | *impositisque rogis iuvenes ante ora parentum;* | *quam multa in silvis* <u>autumni frigore</u> *primo* | <u>lapsa cadunt</u> *folia, aut ad terram gurgite ab alto* | *quam multae glomerantur aves, ubi frigidus annus* | *trans pontum fugat, et terris inmittit apricis* ('Hither rushed all the throng, streaming to the banks; mothers and men and bodies of high-souled heroes, their life now done, boys and unwedded girls, and sons placed on the pyre before their fathers' eyes; thick as the leaves of the forest that at autumn's first frost

drop and fall, and thick as the birds that from the seething deep flock shoreward, when the chill of the year drives them overseas and sends them into sunny lands'). In comparison with the countless multitudes forming the 'tenor' of his predecessors' similes, Ovid's application of the image of numberless leaves to one man's *sparagmos* is indeed bizarre — just *how many* body parts can be generated by even the most conscientious dismemberment? But the rift between human horror show and vindication of divine power is the stake of the myth: the points of view (awful <=> aweful) can't be reconciled, there is in the end only submission. So, now he's made us retch, the poet-priest-hymnodist is here finally to *tell* us wretches that we've been watching, and acting out, 'the natural order' all along. That, however much gentle commentators would like to go easy on you and spare you, bleak 'winter' is where the Ovid set-text 'leaves' us. What it turns out, hereabouts, to be *like*. In Thebes and ...

732–33 talibus ... aras. The subject of all three clauses, which form a *tricolon, is *Ismenides*, 'the daughters of Ismenus', a poeticism for 'the Theban women' (Ismenus being a river in the vicinity of Thebes). *monitae*, which modifies *Ismenides*, takes **talibus exemplis** (referring, in 'poetic' plural, to Pentheus' gruesome demise) as ablative of means. The three main verbs *frequentant* — *dant* — *colunt* are linked by *-que* after *tura* and after *sanctas*). The sense of **tura dant** is 'offer incense'; this forms a *hendiadys with **sanctas... colunt aras**: i.e. the women offer incense on the sacred altars.

In the *Bacchae*, Euripides has Agave return to Thebes proudly bearing Pentheus' severed head, calling for him so that he might nail her trophy — his own head — to the palace doors. Ovid does not attempt to replicate this culminating stroke of tragic irony. He proceeds instead to a moralizing ending which in truth is weird, given that Pentheus was said to be the only one who had not yet joined in the Bacchic revels (513 *ex omnibus unus* with n.). Put differently, the other inhabitants should not really need his ghastly *exemplum* to worship the divinity: they were said to do so joyfully and voluntarily at the outset. But these closing verses serve to set up the opening of Book 4 (rather than conclude Book 3), where the story of reckless defiance continues ...

APPENDICES

1. Versification

One of the great pleasures of reading Ovid's *Metamorphoses* is his verse-craft. His lines flow like those of no other poet — and he is therefore an ideal author for learning how to read and to appreciate Latin hexameters. What follows is a quick overview in the basic principles of hexametric verse.

The Quantitative Basis of Latin poetry

Latin poetry depends for its rhythm on quantity rather than accent. Quantity is the amount of time taken to pronounce a syllable. There are two kinds of syllabic quantity — long and short (defined in the next section). Unlike English poetry, which produces its effect by a sequence of accented and unaccented syllables, Latin poetry uses a predetermined sequence of long and short syllables, a sequence determined by the meter of the poem. Syllables are combined into certain metrical groupings called feet (see section 3), and feet are combined into verses.

Long and Short Syllables

A syllable in Latin poetry is long if it contains a long vowel or a diphthong, or if it contains a short vowel followed by two consonants (one of which may be at the beginning of the following word). Otherwise, it is short. But a syllable containing a short vowel followed by a mute (p, b, t, d, c, g) and a liquid (l, r) may be either long or short, according to the needs of the verse. For example in the line

inque *patris* blandis haerens cervice lacertis
(*Met.* 1.485)

the *a* in *patris* is short by nature. But since it is followed by the mute *t* and the liquid *r* it is common, i.e. it may be either long or short. Since in this case the position in the verse requires a short syllable, it is read as short.

Metrical Feet: Dactyls and Spondees

A given combination of syllables comprises what is known as a foot. In dactylic hexameter, the meter in which Latin epic is written (see next section), two kinds of foot are used: a long syllable followed by two short syllables (e.g. *carmina*), called a dactyl (Greek *dactulos* is itself one); and two long syllables (e.g. *nubes*), called a spondee (the Greek word *spondê* is itself one). Note that the small number of syllabic patterns allowed by the hexameter exclude many words which have intractable combinations. For example, any word in which a single short syllable comes between two long ones (e.g. *iudico*) can never be placed in a hexameter verse. The first syllable of the dactyl and the spondee is always accented: this accent is called the *ictus*. The accented part of a foot is generally known as the *thesis*;[1] the unaccented part as the *arsis*.[2]

Dactylic Hexameter

The meter of Latin epic is known as dactylic hexameter (also sometimes called the Heroic Verse). It is called hexameter (from the Greek 'hex', meaning six) because each line, or verse, contains six feet; and it is called dactylic because the dactyl (long-short-short) is the characteristic foot of the meter and is generally more frequently used than the spondee. The first four feet of the hexameter may be either dactyls or spondees. The fifth foot is almost always a dactyl. The rare verse having a spondee in the fifth foot is called spondaic. An example of a spondaic verse from the set text is 3.669 *pictarumque iacent fera corpora pantherarum*. The sixth foot is always a spondee. The last syllable of a verse may be short in itself; if it is short, it is regarded as long, because a spondee is required

---

[1] *Thesis*/θέσις comes from the Greek *tithemi*/τίθημι, meaning 'to put down' hence 'to stress'.

[2] *Arsis*/ἄρσις comes from the Greek *airo*/αἴρω 'to rise', 'lift up' (in this case after the 'putting down/ stress' of the *thesis*).

in the last foot. Such a syllable is known as the *syllaba anceps* ('either-way syllable').

In general terms, verses that are light and rapid and pleasing to read have a preponderance of dactyls, or at least alternate dactyls and spondees. Speaking broadly, an accumulation of spondees tends to give a slow and laboured movement to the line. This slower movement is, however, often very expressive, as in the following line from the set text:

> illi admirantes remorum in verbere perstant …
> (*Met.* 3.662)
>
> Astonished they persisted in beating their oars (sc. to no avail) …

This ponderous line, with its five spondees nicely conveys the strenuous effort exerted by the Tyrrhenian sailors to set their vessel, which Bacchus has rooted to the spot, back in motion; the effort is of course in vain, and the slow and ponderous versification nicely captures (or self-annotates) this effect.

Among Roman epicists, Ovid is the acknowledged master of light, quick-moving verse, whereas Virgil's verse is more spondaic and hence considered more 'stately'. In their choice of metrical patterns, the silver epic poets adopted various approaches. Valerius Flaccus, for example, followed Ovid in showing a preference for the dactyl over the spondee. Lucan, on the other hand, took on Virgil in exhibiting a decided preference for spondees over dactyls.

Caesura

An examination of any line of verse shows that words often end within a foot. The ending of a word within a foot is called a caesura. In most Latin epic poets, the use of caesurae was considered absolutely necessary for an agreeable cadence. Early Latin hexameter poets, such as Ennius, were regarded in later ages as crude versifiers for failing to recognize this principle. An example of the failure to make use of caesurae is the Ennian verse

> *Romae | moenia | terruit | impiger | Hannibal | armis*
>
> Restless Hannibal threatened the walls of Rome with arms.

where the end of each of the six metrical feet of the hexameter coincides with the end of a word (in an all-out 'busy' effort to stand out, and to *say* so: the *word* | Hannibal | collides with | Rome's | supposedly unshakable | walls |). A given verse tends to have more than one caesura. If there is a particular caesura at the end of an important word or phrase or at a sense pause, it is called *the* caesura. This main caesura is often a help to the sense and should be observed in reading the verse out loud. It may occur after the *thesis* (the so-called masculine caesura), or in the *arsis* of a dactyl (the so-called feminine caesura). The masculine caesura is more common than the feminine.

The more common location of the main caesura is in the third foot, less often in the fourth. Note that the caesura is conventionally indicated by two vertical lines (as opposed to the one vertical line used to indicate the metrical feet):

Talia | dicen | tem || pro | turbat Ech | ione | natus.
(*Met.* 3.526)

As he was saying such things, the son of Echion drives him away.

Here the caesura, which is not a particularly strong one, falls into the third foot and separates the participial construction *talia dicentem*, which refers to Tiresias, from the main verb and the subject of the sentence (*proturbat Echione natus*), which refers to Pentheus. As such, it kick starts the next *action* after the standstill for the *speaking* and is furthermore expressive of the clash between the two characters, though in syntactical terms, the caesura is not strong since *talia dicentem* serves as accusative object of *proturbat*.

Sometimes a verse has two caesurae — usually in the second and the fourth foot — dividing the verse into three parts instead of two. An example (embodying agitation) of this is:

turba fu | rens; || cunc | tae coë | unt || trepi | dumque se | quuntur
(*Met.* 3.713)

The ending of a word with the end of a foot is called diaeresis. In the energetic line from Ennius quoted above, there are thus five diaereseis! When a diaeresis occurs at the end of the fourth foot it is known as a bucolic diaeresis, because it was specially favoured in Greek pastoral poetry. A very expressive example of its use is found early in Book 4:

> saepe, ubi | constite | rant hinc | Thisbe, || Pyramus | illinc
> (*Met.* 4.71)
>
> Often, when they stood there (sc. at the wall), Thisbe here, Pyramus there ...

It comes from Ovid's tale of Pyramus and Thisbe (the ancient archetype of Romeo and Juliet), with the pair of lovers living in adjacent houses separated by a wall and prohibited to meet by their parents. The verse mirrors how Thisbe and Pyramus (each receiving their own foot of the hexameter) tried to get as close to each other as possible (a desire enacted in the verse by the placing of their names right next to one another) by meeting at the wall, which however kept them apart: the bucolic diaeresis after *Thisbe* and before *Pyramus* thus enacts the wall on the level of verse design (as their introduction set out, at 4.55–57. At the death, the two names, his dactyl to her spondee, will get it together arithmetrically: 'Pyram-[id like River]' in one 'Urn [for cremated ashes]', 4.166, una ... *in* urna. ||) In general, however, Latin epic poets used the bucolic diaeresis very sparingly: it was considered to be something of a metrical blemish.

As these examples show, Ovid's handling of the caesura is often expressive and invites interpretation. Consider, for instance, the following two lines:

> at qua | cumque tra | bes ob | structaque | saxa te | nebant
> spumeus | et ferv | ens || et ab | obice | saevior | ibat.
> (*Met.* 3.570–71)

It is difficult to place any significant break (caesura or diaeresis) in line 570 — it is as solid and uninterrupted a hexameter as the (tenacious) barrier to the water it means to describe. The following line features a weak caesura in the third foot (after *fervens*) and is further marked by a pronounced presence of diaereseis: word end and foot end coincide after *spumeus*, *obice*, and *saevior*. This design helps to highlight the fact that the water, 'enraged' by the obstacle, foams emphatically and manages to break through.

Elision and Ecthlipsis

A vowel at the end of a word is usually not pronounced when the next word begins with a vowel or h; this is called elision. For example, in the following verse elision of the final vowel (e) occurs in the second and third foot:[3]

> Taygetenque Hyadasque oculis Arctonque notavi
> (*Met.* 3.595)

Here the syllable *-que* after *Taygeten* is merged with the following word *hyadasque*, and the two syllables would be pronounced as one '-quyh-', and would count as a single short syllable metrically; likewise the (weak) syllable *-que* after *hyadas* is merged with the following word *oculis*, and the two syllables would again be pronounced as one '-quo-', and would count as a single short syllable metrically.

A vowel and *m* at the end of a word are also elided when the next word begins with a vowel or *h*; this specific type of elision is called 'ecthlipsis'. For example, in the following verse ecthlipsis of the second syllable of *quidem* occurs in the second foot (as well as elision of *ego* and *actutum* in the third):

> quem quidem ego actutum (modo vos absistite) cogam
> (*Met.* 3.557)

> quem quidem eg | o actu | tum modo | vos ab | sistite | cogam.

That is, the syllable *-dem* is merged with the following word *ego*, and the two syllables would be pronounced as one '-deg-', and counts as a single short syllable.

Metrical Licenses

Latin epic does not always adhere strictly to the regular norms of hexameter verse. The metrical licenses that occur frequently are as follows:

---

[3] Note that *Taygetenque* scans long (*Ta*) short (*y*) short (*ge*) long (*ten-*), i.e. the *y* is a syllable by itself. Greek proper names often bring exotic sounds and sound-patterns into Latin, not least when myth is handled.

i) Sometimes, a final vowel is not elided when the next word begins with a vowel or *h*; this is called hiatus. Hiatus is especially common before the principal caesura or at a pause in the verse or between proper names. It also occurs regularly with the interjections *o*, *heu* and *pro*. For example in a howling out loud 'Bacchic' line from later in the epic,

> *tympanaque et plausus et Bacchei ululatus*
> (*Met.* 11.17)

hiatus occurs — that is, the diphthong *-ei* at the end of *Bacchei* and the initial vowel *u* in *ululatus* remain unelided and hence are pronounced (and scanned) separately. Note that hiatus tends to occur with long vowels (like the diphthong *-ei* in the line just quoted); hiatus with a short final vowel is very rare.

ii) In certain lines a long vowel or diphthong is made short before a word beginning with a vowel: this is called semi-hiatus.

iii) Occasionally a short syllable is treated as long. This change is known as diastole. One example from the set text occurs at 3.530: *vulgusque proceresque ignota ad sacra feruntur*, where the *-que* after *vulgus* (which is a short syllable) unusually scans long.

iv) A long syllable is sometimes treated as short. This poetic license occurs most often in final vowels or diphthongs. It is called systole or, when it involves the shortening of the second syllable of an iambic word or phrase, correption. In most Latin poetry, correption (i.e. the shortening of the second syllable of an iambic word) was a more accepted poetical practice than systole of longer words.

v) Sometimes a verse ends in a syllable that is elided before the initial vowel of the following verse. Such verses are known as hypermetric, and the elision is called synaphea. The majority of hypermetric verses end in the weak syllable *-que*. An example occurs in a hymn to Bacchus, immediately after the set text:

> turaque dant Bacchumque vocant Bromiumque Lyaeumque
> ignigenamque satumque iterum solumque bimatrem.
> (*Met.* 4.11–12)

> They burn incense, cry 'Bacchus' and 'Bromius' and 'Lyaeus' and 'the offspring of fire' and 'the twice born' and 'the only one born of two mothers'.

Here the -*que* at the end of Lyaeum would open up an impossible 'seventh' foot, but the extra syllable elides with the initial *i* of *ignigenamque* in the following line. Here the hypermeter is expressive of the 'Bacchic enthusiasm' of those who hymn the deity and generate so much energy and ecstasy in doing so that they even make the narrator join in with the racket and burst out of metre...

vi) Two consecutive vowels (or two vowels separated by *h*) belonging to different syllables are sometimes to be pronounced together as one syllable. This contraction of two normally distinct syllables into one is called synizesis (or sometimes synaeresis). Ovid tends to avoid it. (One rare instance occurs at *Met.* 15.718 where *Antium* is to be read as *Antjum*, i.e. di-syllabic.)

Monosyllabic Endings

The last word of a hexameter verse is generally a disyllable or a trisyllable. Two monosyllables at the end of the line are always a special effect, and can be disproportionately striking. For example, in the couplet

> rupit et excussum misisset in aequora, si non
> haesissem, quamvis amens, in fune retentus
> (*Met.* 3.627–28)

si non introduces the protasis of the postpositive protasis of the past counterfactual condition: Acoetes hangs on by two tenuous monosyllables. (The fact that *haesissem* 'hangs over' onto the next line enhances the effect.) A single monosyllable, however, is guaranteed to trigger emphasis — humour or a jolt — at a verse end. The principal exception to this is the word *est*, which often ends a line, and occurs regularly in Silver epic, including the set text, where its vowel is often elided. (This is called prodelision.) See 3.612: ...*in isto est*; 620: ...*cupido est*; 653: ...*rogata est*; 654: ...*vestra est*; 681: ...*cauda est*; 728: ...*nostrum est*.

In general, Ovid's hexameters are pleasingly easy to scan owing to their polished flow: 'In a word, Ovid puts in everything (dactyls, regular pauses, coincidence of ictus and accent, rhyme, alliteration, grammatical simplicity and concision) that will speed up and lighten; leaves out everything (elision, spondees, grammatical complexity, clash of ictus and accent, overrunning of metrical by sense units) that will slow down and encumber his verse'.[4] But as the examples above show, the fluent ease of the metre does not mean the absence of special effects and expressive verse design. Ovid's craft is such that contents and verse-form always work perfectly together — a synergy that significantly enhances the overall impact and resonance of his poetry.

---

4   Otis (1970) 76.

2. Glossary of Rhetorical and Syntactic Figures

This list contains the major rhetorical and syntactic figures identified and discussed in the Commentary. Most of the terms for the figures derive from, or indeed are, either Greek or Latin; we have therefore provided an etymological explanation for each, not least to show that the terminological abracadabra makes perfectly good sense — even if it takes a smattering of ancient Greek and Latin to see this. To facilitate comprehension, the illustrative examples are in English and taken from the Shakespearean corpus. Unless otherwise indicated, they come from the Pyramus-and-Thisbe episode in Act 5 of *A Midsummer Night's Dream*. A good reason for drawing on the oeuvre of an (early) modern author for illustration is to convey a sense of the continuity of classical and classicizing rhetoric in the western cultural tradition. And in Shakespeare, of course, some saw the 'sweet witty soul of Ovid' reincarnated.

alliteration: the repeated use of the same sound at the beginning of words in close proximity.

> *Etymology*: from (un-classical) Latin *alliterare*, 'to begin with the same letter'.

> *Example*: 'Whereat, with blade, with bloody, blameful blade | He bravely broach'd his boiling bloody breast'.

anaphora: the repetition of the same word or phrase at the beginning of several successive syntactic units.

> *Etymology*: from Greek *anapherein*, 'to carry back, to repeat'
>
> *Example*: 'O grim-look'd night! O night with hue so black! O night, which ever art when day is not! O night, O night, alack, alack, alack!'

antithesis: literally 'a placing against'; the (balanced) juxtaposition of contrasting ideas.

> *Etymology*: from Greek *antitithenai*, 'to place (*tithenai*) against (*anti-*)'.
>
> *Example*: ''Tide life, 'tide death, I come without delay'.

apo koinou: two constructions that have a word or phrase in common; or, put the other way around, a word or phrase shared by two different constructions.

> *Etymology*: from the Greek phrase *apo koinou lambanein*, used by ancient grammarians of two clauses taking a word in common (*koinou*, genitive of *koinon* after the preposition *apo*).
>
> *Example*: 'There was a man — dwelt by the churchyard' (*The Winter's Tale*, Act 2, Scene 1).

asyndeton: the absence or omission of conjunctions (see also below *polysyndeton*).

> *Etymology*: from Greek *a-sun-detos*, 'not (*a*-privativum) bound (*detos*, from *dein*, to bind) together (*sun*)'.
>
> *Example*: 'O Fates, come, come, cut thread and thrum; quail, crush, conclude, and quell!'

captatio benevolentiae: a Latin phrase that literally means 'the capture of goodwill', i.e. a rhetorical technique designed to render the audience kindly disposed towards the speaker.

> *(Botched) example*: 'If we offend, it is with our good will. That you should think, we come not to offend. But with good will'.[5]

---

5 Note that (Will) Shakespeare's proxy character here, hilariously, 'translates' the Latin *benevolentia* of the rhetorical figure, but, perversely, refers to the 'good will' of himself, the speaker, rather than that of the audience.

chiasmus: the repetition of a grammatical pattern in inverse order: *a b — b a*.

> *Etymology*: from Greek *chiasmos*, 'a placing crosswise', from the letter X (pronounced *chi*) of the Greek alphabet. (Imagine the two *a* at either end of the first diagonal line of X, and at either end of the second diagonal line the two *b*; then read the top half first and afterwards the bottom half and you get *a b — b a*.)
>
> *Example*: '(a) Sweet Moon, (b) I thank thee ... (b), I thank thee, (a) Moon...'

climax: a series or sequence of units that gradually increase in import or force.

> *Etymology*: from Greek *klimax*, 'ladder'.
>
> *Example*: 'Tongue, lose thy light; | Moon take thy flight: Now die, die, die, die, die' (Pyramus before stabbing himself).

ellipse: the omission of one or more words in a sentence necessary for a complete grammatical construction.

> *Etymology*: from Greek *elleipein*, 'to fall short, leave out'.
>
> *Example*: 'I neither know it nor can learn of him' (*Romeo and Juliet*, Act 1, Scene 1).[6]

hendiadys: one idea expressed by two words joined by 'and', such as two nouns used in place of a noun and an adjective.

> *Etymology*: from Greek *hen-dia-duoin*, 'one thing (*hen*) through (*dia*) two (*duoin*)'.
>
> *Example*: 'The service and the loyalty I owe' (*Macbeth*, Act 1, Scene 4), for 'the loyal service'.

homoioteleuton: similarity of ending in words in close proximity to one another.

> *Etymology*: from Greek *homoios*, 'like', and *teleute*, 'ending'.

---

[6] Filling in the items elided would results in something like 'I neither know it nor can I learn anything about it from him'.

Example: 'My mother weep<u>ing</u>, my father wail<u>ing</u>, my sister cry<u>ing</u>, our maid howl<u>ing</u>, our cat wring<u>ing</u> her hands' (*The Two Gentlemen of Verona*, Act 2, Scene 3).[7]

hyperbaton: dislocation of the customary or logical word order, with the result that items that normally go together are separated.

Etymology: from Greek *huperbaino*, 'to step (*bainein*) over (*huper-*)'. (Imagine, for instance, that if an adjective is placed apart from the noun it modifies you have to 'step over' the intervening words to get from one to the other.)

Example: 'Some rise by sin, and some by virtue fall' (*Measure for Measure*, Act 2, Scene 1).[8]

hyperbole: the use of exaggeration.

Etymology: from Greek *huperballein*, 'to throw (*ballein*, from which derives *bole*, "a throwing") over or beyond (*huper*)'.

Example: 'Will all great Neptune's ocean wash this blood | Clean from my hand? No. This my hand will rather | The multitudinous seas incarnadine, | Making the green one red' (*Macbeth*, Act 2, Scene 2).[9]

---

[7] Note that the last item in the list (wring-ing) contains the -ing sound twice, a stylistic climax that reinforces the climax in content achieved through the anthropomorphism of the cat and the unexpected switch from sound (weeping etc.) to silence (wringing) that coincides with the (humorous) mismatch of creature and activity (cats, not maids, howl; and maids, not cats, wring their hands).

[8] Natural word order would require 'some fall by virtue'. Note that the hyperbaton also produces a chiasmus — Some (a) rise (b) by sin, and some (b) by virtue (a) fall –, which is ideally suited to reinforce the elegant antitheses of sin and virtue, rising and falling. One could further argue that the hyperbaton, which produces disorder on the level of grammar and syntax, is the perfect figure of speech for the basic idea of the utterance: *moral* disorder, which manifests itself in the reward of sin and the punishment of virtue and implies that our universe is devoid of justice, i.e. as chaotic as the hyperbatic word order.

[9] 'To incarnadine' means 'to turn into the colour of flesh (Latin *caro/carnis, carnis*), dye red, redden'. A more familiar term with a similar etymology is 'incarnation'.

hysteron proteron: A Greek phrase, meaning 'the latter (*hysteron*) first (*proteron*)', producing chronological disorder.

> *Example*: 'Th' Antoniad, the Egyptian admiral, | With all their sixty, fly and turn the rudder' (*Antony and Cleopatra*, Act 3, Scene 10).[10]

onomatopoesis/ onomatopoeia: expressions where the sound suggests the sense. (The word sounds like the perfect example of itself.)

> *Etymology*: from Greek *onoma* (genitive *onomatos*), 'word, name', and *poiein* (noun: *poesis*), 'to make'.

> *Example*: 'Sea-nymphs hourly ring his knell | Hark! now I hear them, — Ding-dong, bell' (*The Tempest*, Act 1, Scene 2).

pleonasm: a 'fullness of expression', that is, the use of more words than is strictly speaking necessary to convey the desired meaning.

> *Etymology*: from Greek *pleonazein*, 'to be more than enough or superfluous'.

> *Example*: 'the most unkindest cut of all' (*Julius Caesar*, Act 3, Scene 2, about Brutus' stabbing of Caesar).[11]

polyptoton: the repetition of the same word, variously inflected.

> *Etymology*: from Greek *poluptoton*, 'many (*polu*) cases (from *ptôsis*, i.e. fall, grammatical case)'.

> *Example*: 'Then know that I, one Snug the joiner, am | A <u>lion</u>-fell, nor else no <u>lion's</u> dam'.

---

10 The logical sequence would require 'they turn the rudder and fly'. The example is a beautiful instance of enactment since the *husteron proteron* conveys a sense of how hastily ('heel over head' as it were) everyone is trying to get away.

11 Shakespeare expresses the degree to which Brutus' unkindness outdid that of all the others pleonastically by using both the adverb 'most' and the superlative ending -est.

polysyndeton: the frequent use of conjunctions such as 'and' or 'or' even when they are not required.

> *Etymology*: from Greek *polu-sun-detos*, 'many times (*polu*) bound (*detos*, from *dein*, to bind) together (*sun*)'.

> *Example*: 'Peering in maps for ports *and* piers *and* roads' (*The Merchant of Venice*, Act 1, Scene 1).

tautology: the repetition of the same idea in different ways.

> *Etymology*: from Greek *tauto*, 'the same', and *logos*, 'word, idea'.

> *Example*: 'The ... mouse ... may now perchance <u>both quake and tremble</u> here'.

tricolon: the use of three parallel grammatical units (words, phrases, clauses).

> *Etymology*: from Greek *tri-*, 'three', and *kôlon*, 'limb, member, clause, unit'.

> *Example*: 'Tongue, not a word; | Come, trusty sword; | Come, blade, my breast imbue'.

zeugma: the application of a word (usually a verb or an adjective) to two or more words in different senses.

> *Etymology*: from Greek *zeugma*, 'bond'.

> *Example*: 'Kill the boys and the luggage!' (*Henry V*, Act 4, Scene 7).

Bibliography

Editions, Translations, Commentaries

Anderson, W. S. (ed.) (1997), *Ovid's Metamorphoses Books 1–5* (Norman, OK: University of Oklahoma Press).

Bömer, F. (ed.) (1969), *P. Ovidius Naso Metamorphosen, Buch I-III* (Heidelberg: Universitätsverlag Winter).

— (ed.) (1976), *P. Ovidius Naso Metamorphosen, Buch IV-V* (Heidelberg: Universitätsverlag Winter).

Dodds, E. R. (ed.) (1960), *Euripides Bacchae* (Oxford: Clarendon Press).

Gibson, R. K. (ed.) (2003), *Ovid. Ars Amatoria Book 3* (Cambridge: Cambridge University Press).

Henderson, A. A. R. (ed.) (1979), *Ovid Metamorphoses III* (Bedminister: Bristol Classic Press).

Kenney, E. J. (1986), *Introduction and Notes in* Melville (1986).

Lee, A. G. (ed.) (1953), *Ovid Metamorphoses I* (Cambridge: Cambridge University Press).

Melville, A. D. (tr.) (1986), *Ovid: Metamorphoses* (Oxford: Oxford World's Classics). With Introduction and Notes by E. J. Kenney.

— (tr.) (1995), *Ovid: Sorrows of an Exile* (Oxford: Oxford University Press). With Introduction and Notes by E. J. Kenney.

Richmond, J. A. (ed.) (1962), *The Halieutica Ascribed to Ovid* (London: University of London, Athlone Press).

Schierl, P. (ed.) (2006), *Die Tragödien des Pacuvius* (Berlin: W. de Gruyter).

Tarrant, R. (ed.) (2004), *P. Ovidi Nasonis Metamorphoses* (Oxford: Oxford University Press), http://dx.doi.org/10.1093/actrade/9780198146667.book.1

Turpin, W. (2016), *Ovid, Amores (Book 1)* (Cambridge, UK: Open Book Publishers), freely available at http://www.openbookpublishers.com/product/348

Zissos, A. (ed.) (2008), *Valerius Flaccus: Argonautica Book 1* (Oxford: Oxford University Press), http://dx.doi.org/10.1093/actrade/9780199219490.book.1

Other Literature

Ando, C. (2007), 'Exporting Roman Religion'. In *A Companion to Roman Religion*, edited by J. Rüpke (Malden, MA; Oxford; and Carlton: Blackwell Publishing), pp. 429–45. http://dx.doi.org/10.1002/9780470690970.ch29

Barchiesi, A. (1999), 'Venus' Masterplot: Ovid and the Homeric Hymns'. In *Ovidian Transformations: Essays on the Metamorphoses and Its Reception*, edited by P. Hardie, A. Barchiesi and S. Hinds (Cambridge: Cambridge Philological Society), pp. 112–26.

Barkan, L. (1986), The *Gods Made Flesh: Metamorphosis and the Pursuit of Paganism* (New Haven, CT: Yale University Press).

Brown, S. A. (1999), *The Metamorphosis of Ovid: From Chaucer to Ted Hughes* (London: Duckworth), http://dx.doi.org/10.5040/9781472540324

Cole, S. (2007), 'Finding Dionysus'. In *A Companion to Greek Religion*, edited by D. Ogden (Malden, MA; Oxford; and Carlton: Blackwell Publishing), pp. 325–41, http://dx.doi.org/10.1002/9780470996911.ch22

Currie, H. M. (1981), 'Ovid and the Roman Stage'. *Aufstieg und Niedergang der römischen Welt* II.31.4: 2701–42.

Fantham, E. (2004), *Ovid's Metamorphoses* (Oxford: Oxford University Press).

Farrell, J. (1992), 'Dialogue of Genres in Ovid's Lovesong of Polyphemus (*Metamorphoses* 13.719–897)'. *American Journal of Philology* 113.2: 235–68, http://dx.doi.org/10.2307/295559

Feeney, D. C. (1991), *The Gods in Epic: Poets and Critics of the Classical Tradition* (Oxford: Clarendon Press).

Feldherr, A. (1997), 'Metamorphosis and Sacrifice in Ovid's Theban Narrative'. *Materiali e discussioni per l'analisi dei testi classici* 38.1: 25–55.

— (2010), *Playing Gods. Ovid's Metamorphoses and the Politics of Fiction* (Princeton: Princeton University Press), http://dx.doi.org/10.1515/9781400836543

Fitzgerald, W. (2016), *Variety: The Life of a Roman Concept* (Chicago, IL: University of Chicago Press)), http://dx.doi.org/10.7208/chicago/9780226299525.001.0001

Galinsky, G. K. (1975), *Ovid's Metamorphoses: An Introduction to the Basic Aspects* (Berkeley and Los Angeles, CA: University of California Press).

Gildenhard, I. and A. Zissos (2000a), 'Ovid's Narcissus (*Met.* 3.339–510): Echoes of Oedipus'. *American Journal of Philology* 121.1: 129–47, http://dx.doi.org/10.1353/ajp.2000.0006

— (2000b), 'Inspirational Fictions: Autobiography and Generic Reflexivity in Ovid's Proems'. *Greece & Rome* 47.1: 67–79, http://dx.doi.org/10.1093/gr/47.1.67

— (2004), 'Ovid's "Hecale": Deconstructing Athens in the *Metamorphoses*'. *The Journal of Roman Studies* 94:47–72. http://dx.doi.org/10.2307/4135010

— (2013), 'The Transformations of Ovid's Medea'. In *Transformative Change in Western Thought; A History of Metamorphosis from Homer to Hollywood*, edited by I. Gildenhard and A. Zissos (Oxford: Legenda), pp. 88–130.

Ginsberg, W. (1989), 'Ovid's *Metamorphoses* and the Politics of Interpretation'. *The Classical Journal* 84.3: 222–31.

Görler, W. (1999), 'Rowing Strokes: Tentative Considerations of Shifting Objects in Virgil and Elsewhere'. In *Aspects of the Language of Latin Poetry*, edited by J. N. Adams and R. Mayer (Oxford: Oxford University Press), pp. 269–86, http://www.britac.ac.uk/pubs/proc/files/93p269.pdf

Hardie, P. (1990), 'Ovid's Theban History: The First "Anti-*Aeneid*"?' *The Classical Quarterly* 40.1: 224–35.

— (1992), *The Epic Successors of Virgil* (Cambridge: Cambridge University Press), http://dx.doi.org/10.1017/cbo9781139163743

— (2002a), *Ovid's Poetics of Illusion* (Cambridge: Cambridge University Press).

— (ed.) (2002b), *Cambridge Companion to Ovid* (Cambridge: Cambridge University Press), http://dx.doi.org/10.1017/ccol0521772818

— (2012), *Rumour and Renown: Representations of Fama in Western Literature* (Cambridge: Cambridge University Press).

Harrison, S. J. (2007), *Generic enrichment in Vergil and Horace* (Oxford: Oxford University Press), http://dx.doi.org/10.1093/acprof:oso/9780199203581.001.0001

Hinds, S. (1987), *The Metamorphosis of Persephone: Ovid and the Self-conscious Muse* (Cambridge: Cambridge University Press).

Holzberg, N. (2002), *Ovid: The Poet and his Work* (Ithaca, NY: Cornell University Press).

Inglebert, H. (2014). *Le monde, l'histoire: essai sur les histoires universelles* (Paris: Presses universitaires de France).

James, P. (1993), 'Pentheus Anguigena — Sins of the Father'. *Bulletin of the Institute of Classical Studies* 38.1: 81–93, http://dx.doi.org/10.1111/j.2041-5370.1993.tb00704.x

Janan, M. (2004), 'The Snake Sheds its Skin: Pentheus (Re)imagines Thebes'. *Classical Philology* 99.1: 130–46, http://dx.doi.org/10.1086/423859

Johnson, W. R. (1970), 'The Problem of the Counter-classical Sensibility and Its Critics'. *Classical Antiquity* 3: 123–52, http://dx.doi.org/10.2307/25010603

— (1996), 'The Rapes of Callisto'. *The Classical Journal* 92.1: 9–24.

Keith, A. (2002), 'Sources and Genres in Ovid's *Metamorphoses* 1–5'. In *Brill's Companion to Ovid*, edited by B. W. Boyd (Leiden: Brill), pp. 235–69, http://dx.doi.org/10.1163/9789047400950_009

Knox, P. E. (ed.) (2009), *A Companion to Ovid* (Malden, MA and Oxford: John Wiley & Sons).

Little, D. A. (1970), 'The Speech of Pythagoras in *Metamorphoses* 15 and the Structure of the *Metamorphoses*'. *Hermes* 98.3: 340–60

Lively, G. (2011), *Ovid's 'Metamorphoses': A Reader's Guide* (London: Bloomsbury), http://dx.doi.org/10.5040/9781472539991

Lovatt, H. (2013), *The Epic Gaze: Vision, Gender and Narrative in Ancient Epic* (Cambridge: Cambridge University Press), http://dx.doi.org/10.1017/cbo9781139060080

Mack, S. (1988), *Ovid* (New Haven, CT: Yale University Press).

McNamara, J. (2010), 'The Frustration of Pentheus: Narrative Momentum in Ovid's *Metamorphoses* 3.511–731'. *The Classical Quarterly* 60.1: 173–93, http://dx.doi.org/10.1017/s0009838809990528

Michalopoulos, C. N. (2012), 'Tiresias between Texts and Sex'. *Réseau européen sur les Gender Studies dans l'Antiquité* 2: 221–39, http://eugesta.recherche.univ-lille3.fr/revue/pdf/2012/Michalopoulos-2_2012.pdf

Murnaghan, S. (1987), *Disguise and Recognition in the Odyssey* (Princeton, NJ: Princeton University Press).

Nagy, G. (1979), *The Best of the Achaeans: Concepts of the Hero in Archaic Greek Poetry* (Baltimore, MD: Johns Hopkins University Press).

Orlin, E. M. (2010), *Foreign Cults in Rome. Creating a Roman Empire* (Oxford: Oxford University Press).

Otis, B. (1970), *Ovid as an Epic Poet*, 2nd ed. (Cambridge: Cambridge University Press).

Otto, W. F. (1933), *Dionysos: Mythos und Kultus* (Frankfurt: Vittorio Klostermann).

Schmidt, E. A. (1991), *Ovids poetische Menschenwelt: Die Metamorphosen als Metapher und Symphonie* (Heidelberg: Winter).

Segal, C. (1982), *Dionysiac Poetics and Euripides' Bacchae* (Princeton, NJ: Princeton University Press).

Seidensticker, B. (1972), 'Pentheus'. *Poetica* 5.3/4: 35–63.

Sharrock, A. (1994), *Seduction and Repetition in Ovid's Ars Amatoria 2* (Oxford: Clarendon Press).

Solodow, J. (1988), *The World of Ovid's Metamorphoses* (Chapel Hill, NC: North Carolina University Press) http://dx.doi.org/10.5149/9781469616490_solodow

Thompson, D. L. (1981), 'The Meetings of the Roman Senate on the Palatine'. *American Journal of Archeology* 85.3: 335–39, http://dx.doi.org/10.2307/504178

Tissol, G. (1996), *The Face of Nature. Wit, Narrative, and Cosmic Origins in Ovid's Metamorphoses* (Princeton, NJ: Princeton University Press), http://dx.doi.org/10.1515/9781400864614

Vernant, J. P. (1988), *Myth and Tragedy in Ancient Greece* (New York: Zone Books) [1990 version], https://monoskop.org/images/f/f1/Naquet_Vidal_Pierre_Vernant_Pierre_Jean_Myth_and_tragedy_in_Ancient_Greece_1996.pdf

Verdenius, W. J. (1962), 'AINOS'. *Mnemosyne* 15.1: 389, http://dx.doi.org/10.1163/156852562x00325

Volk, K. (2010), *Ovid* (Malden, MA and Oxford: Wiley-Blackwell), http://dx.doi.org/10.1002/9781444328127

Weber, C. (2002), 'The Dionysus in Aeneas'. *Classical Philology* 97.4: 322–43, http://dx.doi.org/10.1086/449594

Weiden Boyd (ed.) (2000), *Brill's Companion to Ovid* (Leiden: Brill), http://dx.doi.org/10.1163/9789047400950

Wills, J. (1996), *Repetition in Latin Poetry: Figures of Allusion* (Oxford: Clarendon Press).

Zeitlin, F. I. (1965), 'The Motif of the Corrupted Sacrifice in Aeschylus' *Oresteia*'. *Transactions of the American Philological Association* 96: 463–508, http://dx.doi.org/10.2307/283744

— (1990), 'Thebes: Theater of Self and Society in Athenian Drama'. In *Nothing to Do with Dionysos? Athenian Drama in its Social Context*, edited by J. J. Winkler and F. I. Zeitlin (Princeton, NJ: Princeton University Press), pp. 130–67.

— (1993), 'Staging Dionysus between Thebes and Athens'. In *Masks of Dionysus*, edited by T. H. Carpenter, H. Thomas, and C. A. Faraone (Ithaca, NY and London: Cornell University Press), pp. 147–82.

This book need not end here…

At Open Book Publishers, we are changing the nature of the traditional academic book. The title you have just read will not be left on a library shelf, but will be accessed online by hundreds of readers each month across the globe. OBP publishes only the best academic work: each title passes through a rigorous peer-review process. We make all our books free to read online so that students, researchers and members of the public who can't afford a printed edition will have access to the same ideas.

This book and additional content is available at:
http://www.openbookpublishers.com/isbn/9781783740826

Customize

Personalize your copy of this book or design new books using OBP and third-party material. Take chapters or whole books from our published list and make a special edition, a new anthology or an illuminating coursepack. Each customized edition will be produced as a paperback and a downloadable PDF. Find out more at:

http://www.openbookpublishers.com/section/59/1

Donate

If you enjoyed this book, and feel that research like this should be available to all readers, regardless of their income, please think about donating to us. We do not operate for profit and all donations, as with all other revenue we generate, will be used to finance new Open Access publications.

http://www.openbookpublishers.com/section/13/1/support-us

You may also be interested in...

Ovid, Amores (Book 1)
by William Turpin

http://dx.doi.org/10.11647/OBP.0067
http://www.openbookpublishers.com/product/348

Cornelius Nepos', Life of Hannibal': Latin Text, Notes, Maps, Illustrations and Vocabulary
by Bret Mulligan

http://dx.doi.org/10.11647/OBP.0068
http://www.openbookpublishers.com/product/341

Cicero, On Pompey's Command (De Imperio), 27–49. Latin Text, Study Aids with Vocabulary, Commentary, and Translation
by Ingo Gildenhard, Louise Hodgson, et al.

http://dx.doi.org/10.11647/OBP.0045
http://www.openbookpublishers.com/product/284

Tacitus, Annals, 15.20–23, 33–45. Latin Text, Study Aids with Vocabulary, and Commentary
by Mathew Owen and Ingo Gildenhard

http://dx.doi.org/10.11647/OBP.0035
http://www.openbookpublishers.com/product/215

www.ingramcontent.com/pod-product-compliance
Lightning Source LLC
Chambersburg PA
CBHW051806230426
43672CB00012B/2658